Routledge Guides to the Great Books

The Routledge Guidebook to Foucault's
The History of Sexuality

Michel Foucault's *The History of Sexuality* is one of the most influential philosophical works of the twentieth century and has been instrumental in shaping the study of gender theory, feminist theory and queer theory. Foucault's writing can, however, make it a difficult book to grasp, as he assumes a familiarity with the intellectually dominant theories of his time and at times adopts an ironic tone, which renders many passages obscure for newcomers to his work.

The Routledge Guidebook to Foucault's The History of Sexuality offers a clear and comprehensive guide to this groundbreaking work, examining:

- the historical context in which Foucault wrote;
- a critical discussion of the text, which examines the relationship between *The History of Sexuality*, *The Use of Pleasure* and *The Care of the Self*; and
- the reception and ongoing influence of *The History of Sexuality*.

Offering a close reading of the text, this is essential reading for anyone studying this enormously influential work.

Chloë Taylor is Associate Professor of Women's and Gender Studies and Philosophy at the University of Alberta, Canada. She has a PhD in Philosophy from the University of Toronto and was a Tomlinson Postdoctoral Fellow in Philosophy at McGill University.

D0301912

THE ROUTLEDGE GUIDES TO THE GREAT BOOKS

Series Editor: Anthony Gottlieb

The Routledge Guides to the Great Books provide ideal introductions to the texts which have shaped Western Civilization. The Guidebooks explore the arguments and ideas contained in the most influential works from some of the most brilliant thinkers who have ever lived, from Aristotle to Marx and Newton to Wollstonecraft. Each Guidebook opens with a short introduction to the author of the great book and the context within which they were working and concludes with an examination of the lasting significance of the book. The Routledge Guides to the Great Books will therefore provide students everywhere with complete introductions to the most significant books of all time.

Available:

Routledge Guides to the Great Books

The Routledge Guidebook to Foucault's *The History of Sexuality*

Chloë Taylor

LONDON AND NEW YORK

First published 2017
by Routledge
2 Park Square, Milton Park, Abingdon, Oxon OX14 4RN

and by Routledge
711 Third Avenue, New York, NY 10017

Routledge is an imprint of the Taylor & Francis Group, an informa business

© 2017 Chloë Taylor

The right of Chloë Taylor to be identified as the author of this work has
been asserted by her in accordance with sections 77 and 78 of the
Copyright, Designs and Patents Act 1988.

All rights reserved. No part of this book may be reprinted or reproduced or
utilised in any form or by any electronic, mechanical, or other means, now
known or hereafter invented, including photocopying and recording, or in
any information storage or retrieval system, without permission in writing
from the publishers.

Trademark notice: Product or corporate names may be trademarks or
registered trademarks, and are used only for identification and explanation
without intent to infringe.

British Library Cataloguing in Publication Data
A catalogue record for this book is available from the British Library

Library of Congress Cataloguing in Publication Data
A catalog record for this book has been requested

ISBN 13: 978-0-415-71783-0 (hbk)
ISBN 13: 978-0-415-71784-7 (pbk)
ISBN 13: 978-1-315-72715-8 (ebk)

Typeset in Times New Roman
by Out of House Publishing

Printed and bound by CPI Group (UK) Ltd, Croydon, CR0 4YY

CONTENTS

SERIES EDITOR PREFACE

'The past is a foreign country,' wrote a British novelist, L. P. Hartley: 'they do things differently there.'

The greatest books in the canon of the humanities and sciences can be foreign territory, too. This series of guidebooks is a set of excursions written by expert guides who know how to make such places become more familiar.

All the books covered in this series, however long ago they were written, have much to say to us now, or help to explain the ways in which we have come to think about the world. Each volume is designed not only to describe a set of ideas, and how they developed, but also to evaluate them. This requires what one might call a bifocal approach. To engage fully with an author, one has to pretend that he or she is speaking to us; but, to understand a text's meaning, it is often necessary to remember its original audience, too. It is all too easy to mistake the intentions of an old argument by treating it as a contemporary one.

The Routledge Guides to the Great Books are aimed at students in the broadest sense, not only those engaged in formal study. The intended audience of the series is all those who want to understand the books that have had the largest effects.

AJG
October 2012

ACKNOWLEDGEMENTS

To James Merleau, thank you for giving me my first copy of *The History of Sexuality* twenty years ago, when I was twenty, and for half a lifetime of best friendship since then. I am also immensely grateful to Hasana Sharp and Lisa Guenther, for the friendships that have nurtured and inspired my philosophical work and my life for over a decade now. I am also grateful to Ladelle McWhorter, for her support and mentorship over the last ten years. Thanks also to more recent friends and colleagues at the University of Alberta, whose Foucauldian and social justice scholarship has stimulated my own, particularly Danielle Peers, Cressida Heyes and Robert Nichols. I am also deeply appreciative of my colleagues in the Department of Women's and Gender Studies at the University of Alberta – Susanne Luhmann, Lise Gotell, Felice Lifshitz, Michelle Meagher and Philomina Okeke-Ihejirika – for the supportive and stimulating intellectual community that you provide. I am also indebted to two (former, now graduated) feminist philosophy doctoral students at the University of Alberta, Catherine Clune-Taylor and Kristin Rodier. Along with Cressida, you have helped make being a woman in philosophy bearable, and at times even delightful; thanks for your solidarity and brilliance over the last seven years. I am also grateful to feminist philosopher friends whom

I see less often, particularly Alexis Shotwell and Ada Jaarsma. Finally, I am appreciative of Randi Nixon, who read this entire manuscript and provided always helpful and insightful feedback and encouragement along the way. I dedicate this book to Pablo and Artemisia.

INTRODUCTION

In 1950, and again in 1951, Michel Foucault undertook the *agréga-tion de philosophie*, which his biographer David Macey describes as a 'fiercely competitive national examination' and 'one of the most severe forms of intellectual trial by ordeal to have been devised in any country' (Macey, 1993, p. 43). This exam is a requirement for teaching philosophy in France at the *lycée* and university levels, and involves the writing of three day-long papers. If a candidate passes the written exam – which only one out of four typically do (Schrift, 2008) – he or she moves on to two oral exams. In the 1950s the first oral exam was on a topic that the candidate pulled from a basket, while the second oral exam involved a lesson on a fixed theme and three commentaries on texts in French, Latin and either Greek or a modern language. The first time Foucault attempted the *agrégation* he was eliminated in the first oral exam, for which he had pulled the topic 'hypotheses'. The second time Foucault attempted the *agrégation*, after writing papers on expe-rience, theory, Bergson and Spinoza, the topic he pulled from the basket was 'sexuality'. According to Macey, Foucault's 'fluent discussion of [sexuality's] natural, historical and cultural aspects convinced his examiners of his worth', and he was ranked third *ex aequo* in the *agrégation de philosophie* (Macey, 1993, p. 45). Despite his success in passing the exam,

> Foucault was outraged; in his considered opinion, sexuality was not a suitable theme for the *agrégation*. It had been proposed by Canguilhem, despite protests from Davy, on the grounds that the *agrég* topics had not changed since he took his oral in 1927 and that it was time for something new. Besides, argued Canguilhem, all candidates for the *agrégation* had read Freud, and they all talked about sex. Foucault shared Davy's more conservative view, and formally protested to Canguilhem.
>
> (Macey, 1993, p. 45)

At this time, Foucault's academic interests were in the philosophy of Hegel, Husserl and Heidegger, and he felt that the topic of 'sexuality' did not provide him with a serious or appropriate opportunity to demonstrate his intellectual calibre to some of the most senior academics in France.

How did Foucault transition from the apparently conservative young man who considered 'sexuality' to be an inappropriate topic for academic examination to the politically radical and preeminent philosopher in France who would dedicate his last three books to writing a 'history of sexuality'? Should we see in this story a drastic shift from the young Foucault, who was reluctant to talk about sex, to the older Foucault, who would write multiple volumes on the topic? One interpretation of this story is to suggest that, in 1951, Foucault was sexually repressed, but that by the time that he wrote *The History of Sexuality*, in the 1970s and early 1980s, he had lived through the sexual liberation movement and come out as gay, and was thus able to write on this taboo topic. This narrative relies on a common story of sexual repression and liberation that volume 1 of *The History of Sexuality* cautions us against, however. A different interpretation is that the philosopher's anger over being compelled to talk about sex during his 1951 examination resonates with his problematization in volume 1 of *The History of Sexuality* of our compulsory and compulsive production of sexual discourses in the modern era. As a gay youth who had undergone psychiatrization in a homophobic society, by the time of the exam Foucault would in fact have been pressured to talk about sex – and to talk about it to authority figures and academics – continually, with stakes that included his freedom. Volume 1 of Foucault's *The History of Sexuality* asks: why have we come to see sex as so important to who we are? Why has it come to be a topic of authoritative and academic discourse? How have these discourses compelled us to speak about sex, and what power effects have these speech acts had? In volume 1 of *The History of Sexuality* Foucault shows that our compulsory and compulsive talk about sex ironically disproves the 'repressive' and 'liberation' hypotheses implicit in my first interpretation of the *agrégation* anecdote, and that this talk should not be understood as emancipatory but as a discursive act that enmeshes us in networks of power that constitute the kinds of subjects that we are and regulate every aspect of our lives.

As this second interpretation of the *agrégation* story suggests, Foucault's 'history of sexuality' will not be a narrative of sexual acts or sexual pleasures. It is, rather, an analysis of the ways that sex has been caught up with knowledge production and power. In particular, Foucault does not see the increased significance and discursive production around sex to be an indication that we have 'discovered' the importance of sex or that we have become a more 'liberated' society. On the contrary, Foucault interprets these phenomena as indicative of a new form of power – which he calls 'biopower' – that aims to control the life of the human species at both individual and population levels. In particular, having grown up in Nazi-occupied France, Foucault was concerned to explain the emergence of the particular fusion of sex and power that occurred with eugenics, which arose in the nineteenth century and reached its lethal apotheosis under Nazi administration.

In the nineteenth century, Europeans and North Americans grappled with the effects of increased urbanization, including the steady growth of slums inhabited by an underclass of paupers, prostitutes and thieves, many of whom were sickly and, the middle class thought, lazy and immoral. Rates of crime, disease, mental illness, alcoholism, promiscuity and prostitution were rampant in this segment of the population, which was, moreover, reproducing itself more quickly than the middle classes. The result was a growing fear among the bourgeoisie that the 'dregs' of society would eventually overtake them. The middle classes in Western countries began to suspect that their race was degenerating, both because they were not reproducing quickly enough and because the lower classes were reproducing more quickly. These fears were exacerbated in countries such as Britain when studies of the records of the height, weight and health of soldiers throughout the nineteenth century suggested 'a progressive physical degeneracy of race' (Dr Henry Rumsey, cited in Childs, 2001, p. 1). European exploration of non-Western countries also confronted Europeans with races that they deemed inferior but that, because they were believed to have a common ancestry with Europeans in Adam and Eve, were assumed to have 'degenerated' over time, falling from their original (made in God's image) nobility (Childs, 2001, p. 1). The possibility of nationwide racial degeneration was thus posed, and anxiety mounted that Europeans, and settler colonial North Americans, could descend to the level of these 'inferior races' if procreation patterns were not controlled.

In response to these fears, the science of eugenics was born in the late nineteenth century in Britain with the works of the statistician Francis Galton, and reached its height in the first half of the twentieth century throughout the Western world. Galton drew on his cousin Charles Darwin's theory of natural selection and argued that human societies were preventing natural selection, or the 'survival of the fittest', by protecting the sick, the poor and the weak through welfare programmes, charity and medicine. He coined the term 'eugenics' from the Greek roots *eu* (good or well) and *genēs* (born), and described the science as 'the study of all agencies under human control which can improve or impair the racial quality of future generations' (cited in Black, 2004, p. 18). 'Social Darwinists' argued that the 'survival of the fittest' human beings would come about naturally if welfare systems were simply withdrawn: although the poor would continue to have more children than the middle classes, this would be compensated for by higher mortality rates resulting from poverty and lack of medical care. As one social Darwinist, Herbert Spencer, explained:

It seems hard that an unskilfulness... should entail hunger upon the artisan. It seems hard that a laborer incapacitated by sickness... should have to bear the resulting privations. It seems hard that widows and orphans should be left to struggle for life or death. Nevertheless, when regarded not separately but in connexion with the interests of universal humanity, these harsh fatalities are seen to be full of beneficence.

(cited in Childs, 2001, pp. 2–3)

Spencer thus argued that nature should be allowed to run its course, eliminating the weak members of the human species from society. Individuals such as Spencer rejected the argument that improving the environment of the poor might reduce their rates of mental illness, infection, alcoholism, promiscuity and crime. While those advocating environmental reform suggested improvements in education and health care for the urban poor, Social Darwinists opposed such methods, arguing that they would only exacerbate the problem by helping to sustain those segments of society better left to die.

Although Spencer's approach was to let the poor and the weak die out through non-intervention, other eugenicists advocated more active tactics. These tactics were divided into what were called 'negative' and 'positive' eugenics (Withers, 2012, pp. 13–15). 'Negative eugenics,' as the philosopher and eugenist F. C. S. Schiller put it, 'aims at checking the deterioration to which the human stock is exposed, owing to the rapid proliferation of what may be called human weeds' (cited in Childs, 2001, p. 3). This strategy entailed preventing individuals and groups deemed 'degenerate' from procreating through forced sterilization, incapacitation (such as institutionalizing the mentally ill and congenitally disabled in sex-segregated institutions), 'euthanasia' or, as in the case of Nazi Germany, murder and genocide. It has been argued that such negative eugenic tactics continue today through practices such as the mass incarceration of racialized populations in sex-segregated prisons, and routine screenings of foetuses with medical pressure to terminate pregnancies that might result in disabled children (Guenther, 2016). From a eugenical perspective, such 'negative' tactics can only prevent further 'deterioration', however; they cannot actively improve the gene pool, and so strategies of 'positive eugenics' were simultaneously promoted. 'Positive eugenics' involves encouraging or compelling 'genetically advantaged' 'human flowers' to produce large families. Abortion by 'fit' women was illegal in Nazi Germany, and middle-class women who attempted to enter the workforce were discouraged on the grounds that jobs outside the home were 'race-destroying occupations'. Methods of positive eugenics that continue today include targeted financial and political incentives to have children, and the use of medical technologies such as *in vitro* fertilization, gestational surrogacy, pre-implantation genetic diagnosis, egg transplants and cloning.

Eugenics thus attempts to improve the gene pool; what is meant by 'improve' is inevitably socio-culturally defined, however, and has always been informed by classism, racism and ableism (Snyder and Mitchell, 2006). Eugenicists are concerned with increasing the intelligence of the population, for instance, but this concern has tended to promote births in the middle class while preventing them among the working class, as well as to reinforce prejudice against the cognitively disabled – such as the 'simple-minded farmhand' Charles Jouy, discussed in Chapter 1. Racist eugenicists opposed miscegenation, fusing 'scientific' arguments with white suprema-cist assumptions. With the Immigration Act of 1924 in the United States, eugenicists successfully argued against allowing 'inferior stock' from Southern and Eastern Europe into the United States. Laws were written in the late nineteenth century and early twenti-eth to prohibit the mentally ill from marrying and to allow them to be sterilized in psychiatric institutions. These laws were upheld by the US Supreme Court in 1927, and were abolished only in the middle of the twentieth century. As a result, between 1907 and 1974 over 65,000 Americans who were deemed mentally ill were sterilized under state-run eugenics programmes in order to pre-vent them from passing on their genes. As Lisa Guenther notes, however, 'these numbers pale in comparison with the impact of public health and social welfare policies targeting poor people and people of colour. By 1980, an estimated 700,000 people had been sterilized through such policies' (Guenther, 2016, p. 221). The rac-ism of these surgeries is apparent when we consider that, by 1968, the United States had sterilized a third of Puerto Rican women of childbearing age, and by the end of the 1970s more than a quarter of Native American women had had hysterectomies (Guenther, 2016, p. 221). In Canada, Sexual Sterilization Acts were passed in two provinces, resulting in approximately 3,000 sterilizations in Alberta and several hundred in British Columbia between the 1920s and 1970s. As in the United States, the Canadian eugenic programmes targeted people with mental and physical disabilities and people of colour, particularly indigenous and Métis people, and immigrants (Malacrida, 2015). In both the United States and Canada, women were more likely than men to be diagnosed as mentally ill or cognitively deficient, as were poor people compared to middle-class people, immigrants compared to citizens, and non-white people compared to white people.

Following World War II there has been a tendency to repress the fact that other countries besides Germany have histories of eugenics – histories that have quietly continued long after the defeat of the Nazis. Critical race and disability scholars have not only traced the extensive history of eugenics in the Western world, however, but have argued that the contemporary and mostly unquestioned pro-family movement in countries such as the United States and Canada is a mere recasting and extension of the eugenics movement (McWhorter, 2009). Eugenic uses of science continue in the cases of designer babies, genetic counselling, foetal screenings and pre-emptive abortions, and the creation of 'genius sperm banks'. These examples entail the use of new scientific technology to 'improve' the genes of individual babies and of the population as a whole while preventing babies deemed 'unfit' from ever being born. These practices thus further entrench the prejudices of an ableist, white supremacist and classist society while continuing the goals of eugenics.

Volume 1 of Foucault's *The History of Sexuality* culminates in an analysis of the kind of power that underpins eugenics, as it existed in the nineteenth and twentieth centuries and as it continues to thrive in new forms today. In this way, volume 1 provides us with crucial tools for understanding and resisting the forms of sexist, heterosexist, ableist and racist oppression that spur and are extended by eugenic logics and practices. For this reason, volume 1 of *The History of Sexuality* has been extensively mobilized in feminist, queer, critical disability and critical race scholarship, in some cases functioning as a canonical text.

While Chapters 1 to 4 of this book provide detailed explanations and examples of Foucault's arguments in volume 1 of *The History of Sexuality*, Chapters 5 and 6 examine the ways that this volume has been taken up by liberation movements and social justice theories. In particular, Chapter 5 considers the influence of *The History of Sexuality* on feminist theory, and Chapter 6 examines the foundational role of this volume in queer theory. Because volume 1 of *The History of Sexuality* was intended to be a brief 'introduction' and overview for a forthcoming five-volume series of books (none of which were ever written according to Foucault's original plan), it functions at a high level of abstraction, provides few examples or references for its claims, and raises many arguments in a synoptic form. For this reason, in the first four chapters of this book I draw on Foucault's course lectures from the years that he was writing and published volume 1 of *The History of Sexuality*, as well as on the writings of sexual scientists (such as Richard von Krafft-Ebing and Sigmund Freud) whom Foucault had in mind when writing this volume. In this way, I flesh out and provide support for arguments that are made in only nutshell form in *The History of Sexuality* itself. In addition, throughout these chapters I provide applications and examples of Foucault's claims that show the continued relevance of his now forty-year-old work. Finally, Chapter 7 explores the less impactful but still significant final volumes of Foucault's *The History of Sexuality* series, *The Use of Pleasure* and *The Care of the Self*.

1

THE WILL TO KNOW

QUESTIONING THE REPRESSIVE HYPOTHESIS

The History of Sexuality is not a history of sexuality. Rather, as its French subtitle, *La volonté de savoir*, suggests, it is a history of how we came to want to *know* about sex, or how we came to think that sex was such an important thing *to know about*. Beyond this, the first volume of *The History of Sexuality* is a history of the discourses and practices that we have produced to satiate this desire. *The History of Sexuality* is thus a history of knowledgeable discourses about sex, of the invention of sciences of sex and of how we came to believe that these sciences could tell us not only about a particular activity that we may engage in but, more importantly, about *who* we are and *how* we can be happy.

Foucault states in part IV of volume 1 of *The History of Sexuality* that his 'aim' in writing the series of books was '[t]o transcribe into history the fable of *Les bijoux indiscrets*' (Foucault, 1978, p. 77). *The Indiscreet Jewels* was French philosopher Denis Diderot's first novel, published anonymously in 1748. It tells the story of the sultan Mangogul, who procures a magic ring from a genie. This ring, when turned towards a woman, makes her genitals – or 'jewels', as they are called throughout the novel – speak. What the 'jewels' tell when they speak are the secret truths of that woman's sexual thoughts and experiences. These revelations of female desire reveal a promiscuous, libertine society and wreak havoc on relationships throughout the court; as a result, the women of the court – including Mangogul's favourite – live in fear that it will be their genitals that are compelled to speak next. Foucault's statement thus implies that, through some historical process, we have become subjects whose genitals speak, or who involuntarily tell the truths of our sexual desire.

What, though, is the magical ring that has made our genitals speak? For Foucault, the ring is the belief that we have come to hold that our sexual desires are the truths of our selves, and that knowing the truth of these desires is crucial to our self-understanding and happiness. In a previous work, *The Order of Things*, Foucault charts the emergence of the human sciences, or of how humans became not only the subjects of knowledge but the objects of that knowledge as well (Foucault, 1989a). Ten years later, in the first volume of *The History of Sexuality*, he examines how the key to knowing the human – or the key to the human sciences – came to be sex. As Foucault writes, 'Whenever it is a question of knowing who we are, it is this logic that henceforth serves as our master key... Sex, the explanation for everything' (Foucault, 1978, p. 78).

Who exactly thinks that sex is the explanation for everything? While Foucault is suggesting that this is a belief that pervades the modern West, and the human sciences in particular, his most specific target is psychoanalysis. Psychoanalysis is the science (or pseudo-science) of sex that was most influential in France when Foucault was writing, and he notes near the end of the volume that 'the history of the deployment of sexuality' that he has traced 'can serve as an archaeology of psychoanalysis' (1978, p. 130). Archaeology, for Foucault, is an approach to history that shows the conditions of possibility for the present; it can thus be said that what Foucault wants to explain in *The History of Sexuality* is how we came to be the kinds of subjects that psychoanalysis could explain, or how we became subjects with psyches whose secrets were unlocked by sex. Sigmund Freud had, after all, scan-dalized his contemporaries with his 'pan-sexualism' – his belief that sex was at the root of all psychological ills and psychosomatic illnesses, and that all psychological phenomena could be inter-preted through its lens. For Freud, famously, a pipe was never just a pipe; a pipe necessarily represented a penis, and knowing this truth was necessary to interpret not only our fantasies and dreams but our psyches and selves. Foucault writes:

> We must write the history of this will to truth, this petition to know that for so many centuries has kept us enthralled by sex: the history of a stubborn and relentless effort. What is it that we demand of sex, beyond its possible pleasures, that makes us so persistent? What is this patience or eagerness to constitute it as the secret, the omnipo-tent cause, the hidden meaning, the unremitting fear? And why was the task of discovering this difficult truth finally turned into an invi-tation to eliminate taboos and break free of what binds us? Was the labor then so arduous that it had to be enchanted by this promise? Or had this knowledge become so costly – in political, economic, and ethical terms – that in order to subject everyone to its rule, it was nec-essary to assure them, paradoxically, that their liberation was at stake?
> (Foucault, 1978, pp. 79–80)

The History of Sexuality is thus a history of a desire: the desire not so much to *have* sex as to understand it; and, for contempo-rary Western subjects, Foucault claims, sex is no longer about acts or pleasures so much as it is about desire (1983).

Finally, and most importantly, *The History of Sexuality* is a history of the power effects that these discourses and practices of producing sexual knowledge have had. These power effects are significant; they include the constitution of sexualities, an inva-sive medicalization of human life, a transformation of the institu-tion of the family, new relations towards death, biological racism and modern forms of war. The French subtitle of volume 1 of Foucault's *The History of Sexuality*, *La volonté de savoir* (*The Will to Know*), is intended to call to mind Friedrich Nietzsche's *Will to Power*: as Foucault argues, the will to know about sex is intricately caught up with power relations and their effects.

Perhaps the most pressing philosophical question that Foucault poses in *The History of Sexuality* is this: what must modern power be like to have produced these kinds of relations and effects?

The History of Sexuality is history in the sense of genealogy. For Foucault, following Nietzsche, a genealogy is a counter-history, a refutation of a dominant story that we tell about an institution (such as the prison), a phenomenon (such as madness), a set of beliefs (such as morality) or a practice (such as psychiatry) (Foucault, 1984). A genealogy refutes either teleological histories (such as the 'progress' stories about mental illness and punishment, refuted in Foucault's *History of Madness* and *Discipline and Punish*) or universalizing histories (such as the history of morality, refuted by Nietzsche's *On the Genealogy of Morality*). Genealogies focus on discontinuities, contingencies and power struggles in order to demonstrate that the past was different from the present, the present could have been otherwise and thus the future may also be otherwise. Genealogies are political: they aim to disrupt, to open up spaces for social change.

What, then, is the dominant story about sexuality that Foucault's *The History of Sexuality* is disrupting? What are the current assumptions about sex that his genealogy challenges? Foucault identifies his target at the outset of *The History of Sexuality* as 'the repressive hypothesis'. The 'repressive hypothesis' is the story according to which sex was once free, but 'twilight soon fell upon this bright day' (Foucault, 1978, p. 3), at which point – first with Christianity and then again with Victorianism – sex was repressed, and we are still struggling to free ourselves of this repressive heritage. The repressive hypothesis is *teleological* because it has an idea of the sexually liberated society towards which we are striving: a society of free love in which we can express our sexuality both in acts and words, without the baggage of Christian morality and Victorian prudishness. The sexual liberation movement has embraced this narrative and sees itself struggling to bring back the 'bright day' when, at last, 'sex will be good again' (Foucault, 1978, p. 7). The 'repressive hypothesis' is also a *universalizing* history of sex, since it assumes that repression works on a sexuality that was always already there, that is an innate, primordial and static drive. Both the universalizing view of sex and the teleological view of sexual liberation are called into question by *The History of Sexuality*; for Foucault, sex is a socially constituted phenomenon, thoroughly cultural, contingent and caught up in shifting forms of knowledge/power that the sexual liberation movement has extended rather than escaped.

Who actually upholds the repressive hypothesis? Foucault's most direct target is the Marxist-Freudians, such as the German psychiatrist Wilhelm Reich and social theorist Herbert Marcuse, who are named at a few points in Foucault's introductory volume (1978, p. 131). Reich and Marcuse's writings from the 1920s to the 1950s influenced the counter-cultural class struggles and sexual liberation movements of the 1960s and 1970s, as well as works such as Jos van Ussel's 1970 *History of Sexual Repression* (Reich, 1945; Marcuse, 1955; 1964; van Ussel, 1970).[1] Marxist-Freudians responded critically to volumes such as *Civilization and Its Discontents* (Freud, 1990), in which Freud argues that sexual repression is necessary for civilization. For Freud, most sexual urges are necessarily sublimated into the energy needed for work and progress. Although psychoanalysis could bring sexual repressions to light, its ultimate goal was not to abolish all repressions but to eliminate only a select few, while fortifying the rest. For Freud, analysis should aim not to liberate sexual instincts but to domesticate them (Freud, 1964, p. 227). Marxist-Freudians such as Marcuse disagreed. In *Eros and Civilization* (Marcuse, 1955), Marcuse argues that it was specifically the sexual lives of the working class that were being repressed, so as to be channelled into *alienated* labour. For Marcuse, Freud had failed to think beyond the bourgeois morality of his time, and the role of psychoanalysis should be to help patients overcome sexual repression, to bring about a non-repressed civilization characterized by non-alienated libidinal work and non-repressive sublimation.

While the most direct target of Foucault's argument is the Marxist-Freudians – and he is concerned to refute both Marxist ideas about power and psychoanalytic notions about sex throughout his book – he also thinks that, more generally, almost everyone at this time, even if not a card-carrying Marxist or Freudian, held a certain view of sexual repression. This was the view of the 'sexual liberation movement' of the 1960s and 1970s, and it still holds true today. Although historians of the nineteenth century have refuted this view of Victorian sexuality (Gay, 1984), we continue to think that the Victorian age entailed a new prudishness and that it was only in the late twentieth century that people began to break free of this sexual repressiveness. According to the repressive hypothesis, although the sexual liberation movement is well underway, there is still work to be done: we are still 'other Victorians', inheritors of a sexually repressive legacy.

In case we question whether the repressive hypothesis remains alive and well, we can consider a recent example of the hypothesis in the work of contemporary sexual scientist Leonore Tiefer. Throughout her 2004 book *Sex Is Not a Natural Act*, Tiefer, a sex therapist, insists that sex, frank conversation about sex, sex education and sex research are censored, forbidden, underfunded, treated with moral disapprobation and ridiculed (Tiefer, 2004, pp. xi, xii, xiv, 8, 15, 110). So difficult do we find it to talk about sex in the twenty-first century, Tiefer claims, that half her job is just getting clients to 'talk calmly and frankly about their sex lives' without becoming tongue-tied or giggly (p. xiv). In particular, 'women's sexuality has been repressed, suppressed, and oppressed' (p. 139). Of a forty-five-minute sexological interview, Tiefer writes, '[s]ince this is Nicole's only opportunity (maybe in her whole life) for an extensive sex discussion with a person comfortable talking about sex, the brevity is a tragic tease' (p. 265). So sexually repressed are we, this statement suggests, that the only people 'comfortable talking about sex' are professional sex therapists, and thus the only way we are likely to have a frank conversation about sex in our entire lives is by hiring a medical professional with whom to have it. From these passages we see that Tiefer assumes that there is something – sexuality, and especially women's sexuality – that exists pre-discursively in order to be repressed, censored or silenced. Although she thinks that reading more books about sex and watching more sex videos will help, it seems that the best cure for sexual repression is to speak to a sexual scientist. Thus, having only a forty-five-minute interview with a sexologist in a lifetime is 'tragic'.

Against this view, Foucault wants to point out the irony of the fact that we live in a society in which people such as Tiefer can make a good living and have prestigious careers talking about sex, can spend forty hours a week listening to people talk about sex and yet still claim that we don't talk about sex and that sex talk is undervalued and censored in our society. Indeed, far from being a forbidden activity, speaking about sex has gained a historically unprecedented legitimacy, enough so that it can have been enshrined in academia and made into science. Talking about sex is in fact *so* legitimated today that such talk even has a 'market value':

> Ours is, after all, the only civilization in which officials are paid to listen to all and sundry impart the secrets of their sex: as if the urge to talk about it, and the interest one hopes to arouse by doing so, have far surpassed the possibilities of being heard, so that some individuals have even offered their ears for hire.
>
> (Foucault, 1978, p. 7)

For Foucault, the very existence of psychoanalysis, sexology and sex therapy – or the fact that the act of listening to sexual confessions can have been commodified – indicates not so much that sex is repressed or silenced but that we talk so much about sex that there are not enough people to listen.

In 1929 Virginia Woolf wrote *A Room of One's Own*, in which she anticipates Foucault's argument that, far from sex being silenced in her era (let alone today), there was a proliferation of texts on sexuality in the nineteenth and early twentieth centuries, and of scientific texts in particular (Woolf, 1957). Woolf describes going to the British Museum to do research on the female sex and being astounded by the numbers of books she found. Woolf draws attention to the fact that these books were being written *about* women *by* male scientists. She addresses her female audience by asking:

> Have you any notion how many books are written about women in the course of one year? Have you any notion how many of them were written by men? Are you aware that you are, perhaps, the most discussed animal in the universe? [...] Sex and its nature might well attract doctors and biologists; but what was surprising and difficult

of explanation was the fact that sex – women, that is to say – also attracts agreeable essayists, light-fingered novelists, young men who have taken the M.A. degree; men who have taken no degree; men who have no apparent qualification save that they are not women. Some of these books were, on the face of it, frivolous and facetious; but many, on the other hand, were serious and prophetic, moral and hortatory. Merely to read the titles suggested innumerable schoolmasters, innumerable clergymen mounting their platforms and pulpits and holding forth with a loquacity which far exceeded the hour usually allotted to such discourse on this one subject. It was a most strange phenomenon; and apparently... one confined to the male sex. Women do not write books about men – a fact that I could not help welcoming with relief, for if I had first to read all that men have written about women, then all that women have written about men, the aloe that flowers once in a hundred years would flower twice before I could set pen to paper.

(Woolf, 1957, pp. 26–7)

Woolf points out that professionals and non-professionals alike, so long as they were men, felt authoritatively positioned to produce books about sex in her age, and about the sexuality of the female human in particular. To some degree, simply belonging to the male sex made these authors feel like experts on the female sex. Woolf scoffs at men who did not have a graduate degree who nevertheless felt qualified to write about sex. In this attitude we see that sex has become the proper domain of academics, or that the legitimate discourse on sex in the modern West had become that of science. The reason women were not writing books on sex is that women were rarely academics at this time, as is clear from Woolf's account of being harassed on her way to the library. Today, when women have gained access to the academy, we *are* writing books about sex. Since *A Room of One's Own*, the proliferation of texts on sex has only grown, and Woolf might have been appalled to know that we now have departments of sexology, psychology, women's studies, sexuality studies and gender studies that are largely populated by women, many of whom are writing about sex.

For Foucault, what this indicates is that sex has become some-thing 'to be put into words'. Far from being silent on sex, we talk about it constantly, even if the *way* we talk about it has changed. We now talk about sex in ways that are informed by authoritative dis-courses. Thus, even when we exchange sexual secrets with friends and lovers we take up expert discourses: we engage in analysis and self-analysis; we taxonomize our sexualities, giving ourselves ever more refined sexual labels ('switches', 'power bottoms'); we see sex as a health issue (frequent ejaculations prevent prostate cancer, lack of interest in sex is 'hypoactive sexual desire dysfunction'); we are concerned with what is sexually normal – indeed, this is the *primary* concern that is addressed to sex therapists (see Taylor, 2015); and we talk about sex as if we are describing something important. Speech about sex is understood as a quasi-scientific and confessional revelation of who we are, a way to understand and describe our nature, character and identity.

It is odd, for Foucault, that we believe in the 'repressive hypoth-esis', because it is clear that we live in a society inundated with sexual discourses. Today sex is an omnipresent theme in television, film and advertising; pornography occupies the majority of the internet; sexologists are continually on radio and talk shows; we have sex education for adolescents; we devote courses to sex at uni-versities; and even offer sexuality studies diplomas, certificates and PhDs. Despite all this evidence to the contrary, however, we still frequently hear people talk about sex as if it were repressed. Why would the 'repressive hypothesis' have such staying power even though it is refuted by so much evidence around us? Foucault's response is: 'This discourse on modern sexual repression holds up well, owing no doubt to how easy it is to uphold' (1978, p. 5). This theory is 'easy to uphold' for two reasons.

First, by placing the dawn of sexual repression at the beginning of the seventeenth century, we make sexual repression correspond with the rise of capitalism. It is then easy to argue that the only kind of sex that would be permitted – especially for the prole-tariat – would be the kind that reproduces the labour force. The repressive hypothesis assumes a negative relation between sex and power. Power is thought to forbid sex, to deny the very existence of many kinds of sex, to try not to see it or talk about it, to censor and silence sex. The only kind of sex that is permitted is between heterosexual, married people, and even this should be discreet, utilitarian and (re)productive. These are 'the monotonous nights of the Victorian bourgeoisie' in which there is 'a single locus of sexuality... the parents' bedroom' (Foucault, 1978, p. 3).

This Marxist explanation is *too simplistic* for Foucault. In the 'Periodization' section of part IV of *The History of Sexuality*, Foucault rejects the Marxist interpretation of sexual repression by showing that power is not (only) inflicted from above on those below. On the contrary, 'the working classes managed for a long time to escape the deployment of "sexuality"' (1978, p. 121). In the era that saw the rise of capitalism, the bourgeoisie directed their sexual enquiries and ethics primarily towards themselves rather than the proletariat (pp. 121–4). The bourgeoisie submitted themselves to scientific study, subjected their own wives and children to psychiatric and pedagogical forms of disciplinary power. They did not send their workers to psychiatrists or prevent the proletariat's children from masturbating. As Foucault writes,

> The living conditions that were dealt to the proletariat, particularly in the first half of the nineteenth century, shows that there was anything but concern for its body and sex: it was of little importance whether those people lived or died, since their reproduction was something that took care of itself in any case.
>
> (Foucault, 1978, p. 126)

For Foucault, modern power does not primarily move from above to those below but circulates, and usually it is those who try to wield power who are the first to be submitted to it: the prison warden is himself subjected to intense surveillance, psychoanalysts must undergo extensive analysis, and the clergy who insist that everyone must confess are the very people who are obliged (and tend) to confess most frequently. Similarly, and contra Marcuse, the bourgeois scientists who examine sexuality were affected by the power effects of their studies long before the working classes. Consequently, Foucault writes that 'sexuality is originally, historically bourgeois, and that, in its successive shifts and transpositions, it induces specific class effects' (1978, p. 127).

The second reason that the 'repressive hypothesis' is easy to uphold is that *it is gratifying*. This is what Foucault calls the 'speaker's benefit'. By describing sex as repressed, we make speaking about sex transgressive. A person who speaks about sex feels that

> he upsets established law; he somehow anticipates the coming freedom... [W]e are conscious of defying established power, our tone of voice shows that we know we are being subversive, and we ardently conjure away the present and appeal to the future, whose day will be hastened by the contribution we believe we are making.
>
> (Foucault, 1978, pp. 6–7)

By positing sex as repressed, we derive the benefit of feeling that we are engaged in a serious, therapeutic and emancipatory political task when we talk about sex. Moreover, we get to feel that we are contributing to the generation of knowledge. Just by speaking of sex we are therefore able to believe we are contributing to science, liberating ourselves and our society from an oppressive sexual censorship and paving the way to a happier future. With these three positive ends, talking about sex becomes a laudable activity.

Despite these reasons to be sceptical of the repressive hypothesis, Foucault does not want to deny that there was ever any censorship of sex. It is clear that these forms of repression have existed and continue to exist, and we can point to any number of examples. As Foucault emphatically states:

> Let there be no misunderstanding: I do not claim that sex has not been prohibited or barred or masked or misapprehended since the classical age; nor do I even assert that it has suffered these things any less from that period on than before. I do not maintain that the prohibition of sex is a ruse; but it is a ruse to make prohibition into the basic and constitutive element from which one would be able to write the history of what has been said concerning sex starting from the modern epoch. All these negative elements – defenses, censorships, denials – which the repressive hypothesis groups together in one great

central mechanism destined to say no, are doubtless only component
parts that have a local and tactical role to play in a transformation into
discourse, a technology of power, and a will to knowledge that are far
from being reducible to the former.

(Foucault, 1978, p. 12)

What Foucault wants to argue, in other words, is that, although
we can point to endless instances of sexual censorship and prohibition over the past few centuries, the relationship between sex
and power in this period has been much more complicated and
creative than these instances of prohibition. Moreover, even these
instances of repression have had productive effects. For instance,
although sexually explicit writings and images have often been
censored, history has shown again and again that censorship is the
best advertisement for a product: censorship of sexually explicit
material draws attention to those works that are censored, creating
more curiosity and desire to consume them. Censorship, or repression, does not actually negate desire; on the contrary, it produces
more desire and new forms of desire. The relationship between
sex and power is not *fundamentally* characterized by negation
and silence, therefore; rather, what is remarkable, what we need
to attend to, is the fact that there has been a proliferation of new
practices and discourses about sex, and these discourses have been
constitutive or have had productive effects. Ultimately, Foucault
argues that they have *created* sexualities rather than (or even
while) prohibiting them. Thus, the really interesting questions, for
Foucault, are not 'Why are we repressed?' but, rather: 'Why have
we in fact spoken so much about sex and about sexual repression
in the last few centuries?'; 'Which institutions prompted people to
speak?'; 'How was sex spoken about?'; 'What was said?'; 'What
kind of knowledge was developed about sex?'; and 'What sort of
power effects has this knowledge had?' (Foucault, 1978, pp. 8–9).

Far from sex being taboo, for power to get a hold on sex it
required data, which meant that it required people to speak. The
sciences of sex thus rely on sexual confessions – which, ironically, are exactly what the sexual liberation movement provided.
Misunderstanding the relation between sex and power as repressive, the sexual liberation movement incites us to 'come out of the

closet', to 'break the silence', to tell the secrets of our sex. This has not so much been a resistance to power, however, as an extension of power; Foucault argues that such comings-out-of-closets are exactly what needed to take place for power to take hold of our bodies and the population.

Foucault thus writes that '[o]ne can raise three serious doubts concerning' the repressive hypothesis, including whether it is 'truly an established historical fact', whether repression is really how power functions and, finally,

> Did the critical discourse that addresses itself to repression come to act as a roadblock to a power mechanism that had operated unchallenged up to that point, or is it not in fact part of the same historical network as the thing it denounces (and doubtless misrepresents) by calling it 'repression'?
>
> (Foucault, 1978, p. 10)

Foucault's response to this last doubt is that the discourses that are critical of sexual repression – the sexual liberation movement and Marxist-Freudianism, for instance – did not so much act as an impediment to the power mechanisms that constrain sex as they extended these power mechanisms by providing one more incitement to produce the sexual discourses that power required.

CONFESSION

Although the 'repressive hypothesis' assumes that the two great causes of our supposed sexual silence were Christianity and Victorianism, in fact, for Foucault, the Counter-Reformation and the nineteenth century were remarkable for having produced compulsory technologies of sexual confession (Foucault, 1978, p. 116). In the middle of the sixteenth century, the Council of Trent ordered all Christians to confess to their local parish priest at least once a year. Confession had already been a practice of the Christian Church for centuries, but other than in monasteries it was not practised frequently (Taylor, 2009a, pp. 13–65). When practised at all, it was usually reserved for very serious sins or for a sacrament on one's deathbed. Many Christians would never have confessed at all. The Counter-Reformation Catholic Church mandated annual confession at Lent, but it responded to Reformation critiques of the practice by insisting that priests abstain from using certain words and from enquiring into specific acts and positions. Although we might be inclined to say that there was a sexual censorship here, what this circumspection in language actually enabled was greater numbers of sexual interrogations and confessions. Censorship did not contradict the increase in sexual discourses but, rather, facilitated that increase.

Confession did not begin willingly. The Council of Trent decreed that anyone who did not confess annually be excommunicated. There was mass resistance to this order on the parts of priests, the laity and theologians (Foucault, 2007, p. 194; Taylor, 2009a, pp. 52–5). Nevertheless, over generations and centuries the habit of confession was successfully inculcated in most Christians, to the extent that it became a desire. For Foucault, this is how discipline works: first a practice is forced on you, but if you repeat it enough times it becomes a habit, and eventually a habit becomes a desire. At this point, one ceases to see the practice one desires as an effect of power. Thus, over time, confession came to feel like a psychic need, and confession manuals came to complain of 'scrupulous' penitents who confessed too often, who irritated and exhausted priests because they came every day and could never confess enough (Taylor, 2009a, pp. 55–63).

According to Foucault, an important effect of the Council of Trent was that it shifted 'the most important moment of transgression from the act itself to the stirrings – so difficult to perceive and formulate – of desire' (1978, pp. 19–20). For the Church, it was not just adultery that was a sin but even the glimmer of desire for an adulterous act. Such mental states are often difficult to perceive and formulate. This means two things: first, the analysis of one's mind can be endless; second, we require an expert to help us discover and interpret the truth of our inner states. This role of expert was first fulfilled by priests and later by medical experts such as psychiatrists, psychologists and psychoanalysts. In these ways, sex became something complicated: it was no longer a matter of acts of which the actor was fully aware. Rather, sex came to be about subtle mental temptations that might come from the devil, desires that might be unconscious, or whose causality might have unconscious sources. In each case, a certain expertise in deciphering them was required, placing the sexual subject in the hands of priests and, later, of doctors and therapists.

Although the Catholic Church initially found confession difficult to enforce, once the compulsion to confess was internalized in Western subjects it not only produced scrupulous confessants but also spread to secular domains, such as erotic writings and psychoanalysis. Foucault takes as examples the confessional writings found in *My Secret Life* (anon, 1966) and the works of the Marquis de Sade. Of the author of *My Secret Life*, he writes: 'This nameless Englishman will serve better than his queen as the central figure for a sexuality whose main features were already taking shape with the Christian pastoral' (Foucault, 1978, p. 22). To take a random but typical passage from the thousands of pages of *My Secret Life*, the author writes:

> The next night she met me veiled as before, stripped to her chemise, and seemed to like it. She had fine big breasts, large arms and thighs, and her motte was covered with thick sandy coloured hair, her cunt was fat lipped and I guessed her twenty-eight. – Yes, her exact age, she said. – She didn't much like my looking at her cunt, and refused altogether to turn bum upwards. – She was very poorly dressed, and had common stockings and boots on. – Was she often about here – 'No.' – 'Where then?' 'Nowhere.' 'I'll meet you if you write,' and she told me where to – it was two or three miles off. – I could not make her out but risked a question. 'You're gay [a prostitute]?' 'No,' said she laughing. 'You don't want money then.' 'I shouldn't be here if I didn't,' and still she laughed. – This was after our fuck, and I was lying by her side on the bed.
>
> Whatever she might have met me for, she was determined to have fucking enough, and didn't want to talk. We had been quick about the first spend, – lust allayed, I wanted a look at her cunt. 'No it's nasty.' 'But wash it, I want to look; it's a lovely yellow haired cunt.' 'Yellow haired cunt,' she repeated, laughing as if I had made a good joke.
>
> Altho the same in the essentials, tho the end of it must be the insertion of the prick in the cunt, how varied are the manners and words of different women on the approach to that end. It is that variety which

so charms me. – 'Well – wash it – do.' 'Presently, you'll do it again to me soon, I'll wash after.' – And putting her mouth to mine, she put out her tongue, and clutched my prick with vivacity, and evident intention to make me stroke her again, as soon as she could. She was one of those who do not rely on words to excite a man, but did it by kissing, tonguing and squeezing my prick and handling my balls, and soon was successful. She had put a towel under her backside at the first fuck, but I had not spent as much as on the night previously, when my spermatic accumulators were full. After fucking her a third time we parted, but not till I had a better look at her cunt, and found the lip lining and clitoris pink rather than red, which I don't recollect having seen in the cunt of a woman of her age and size before.

(anon, 1966, p. 1045)

For Foucault, the author of this autobiographically pornographic work, offered up as a quasi-scientific contribution to human knowledge, supplants Queen Victoria as exemplary of the modern age. We are not so much 'other Victorians' as we are beings who compulsively turn sex into discourse, who see sex as *the secret* that, ironically, can never be spoken of enough.

One explanation for the spread of sexual confession from a religious to a secular practice is that, once Western subjects had internalized the habit of confession, they would feel a need to create new outlets for this habit as the Church became less central to their lives (Berggren, 1975, pp. 8–9). Foucault argues, however, that the secularization of confession also occurred because of the creation of new technologies to elicit confessions outside the Church. These arose as a result of the vested interests that scientists and the state came to have in hearing people speak about sex. Foucault writes: 'Toward the beginning of the eighteenth century there emerged a political, economic, and technical incitement to talk about sex' (1978, p. 23). Sex became 'in the nature of a public potential; it called for management procedures' (p. 24). For the first time, states needed to know how many children were being born within their borders, and in what contexts. How many are legitimate and how many are illegitimate? Who is raising them? Are people using birth control? How many people are having non-reproductive sex or are in non-reproductive relationships? At what age are people having children? What groups of people are having the most children? How many children are people having on average? How much perversion is there in the country? Is the population degenerating, decadent or in decline? All this was necessary to forecast labour and military power, or was caught up with political and economic concerns. The result of these concerns was a new fervour to gather information about sex. For the first time, demographers were sent out to ask people about their sexual practices, and statistics were generated.

Beyond these demographic enquiries, sexual confessions were elicited by scientists, by doctors and by lawyers and judges. In all these cases sex was presented as dangerous, and this was purportedly why experts needed to know about it. Much as the Church had used the sinfulness of sex – or the dangerousness of sex to one's immortal soul – so nineteenth-century doctors used the dangerousness of sex to health and the population as an excuse to enquire into it. Sex could endanger individuals in the form of diseases and unwanted pregnancies, and it could endanger populations should the wrong people reproduce. If sex was not monitored, the wrong kinds of genes could swamp the nation, resulting in a degenerate population. For all these reasons, doctors felt they were justified to ask about sex so that they or others could intervene for the good of the individual and society. Just as Christians in the sixteenth century initially resisted the order to confess to priests, however, so Foucault observes that patients were at first wary of the obligation to confess their sexual lives to doctors. While we have today become used to doctors questioning us about our sexuality, nineteenth-century patients, for whom sex was not yet positioned in the domain of health, would not have immediately seen why such intrusive enquiries were justified. Foucault describes five methods that doctors developed to quell these suspicions.

First, doctors employed a 'clinical codification of the inducement to speak' (Foucault, 1978, p. 65). This is similar to the 'neutralization' of language in the Catholic confessional after Reformation critiques, and in the sexual education courses of which Foucault writes (pp. 28–9). Against allegations of sexual curiosity, priests were instructed to keep their interrogations into the sexual lives of confessants vague and couched in codified language. Similarly, patients were reassured that the questions of doctors were professional and of scientific interest by their use of technical terminology. Something akin to this also occurred in education, when the use of clinical language allowed sex to become a pedagogical domain – 'sex education' – while remaining in the bounds of professional propriety.

Second, and perhaps most importantly, medical interrogations into patients' sex lives were justified through 'the postulate of a general and diffuse causality' (1978, p. 65). As Foucault writes, 'Having to tell everything, being able to pose questions about everything, found their justification in the principle that endowed sex with an inexhaustible and polymorphous causal power' (p. 65). A striking example of such diffuse causal power being attributed to sexual acts is the case of masturbation. Well into the twentieth century, parents and children were instructed by doctors that masturbation could cause paleness, sweating, trembling, bags under the eyes, difficulties in concentration and troubles in equilibrium, and eventually led to the softening of the brain, lesions to the bone marrow, epileptic fits, loss of consciousness, insanity and premature death (Bergman, 1987). As will be discussed in Chapter 3, sexual scientists also warned parents that masturbation could result in homosexuality (Krafft-Ebing, 1894, p. 188). As a sin of youth, masturbation threatened to undermine the entire fabric of society, or was a serious threat to the population. Private sexual acts such as masturbation thus took on enormous proportions in the modern imaginary. The positing of such dramatic dangers to a child's health and to the nation's future justified a doctor questioning a child about his masturbatory habits, just as, centuries earlier, the understanding of masturbation as a mortal sin permitted intrusive soliciting of sexual confessions from adolescents on the part of priests. As Foucault writes,

> Educators and doctors combatted children's onanism like an epidemic that needed to be eradicated. What this actually entailed, throughout this whole secular campaign that mobilized the adult world around the sex of children, was using these tenuous pleasures as a prop, constituting them as secrets (that is, forcing them into hiding so as to make

possible their discovery), tracing them back to their source, tracking them from their origins to their effects, searching out everything that might cause them or simply enable them to exist. Wherever there was a chance they might appear, devices of surveillance were installed; traps were laid for compelling admissions; inexhaustible and corrective discourses were imposed; parents and teachers were alerted... they were kept in readiness in the face of this recurrent danger; their conduct was prescribed and their pedagogy recodified; an entire medico-sexual regime took hold of the family milieu.

(Foucault, 1978, p. 42)

It was '[t]he limitless dangers that sex carried with it [that] justified the exhaustive character of the inquisition to which it was subjected' (Foucault, 1978, p. 66).

Dangers were falsely attributed to a wide variety of other sexual activities, and also to bodily functions such as menstruation (Laqueur, 1990, p. 218). Menstruation was described by nineteenth-century doctors as both physically devastating, 'leaving behind a ragged wreck of tissue, torn glands, ruptured vessels, jagged edges of stroma, and masses of blood corpuscles, which it would hardly seem possible to heal satisfactorily without the aid of surgical treatment' (Laqueur, 1990, p. 221), despite women's claims to the contrary. Menstruation was also described by doctors as psychologically traumatizing, and was regularly compared to heat in non-human animals. Menstruation was thus seen as debilitating to women's moral and mental faculties, and hence dangerous to both the individual menstruator and society. While we might be tempted to read this medical hysteria around menstruation, like the medical combat against childhood masturbation, as repressive, what Foucault thinks we should attend to is the considerable production of discourse around sex that these phenomena necessitated and allowed, and the novel kinds of power relations that these discourses made possible: these include a medical infiltration of the school and the family and the medicalization of children's and women's bodies. Today we realize that nineteenth-century doctors were mistaken about the debilitating effects they attributed to many sex acts and reproductive functions, but by now we are so used to intimate confessions being required of us that we give them willingly, and the postulate of a 'general and diffuse causality' has done its work.

The third justification for inquisitiveness on the part of nineteenth-century doctors was 'the principle of a latency intrinsic to sexuality' (Foucault, 1978, p. 66). This was seen, for instance, in the relegation of sexual impulses to the unconscious by Freud. Similarly, the fourth reason Victorian doctors had to extract sexual confessions was that sexuality was now known to be extremely complex, and to require experts to interpret it. We see both the new complicatedness of sexuality and its latency in Freud's 'The psychogenesis of a case of homosexuality in a woman' (Freud, 2001). Here, he accounts for an eighteen-year-old woman's romantic love for another woman as follows:

> It was just when the girl was experiencing the revival of her infantile Oedipus complex at puberty that she suffered her great disappointment. She became keenly conscious of the wish to have a child, and a male one; that what she desired was her *father's* child and an image of *him*, her consciousness was not allowed to know. And what happened next? It was not *she* who bore the child, but her unconsciously hated rival, her mother. Furiously resentful and embittered, she turned away from her father and from men altogether. After this first great reversal she forswore her womanhood and sought another goal for her libido... the search for a substitute mother to whom she could become passionately attached.
>
> (Freud, 2001, pp. 157–8, italics in original, emphasis added by author)

As Freud makes clear, this patient was not conscious of either her desire for her father's child or of her matricidal hatred, and nor did she realize that she was seeking a mother figure in her romantic relationships. For Freud, sex was not only dangerous but required medical expertise to be understood: if there was any hope of homosexuals such as this one being 'cured', doctors were required to extract sexual confessions and to intervene on the basis of these speech acts.

Finally, having doctors listen to sexual confessions was scientifically justified 'through the medicalization of the effects of confession' (Foucault, 1978, p. 67). Patients came to believe that just talking about sex with an expert could be therapeutic not only for their sexual problems but for all the other problems to which sex was tenuously linked as well. This is an assumption that Freud and Joseph Breuer would elaborate when they wrote about the 'talking cure' in their *Studies on Hysteria* (Freud and Breuer, 1978). In this early work, Freud and Breuer claim that the act of patients confessing to them led to them being cured of their psychological and hysterically physiological ailments: confession served as 'chimney sweeping', and the psyche was clean afterwards. Freud quickly rejected the notion of confession as magically cathartic, however, and realized that talking could repeat rather than heal trauma within a relation of transference (Freud, 1964). The transference relation, and not mere confession, was also the means through which healing could occur. Despite Freud's later and more nuanced view, it is the early and immature psychoanalytic notion of a 'talking cure' that has remained influential in popular psychology: we believe that speaking is therapeutic and silence always indicates oppression. The popularization of the notion of a 'talking cure' is an enormous incitement to confessional discourse today, even though it was almost immediately rejected within psychoanalytic theory itself.

As a result of these incitements, Foucault writes that there has been a 'radiation' of discourses about sex throughout society. The effects of these radiating discourses are a medicalization of sex and a society convinced of the importance and dangers of sex, vigilant in the need to talk about sex and to report anything abnormal to authorities. As a result, Foucault describes the modern Western subject as a 'confessing animal' (*bête d'aveu*) (1978, p. 80). Significantly, Foucault uses the word *bête* rather than *animal* in this phrase. *Bête* can be translated as 'beast', and indicates stupidity, mistakes and foolishness, as in the expression *faire une bêtise* ('to make a mistake', 'to mess up'). Foucault's use of the term *bête* thus suggests a greater lack of agency than if he had written *animal*: while *animal politique* is the translation of Aristotle's 'political animal', a *bête politique* is someone who compulsively follows politics. Likewise, we might say that, while an *animal d'aveu* is an animal whose *telos* or flourishing involves confession, a *bête d'aveu* is a creature who confesses compulsively, foolishly, in error or without agency.

This transformation of the Western subject into a *bête d'aveu* has meant not only a change in how we talk to doctors and lovers but transformations in literature, politics, philosophy and, ultimately, human subjectivity. Modern human beings have invented confessional genres; we are prolific writers of autobiographies, memoirs, diaries and letters; we are increasingly habituated to the confessions of politicians and other public figures; we are consumers and producers of reality television, confessional talk shows, social networking and blogs; we photograph, video, post to Facebook, tweet, text and Instagram every thought and activity of our day. This compulsive self-reporting has entailed a drastic and 'voluntary' increase in how easily we may be monitored by our partners, lovers, family members, peers, employers and the state, and thus a decrease in freedom, a tightening of nets of control. At the same time, philosophers have turned inwards to find the truth: we have ceased to seek answers about the cosmos, God, space and time, and instead seek the truths of our selves – indeed arguing, in the Kantian and phenomenological traditions, that these are the only kinds of truths that we *can* find. In the seventeenth century, René Descartes sat by the fire in his dressing gown and meditated on the contents of his own mind to draw conclusions about God and knowledge. Some 130 years later, Jean-Jacques Rousseau would write his *Confessions* (Rousseau, 1953), and these begin with an exploration of his sexual masochism. As Foucault argues, and as Rousseau's *Confessions* illustrate, sex is not what we are secretive about; on the contrary, sex is what we confess.

THE SOCIAL CONSTRUCTION OF SEXUALITIES

Foucault gives an example of compulsory medical confession and its power effects in what has proved to be a highly controversial discussion of Charles Jouy (1978, pp. 31–2). As Foucault describes the situation, Jouy was a cognitively disabled (or 'somewhat simple-minded') peasant, living in Lapcourt, France, in the middle of the nineteenth century, who did odd jobs for scant pay and slept in barns. Because he was poor and homeless, Jouy could not afford a wife or court a woman his own age. It was due to this context, for Foucault, that, '[a]t the border of a field, he had obtained a few caresses from a little girl' (p. 31). Infamously, Foucault makes light of this incident of adult–child sex, emphasizing that such events were common in village life, that Jouy had done this before and seen it done by others, and that such exchanges were a 'familiar game' for 'village urchins'. While the repercussions of these events were, by twentieth- and twenty-first-century standards, not entirely surprising, Foucault emphasizes that they were extraordinary in their historical context: Jouy was reported to the village mayor by the girl's parents, the mayor had him arrested by the police, who turned over to psychiatrists. These psychiatrists subjected Jouy to examinations and deemed him a danger to society. As a result, Jouy spent the rest of his life in a psychiatric asylum, where he underwent extensive medical evaluations. Foucault notes that, in a period when children would have been instructed for the first time in history to not speak about sex, Jouy was obliged to confess his sexual desires at length to doctors, who published medical studies on his case. For Foucault, Jouy was a victim of a new, scientific will to know about sex, and his life was sacrificed to this will. While many contemporary readers are likely to understand Jouy as a child molester, paedophile or sex offender, and thus to deem his arrest, psychiatric evaluation and detention by doctors who judged him likely to reoffend to be legitimate juridico-medical responses to a serious situation, Foucault expresses disgust at 'the pettiness of it all'. For Foucault, it was outrageous that a man should have lost his freedom for what were, in his mind, 'inconsequential bucolic pleasures' (*ces infimes délectations buissonnières*) (Foucault, 1978, p. 31; 1976, p. 44). The word that is translated as 'inconsequential' in this passage, *infimes*, could also be translated as 'tiny', 'minuscule' or 'unimportant'. Foucault's trivialization of – or outright disbelief in – the harms of child–adult sex could not be clearer.

In *Abnormal,* the volume of lectures from the Collège de France that he was giving at the same time that he wrote *The History of Sexuality*, Foucault describes the Jouy case in greater detail (Foucault, 2003a, pp. 292–303). Here we learn that Jouy was an illegitimate child and orphaned young. He was forty years old at the time of the events and had received little education. He had survived as best he could by doing the worst kinds of

work in the village for the least pay, but was friendless and marginalized in village life and often drunk. As Foucault notes, Jouy earned
only a quarter of what agricultural workers earned in this period,
and so would have been poor indeed. We also learn more in this
lecture about the nature of the events that Foucault briefly glosses as
'a few caresses' in *The History of Sexuality*. In fact, the girl, whose
name was Sophie Adam, had masturbated Jouy on two occasions in
the presence of another girl. This was followed by a third incident, in
which, at the side of a country road, the sexual interaction between
Jouy and the 11-year-old girl escalated to what would today be considered sexual assault, given the ages of those involved, although the
contemporary medical report describes Jouy as 'gentle' and Adam
as 'consenting' (Bonnet and Bulard, 1868; Rehn-DeBraal, 2013).
After this last event, Jouy gave Adam some coins. Foucault expresses
no disapprobation of Jouy for what contemporary readers are likely
to see as the assault of Sophie Adam, and, indeed, he consistently
belittles and doubts that a rape occurred, writing of 'almost rape,
perhaps', and joking that maybe it was the young girl who dragged
the adult man into the ditch. Astonishingly, although perhaps referring to the peasant's poverty, Foucault describes Jouy's act of giving
Adam some coins after 'almost raping' her as 'very decent' (2003a,
p. 292). Foucault tells us that Adam went to a fair after she left Jouy
and spent the coins on almonds, and he takes this to indicate that
she was not bothered by what had occurred and that adults made
too much commotion about it. Foucault explains that Adam did not
tell her parents about (what would now be considered) the assault
for fear of getting 'slapped', but her mother guessed what had happened some days later when she found stains on her daughter's laun-
dry. Presumably these stains were either semen or blood, or both. As
in *The History of Sexuality*, Foucault is at pains to trivialize what
happened to Sophie Adam in his *Abnormal* course lecture, speaking, for instance, of 'an everyday offense' (2003a, p. 293). Beyond
joking that it may have been the girl who raped the forty-year-old
man, Foucault writes: 'The young girl more or less lets it happen;
she seems to receive a few *sous* quite naturally and runs to the fair
to buy some roasted almonds' (p. 292). The fact that the girl had
had prior sexual experiences and takes the money – or was not what
feminists have called an 'ideal victim' – appears to invalidate the

seriousness or factuality of rape or adult-child sex for Foucault, in a way that is all too familiar to feminist readers.[2]

What is important about this case, for Foucault, is not what happened to Sophie Adam but that it demonstrates the emergence of a new form of power that is vested in regulating sex, and the consequences this would have for 'abnormal' subjects such as Charles Jouy. While Adam expected to be beaten if her parents found out about her sexual interactions with Jouy, the case reveals that the form of power that would have spelled corporeal punishment such as this for Adam – a form of power that will be described in later chapters as 'sovereign power' – had already been supplanted by a new form of power, 'disciplinary power', and this would mean far graver consequences than a few blows to a girl's body (Foucault, 2003a, pp. 295–6). Disciplinary power would entail the taxonomization and pathologization of sexual deviances that had formerly been tolerated, and would have far-reaching, constitutive effects: it would produce individuals with 'sexualities' and a eugenic, sexually confessional society.

Not surprisingly – and whether or not they appreciate the larger objectives of Foucault's studies in question – feminist philosophers have extensively criticized these sections of *The History of Sexuality* and *Abnormal* (Plaza, 1978; Woodhull, 1988; Hengehold, 1994; Alcoff, 1996; Cahill, 2000; Sawicki, 2005; Taylor, 2009b; Ball, 2013; Rehn-DeBraal, 2013). They have, for instance, objected to Foucault's use of euphemisms to describe what they view as sexual assault, as when he writes of an adult 'obtaining a few caresses from a little girl', and 'these timeless gestures, these barely furtive pleasures between simple-minded adults and alert children'. They have criticized Foucault's use of the term 'alert' to describe Sophie Adam, which seems to responsibilize the child for her rape. They have been angered by Foucault's trivializing of the rape as 'inconsequential' and 'bucolic', and by his description of it as 'pleasure between' an adult and child, rather than the pleasure of an adult taken at the expense of a child. Feminists have also criticized Foucault for his exclusive concern for the adult man in this case, and his lack of sympathy for the little girl. Feminist sympathies have tended to focus on Sophie Adam, with little to spare for the orphaned, homeless and marginalized Jouy. Nonetheless, a recent article by feminist disability studies scholar Shelley Tremain has urged feminist readers to consider the Jouy case from a critical disability studies perspective; doing so allows us to return to the situation of the cognitively disabled peasant with concern for his plight as well as that of Adam (Tremain, 2013).

Granting the problematic nature of Foucault's discussion of the case, it is nevertheless true that we can witness a significant historical shift in the history of sexuality in the case of Charles Jouy. Foucault is correct that events such as the rape of Sophie Adam had occurred regularly throughout history, and no one had paid much attention to these incidents previously (Vigarello, 1998; Ruggiero, 1980; 1995). In the middle of the nineteenth century, however, Jouy was not only apprehended by the police for his act but, significantly, he was handed over to doctors. These doctors subjected Jouy to medical tests, wrote a detailed report on his case and incarcerated him for the rest of his life. Jouy's sexual acts were not interpreted as arising from his situation – that he was impoverished and thus could not find a sexual partner of his own age – but as an expression of his essential being. Although, as Tremain has noted, the term 'paedophile' would not be invented for a few more years, Jouy was deemed by doctors to be sexually dangerous, and thus it was decided that he could never be released from hospital, even though, as a diagnosed 'idiot', he was technically innocent. According to his doctors, Jouy was innately disposed to predate sexually on children, since his intelligence level was that of a child even while his sexual development was that of a man.

With respect to cases such as Jouy's, Foucault argues that nineteenth-century psychiatry was not so much about repressing perversions as 'implanting' and 'incorporating' them into individuals. Even if scientists spoke of these perversions with disapprobation and disdain, their objective was not so much prohibition as understanding: they wanted to categorize perversions, to know what gave rise to them and what their characteristics were. In this taxonomical fervour, 'to marry a close relative or practice sodomy, to seduce a nun or engage in sadism, to deceive one's wife or violate cadavers, became things that were essentially different' (Foucault, 1978, p. 39). Although these acts were not novel, what was new to the nineteenth century was the interpretation of these acts as revelatory of identities. As Foucault writes:

It is possible that the West has not been capable of inventing any new pleasures, and it has doubtless not discovered any original vices. But it has defined new rules for the game of powers and pleasures. The frozen countenance of the perversions is a fixture of this game.

(Foucault, 1978, p. 48)

Previously, Foucault argues, the perpetrator of a forbidden act 'was nothing more than the juridical subject of them' (p. 43). In contrast, taking the example of homosexuality, Foucault writes:

The nineteenth-century homosexual became a personage, a past, a case history, and a childhood, in addition to being a type of life, a life form, and a morphology with an indiscreet anatomy and possibly a mysterious physiology. Nothing that went into his total composition was unaffected by his sexuality. It was everywhere present in him at the root of all his actions because it was their insidious and indefinitely active principle; written immodestly on his face and body because it was a secret that always gave itself away. It was consubstantial with him, less as a habitual sin than as a singular nature.

(Foucault, 1978, p. 43)

Foucault notes that (what we now call) 'homosexuality' in this period was 'characterized... less by a type of sexual relation than by a certain quality of sexual sensibility, a certain way of inverting the masculine and the feminine in oneself' (p. 43). Homosexuality – like other sexualities – was not so much about what sexual actions individuals had performed as it was about the kind of being that they were, and this being was defined by their desires. As a result, in one of Foucault's most famous phrases, '[t]he sodomite had been a temporary aberration; the homosexual was now a species' (p. 43).

THE PERVERSE IMPLANTATION

How does the perverse implantation occur? It is one thing to note that scientists labelled individuals according to their so-called perversions in the nineteenth century, but how did those individuals incorporate those labels as who they were? Why did we submit to medical power such that we have long since accepted the view that we *have* sexualities, and that these sexualities *characterize* us in significant ways? One explanation is that, if a person is spoken about in a certain way and made to speak about herself in that way, she will eventually come to see herself that way, at which point she will act according to how she has come to see herself. If a child is continually told that she is 'no good', she will eventually *believe* she is 'no good' and then she will probably act in ways that confirm this judgement. We can see this both as a submission to power – she submits to being what she is told that she is – and as an unintentional resistance to power: the child is being chastised as 'no good' in order to make her behave better, and yet the end result is more bad behaviour on her part.

This process of internalizing what we are told we are is particularly predictable when it is people in positions of authority who label us, and scientists and doctors are the authorities par excellence of our time. Indeed, Foucault argues in his *History of Madness* that madness was vanquished because the mad respected the authority of doctors and thus accepted the doctors' view that they were mentally ill (Foucault, 2006a). In this way, former madmen became so mentally enchained by psychiatry that they could be released from their physical chains within psychiatric asylums and, eventually, from the asylums themselves. We become chained to what doctors say about us because we give their discourses authority. While Foucault's focus in *The History of Sexuality* is the implantation by medicine of sexual identities, Foucauldian scholars such as Ian Hacking have discussed the ways that other medical and pathologizing labels – such as those of mental illness – have been implanted in individuals and internalized by them as identities (Hacking, 1995a; 2002). We believe what doctors say about us and accept the labels they give us because they have medical licences and educations, though Foucault's claim is consistently that what psychiatrists are doing has nothing to do with medicine and does not draw on a medical education at all (Foucault, 1988a; 1988b; 2003a; 2006a; 2006b). Psychiatry, for Foucault, has always been social hygiene, and has always had more to do with morality and social norms than science.

Another reason, according to Foucault, that subjects internalize the labels that are assigned to them is that this very categorization of sexualities has become an erotic act; although he contrasts the *scientia sexualis* of the West with the *ars erotica* of the East, he also argues that the sexual sciences have made confession into an erotic art of their own (Foucault, 1978, pp. 57–8, 71–2). What this means is that the acts of sexual labelling and self-labelling – and hence the interactions between doctors and patients, confessors and confessants – have been eroticized. As Foucault writes:

> [T]his form of power demanded constant, attentive, and curious presences for its exercise; it presupposed proximities; it proceeded through examination and insistent observation; it required an exchange of discourses, through questions that extorted admissions, and confidences that went beyond the questions that were asked. It implied a physical proximity and an interplay of intense sensations. The medicalization of the sexually peculiar was both the effect and the instrument of this... The power which thus took charge of sexuality set about contacting bodies, caressing them with its eyes, intensifying areas, electrifying surfaces, dramatizing troubled moments. It wrapped the sexual body in its embrace.
>
> (Foucault, 1978, p. 44)

Foucault describes the new role of medicine in eliciting sexual confessions in consistently sexual language. Medicine enquires into people's intimate lives, into the secrets of their bodies and souls, and as a result medicine becomes sex, doctors take on erotic roles. Priests, teachers and psychiatrists, like doctors, have been similarly eroticized as a result of their roles in eliciting sexual confessions and the prohibition on sexual relations with them. Foucault writes:

> There was undoubtedly an increase in effectiveness and an extension of the domain controlled; but also a sensualization of power and a gain of pleasure... Pleasure spread to the power that harried it; power anchored the pleasure it uncovered... The medical examination, the psychiatric investigation, the pedagogical report, and family controls may have the over-all and apparent objective of saying no to all wayward or unproductive sexualities, but the fact is that they function as mechanisms with a double impetus: pleasure and power. The pleasure that comes of exercising a power that questions, monitors, watches, spies, searches out, palpates, brings to light; and on the other the pleasure that kindles at having to evade this power, flee from it, fool it, or travesty it... Power asserting itself in the pleasure of showing off, scandalizing, or resisting. Capture and seduction. Confrontation and mutual reinforcement, parents and children, adults and adolescents, educator and students, doctors and patients, the psychiatrist and his hysteric... all have played this game continually since the nineteenth century. These attractions, these evasions, these circular incitements have traced around bodies and sexes, not boundaries not to be crossed, but perpetual spirals of power and pleasure.
>
> (Foucault, 1978, pp. 44–5)

We see the sexualization of confession in James Joyce's *Portrait of an Artist as a Young Man*. Here, Joyce's autobiographical character, Stephen Dedalus, is tempted to become a priest because of the sexual allure of the confessional:

> He would know obscure things, hidden from others, from those who were conceived and born children of wrath. He would know the sins, the sinful longings and sinful thoughts and sinful acts, of others, hearing them murmured into his ears in the confessional under the shame of a darkened chapel by the lips of women and of girls... He would hold his secret knowledge and secret power, being as sinless as the innocent.
>
> (Joyce, cited in Brooks, 2000, p. 88)

Dedalus is drawn to the intense sexuality that hearing confessions endows on the priesthood, despite its vow of chastity. As confessors,

celibate priests are sexualized rather than asexual figures. We may say
something similar about doctors and psychiatrists, who are also 'off
limits' to their patients sexually. As these examples suggest, sexual
confessions are pleasurable; they are sex acts in themselves. Often they
are foreplay, and often they are seductions. We then believe in the
tales we tell, and tell them again, because we are erotically invested in
them. Foucault thus writes: 'The growth of perversions is not a moralizing theme that obsessed the scrupulous minds of the Victorians. It
is the real product of the encroachment of a type of power on bodies
and their pleasures' (1978, p. 48). What this means is that perversions
are not resistances to power but the effects of power.

Importantly, the perverse implantation also functioned
because of what Foucault describes in volume 1 of *The History of
Sexuality* as the production of a 'reverse discourse'. As he writes:

> There is no question that the appearance in nineteenth-century psy-
> chiatry, jurisprudence, and literature of a whole series of discourses
> on the species and subspecies of homosexuality, inversion, peder-
> asty, and 'psychic hermaphrodism' made possible a strong advance
> of social controls into this area of 'perversity'; but it also made pos-
> sible the formation of a 'reverse' discourse: homosexuality began to
> speak in its own behalf, to demand that its legitimacy or 'naturality' be
> acknowledged, often in the same vocabulary, using the same catego-
> ries by which it was medically disqualified.
>
> (Foucault, 1978, p. 101)

In other words, accepting and internalizing the labels ascribed
to them by doctors allowed individuals to resist some of the
claims that doctors were making about them and the social and
legal effects that these claims had. For example, individuals might
accept that they were indeed 'homosexuals', and that much of
what doctors said about 'homosexuals' was true, precisely in order
to be in a position to resist the pathologization and criminalization of people given this label. Accepting 'homosexual' as an
identity category allowed people with this label to form a sense
of group identity or solidarity, and this in turn allowed people
to speak authoritatively from the position of their sexual identity in order to resist some aspects of what doctors were saying

about them. Accepting the labels originally coined by doctors also allowed the formation of communities, meeting places and resistance movements for people who congregated around these labels. As Tamsin Spargo writes,

> It is possible to see in this model of reverse discourse the germ of identity politics. Those who were produced as deviant subjects, 'homosexuals,' may find a common cause, a common dissenting voice that turns confession to profession. The discourse of sexology, for example, produced the identity category of the 'invert' as an aberration from the norm, but it might also enable that individual to question his or her social and political position. It provided a vocabulary and knowledge which could be strategically used by its subjects. As recent work has revealed, there were a number of explicit attempts to redeploy the knowledge and rhetoric of inversion and of homosexuality to appeal for decriminalization in the late 19th century.
>
> (Spargo, 1999, p. 22)

It is in fact questionable whether same-sex sexual and romantic relations could ever have become as socially accepted as they are today if the label 'homosexual' – originally intended to repress that form of sexuality – had not been implanted in, internalized by and redeployed by those so labelled. While 'reverse discourses' allow subjects to resist some aspects of the original discourses that categorize and describe them, it is important to recognize that they do so only by conceding to these discourses to a great extent. A 'reverse discourse' does not set one apart from power or overthrow power, but it does negotiate and resist power.

Needless to say, the 'perverse implantation' and such 'reverse discourses' as those of gay liberation and pride were *not* what was intended by sexual scientists when they diagnosed individuals as, for instance, 'homosexuals'. Scientists had a will to *know* about sex, to taxonomize sexual perversions and perhaps to 'cure' them. Their wish was never to *produce* perversions, however, and to *incorporate* these products into patients, let alone for those 'perverts' to redeploy the discourses of science for their own, emancipatory political ends. These unintended effects of the interpenetration of pleasure and power illustrate two points that Foucault makes in volume 1 of *The History of Sexuality*: resistance follows from power, and power is always in excess of the intentions of those who try to wield it. The following chapter provides a detailed discussion of Foucault's study of power in this volume.

NOTES

1 Foucault references van Ussel's Marcuse-inspired work when discussing the theory of sexual repression in his 5 March 1975 lecture, published in *Abnormal: Lectures at the Collège de France 1974–1975*: Foucault (2003a, p. 236).

2 Foucault engages in what feminists have described as 'victim blaming' or 'slut shaming'. This victim-blaming logic has been observed frequently in rape trials, when a woman's sexual history is used to deny that a rape occurred or to blame the woman for her own rape. See Larcombe (2002).

SUGGESTIONS FOR FURTHER READING

Falzon, Chris, Timothy O'Leary and Jana Sawicki (eds.). 2013. *A Companion to Foucault*. Malden, MA: Blackwell.

Hacking, Ian. 2000. *The Social Construction of What?* Cambridge, MA: Harvard University Press.

Lawlor, Len, and John Nale. 2014. *The Cambridge Foucault Lexicon*. New York: Cambridge University Press.

Oksala, Johanna. 2007. *How to Read Foucault*. New York: Norton.

Taylor, Dianna (ed.). 2011. *Foucault: Key Concepts*. Durham: Acumen.

2

POWER OVER LIFE

OBJECTIVE: REGICIDE

In volume 1 of *The History of Sexuality* and in his course lectures from the same period, Foucault traces the shift from what he alternately calls 'juridico-legal' or 'sovereign' power to two typically modern forms of power – discipline (which he described in his previous book, *Discipline and Punish*) and biopolitics – as a shift from a right of death to a power over life. As he writes: '[I]n the classical theory of sovereignty, the right of life and death was one of sovereignty's basic attributes... The right of sovereignty was the right to take life or let live. And then this new right is established: the right to make live and to let die' (Foucault, 2003b, pp. 240–1). Sovereign power is a power that deduces. It is the right to take away not only life but wealth, services, labour and products. As Foucault writes:

> The sovereign exercised his right of life only by exercising his right to kill, or by refraining from killing; he evidenced his power over life only through the death he was capable of requiring. The right which was

> formulated as the 'power of life and death' was in reality the right to *take* life or *let* live. Its symbol, after all, was the sword.
>
> (Foucault, 1978, p. 136, emphasis in original)

Sovereign power's only power over life is to seize that life, to end, impoverish or enslave it; what it does not seize it leaves alone.

The seventeenth-century English political philosopher Thomas Hobbes illustrates Foucault's points, writing in the *Leviathan*:

> For seeing there is no Common-wealth in the world, wherein there be Rules enough set down, for the regulating of all the actions, and words of men, (as being a thing impossible:) it followeth necessarily, that in all kinds of actions, by the laws praetermitted, men have the Liberty, of doing what their own reasons shall suggest, for the most profitable to themselves.
>
> (Hobbes, 1981, p. 264)

As this quotation shows, Hobbes envisages power only in the form of rules or laws laid down by the sovereign. Moreover, he believes that any aspect of life that is not restricted by such rules or laws is, by definition, free. Finally, Hobbes believes that, since there could *never* be enough laws to regulate *all* our actions, it follows that at least *some* actions are always free or that all subjects are free to some extent. Hobbes thus argues that, so far as 'corporall Liberty' is concerned, subjects of any commonwealth are free: 'For if wee take Liberty in the proper sense, for corporall Liberty; that is to say, freedome from chains, and prison, it were very absurd for men to clamor as they doe, for the Liberty they so manifestly enjoy' (p. 264). Hobbes goes on to note that it would be ludicrous for a sovereign to regulate (or lay down laws regarding) the corporeal dimensions of a subject's existence, and hence no covenant with the sovereign could be concerned with these aspects of a subject's life. For Hobbes, it would be *absurd* to imagine certain mundane aspects of life, such as liberty over one's body and private life, being the subject of such laws or covenants. Hobbes cannot *imagine* these aspects of life being of interest to the king or to the commonwealth, or extra-legal mechanisms of power that might function at their level. He elaborates:

> The Liberty of a Subject, lyeth therefore only in those things, which in regulating their actions, the Soveraign hath praetermitted: such as is the Liberty to buy, and sell, and otherwise contract with one another; to choose their own aboad, their own diet, their own trade of life, and institute their children as they themselves think fit: & the like.
>
> (Hobbes, 1981, p. 264)

For Hobbes, 'Lawes are of no power... [w]ithout a Sword in the hands of a man, or men, to cause those laws to be put in execution', and he assumes that mundane and bodily concerns such as dwelling, diet and childcare could never warrant the wielding of a sword or the exercise of law. Sovereign power is, then, a juridico-legal power to kill that leaves the daily life of the body alone. In those realms in which one would not wield a sword or the force of law, one is free or escapes from power. In particular, Hobbes thinks that, since there are no laws dictating how we should walk, sit, sleep, eat, drink, talk, gesticulate and so forth, our bodies are free, or that we have 'corporall Liberty', unless the sovereign has us literally in chains.

Sovereign power's right over life is merely the right of subtraction, as opposed to regulation or control. Foucault argues that slavery is an example of sovereign power, because it entails bodies being seized, time being seized, labour being seized, life itself being seized, and this power is maintained through the threat of violence and death (2006b, pp. 67–8). Under disciplinary power, an example of which is colonization, the soul is occupied, refashioned and transformed, and so, ultimately, there is less need for physical violence. Those subjected to sovereign power submit through fear of pain and death, but their minds do not submit as under disciplinary power, which colonizes and constitutes subjects. As Western societies have become increasingly biopolitical, Foucault argues that power now administers life rather than having a right of death. In contrast to sovereign power, which could '*take* life or *let* live', biopower is the power 'to *foster* life or *disallow* it to the point of death' (Foucault, 1978, p. 138, emphasis in original). He writes,

> Power would no longer be dealing simply with legal subjects over whom the ultimate dominion was death, but with living beings, and

the mastery it would be able to exercise over them would have to be
applied at the level of life itself: it was the taking charge of life, more
than the threat of death, that gave power its access even to the body.

(Foucault, 1978, pp. 142–3)

While Hobbes deems corporeal aspects of life such as housing
(abode), desires (what we want to purchase and consume), the
care of the body (diet), childcare and education, and the ways
that we walk, move, talk and otherwise comport our bodies to be
outside the interests of the sovereign and hence free, for Foucault
these aspects become some of the privileged loci of the mechanisms of modern power, indicating a transformation of power
that Hobbes would have deemed 'a thing impossible'.[1] Biopolitics
and disciplinary power are able to access the body because they
function through norms rather than laws – and, while there may
not be laws about how we walk, comport our bodies, gesticulate,
speak, eat, sleep and so forth, there *are* norms about each of these
mundane practices. Biopolitics and disciplinary power are also
able to access the body because they are internalized by subjects
rather than exercised from above through acts or threats of violence, and because they are dispersed throughout society rather
than located in a single individual or government body. While the
sovereign power that Hobbes describes could only seize life or
kill, Foucault writes of 'a very profound transformation of these
mechanisms of power', in which 'deduction' would be replaced
by a power 'working to incite, reinforce, control, monitor, optimize, and organize the forces under it: a power bent on generating forces, making them grow, and ordering them, rather than one
dedicated to impeding them, making them submit, or destroying
them' (1978, p. 136).

In his 1977–8 Collège de France course, *'Security, Territory,
Population'*, Foucault took the example of a prohibition such
as 'Do not steal' or 'Do not murder' to illustrate the differences
between sovereign power, disciplinary power and biopolitics
(Foucault, 2007, pp. 4–5). Under sovereign power, which pre-
dominated until the second half of the seventeenth century,
when Hobbes was writing, an individual who transgressed these
prohibitions against theft and murder would be subjected to the

law and punished solely on the basis of his crime; he might, for instance, be executed, flogged, exiled or fined. Under disciplinary power, which emerged in the eighteenth century, the criminal will still be subjected to the law or punished, but it will no longer be a mere matter of his crime. Rather, power will now be at least as interested in the thief's or murderer's character. The conditions, both material and psychological, under which the individual committed his crime will now be of crucial interest. This information will be deemed important in order to anticipate and intervene in the likelihood that the criminal reoffends. To predict and control the individual's chance of recidivating, the criminal needs to be subjected to psychological examinations, surveillance and rehabilitative practices unknown under sovereign power. For this reason, the punishment is less likely to put an end to the criminal's life and more likely to control it through tactics such as prison, psychiatric treatment, parole and probation. Finally, under biopolitics, which emerged later in the eighteenth century, the focus and target of power becomes the numbers of thefts and murders occurring in the population. Power now takes an interest in whether crime rates are rising or falling, in which demographic groups particular crimes are predominant and how crime rates can be optimally controlled or regulated. While many of the same tactics will be employed under biopower as under disciplinary power, the focus will now be on the population rather than the individual.

If at times Foucault describes discipline and biopower as two distinct (although intersecting and overlapping) forms of power (Foucault, 2007), at other times he includes discipline *within* biopower, or describes discipline as one of the two levels at which biopower works. Biopower is a power over *bios*, or life, and lives may be managed on both individual and group levels. While at one level disciplinary institutions such as schools, workshops, prisons and psychiatric hospitals target individuals as they deviate from norms, at another level the state is concerned with knowing and administrating the norms of the population as a whole and with understanding and regulating 'the problems of birthrate, longevity, public health, housing, and migration' (Foucault, 1978, p. 140). Disciplinary power works primarily through institutions and through tactics such as incarceration and surveillance, while biopolitics works primarily through the state and through tactics of governmentality; that said, the state is also directly involved in many institutions, such as the prison, the army and the school. In *The History of Sexuality*, Foucault writes of biopower:

> [T]his power over life evolved in two basic forms; these two forms were not antithetical, however; they constituted rather two poles of development linked together by a whole intermediary cluster of relations. One of these poles – the first to be formed, it seems – centered on the body as a machine: its disciplining, the optimization of its capabilities, the extortion of its forces, the parallel increase of its usefulness and its docility, its integration into systems of efficient and economic controls, all this was ensured by the procedures of power that characterized the *disciplines: an anatomo-politics of the human body*. The second, formed somewhat later, focused on the species body, the body imbued with the mechanics of life and serving as the basis of the biological processes: propagation, births and mortality, the level of health, life expectancy and longevity, with all the conditions that can cause these to vary. Their supervision was effected through an entire series of interventions and *regulatory controls: a bio-politics of the population.*
>
> (Foucault, 1978, p. 138, emphasis in original)

Discipline (or anatomo-politics) may be seen as biopower that targets the individual body, therefore, while another level of biopower (biopolitics) targets the species body. Foucault describes these two levels as 'the two poles around which the organization of power over life was deployed' (p. 138). These two levels of power are necessarily intertwined, since bodies make up populations and populations are made up of individual bodies. In *'Society Must Be Defended'*, Foucault insists that a biopolitics of the population

> does not exclude disciplinary technology, but it does dovetail into it, integrate it, modify it to some extent, and above all, use it by sort of infiltrating it, embedding itself in existing disciplinary techniques. This new technique does not simply do away with the disciplinary technique, because it exists at a different level, on a different scale, and

> because it has a different bearing area, and makes use of very different
> instruments.
>
> (Foucault, 2003b, p. 242)

One way of conceptualizing the point of this passage is to say that discipline is the micro-technology and biopolitics is the macro-technology of the same power over life.

According to Foucault, biopower administers life, and, in order to do this, it was important for the state to obtain forecasts and statistical estimates concerning such demographic factors as fertility, natality, immigration, dwelling and mortality rates (1978, p. 25). For this reason, an important moment in the history of biopower was the development of the modern census. While inventories of heads of households, property and men who could serve in the military were taken in ancient Rome, China, Palestine, Babylonia, Persia and Egypt, they were almost unknown throughout the Middle Ages (an exception being William the Conqueror's Domesday Book in England), and differed from the modern census in that they did not attempt to gather information about the entirety of the population but only about specific types of individuals: those who could be taxed, drafted or forced to work. The idea of enumerating the entirety of a population was introduced in Western countries only at the end of the seventeenth century, and it became increasingly detailed in the centuries that followed. Soon the census secured data on dates and places of birth, marital status and occupations. Modern states recognized the necessity of understanding the characteristics, structures and trends of their populations in order to manage them or to compensate for what they could not control.

We can think of any number of examples of biopower with which we are familiar, even if we did not previously recognize them as such. For instance, one subject of biopolitical concern is the age of a population, 'together with a whole series of related economic and political problems' (Foucault, 2003b, p. 243). The state is concerned with those demographic forecasts that foresee a 'sapp[ing of] the population's strength, [a] shorten[ing of] the working week, wasted energy, and cost money...' (p. 244). We often hear of the ageing of the 'baby boomer' generation, for instance, when a large segment of the population will retire from the workforce and may require expensive geriatric care. A 'sapping' of both the labour force and medical resources is predicted as a result, and needs to be compensated for, while retirement and geriatric care facilities will have to be established and staffed in anticipation of this event. Another area of biopolitical study and intervention is the health and survival of neonates, managed, for instance, through government-sponsored breastfeeding advocacy campaigns (Kukla, 2005). States may also be concerned with monitoring and manipulating which demographic groups babies are being born into. The French Canadian province of Quebec has a profound interest in keeping the French language alive in its territory, for instance, and is thus concerned with increasing its francophone population. Since the census reveals that French Canadians have fewer children than English Canadians, 'allophones' and immigrants, the province compensates with targeted pro-natal policies, by promoting immigration from francophone countries through financial incentives and by promoting immigration in general (through attractions such as inexpensive daycare) while obliging children of non-francophone families to attend French-language schools.

As Foucault writes in *The History of Sexuality*, 'At the heart of this economic and political problem of population was sex... It was essential that the state know what was happening with its citizens' sex, and the use they made of it... Between the state and the individual, sex became an issue, and a public issue no less' (1978, p. 26). Although non-reproductive sexual acts had long been considered sinful, since the eighteenth century they had come to be seen as a threat to society. At the disciplinary level, individuals engaging in non-reproductive sex acts and women uninterested in procreative sex have been medically treated for perversion, frigidity and sexual dysfunction (Taylor, 2015). At the biopolitical level, non-reproductive sex acts and the rejection of reproductive sexuality are issues that need to be managed through measures such as financial incitements to procreate and the encouragement of certain forms of immigration. It is necessary to know the proportion of the population that is engaging in specific sexual acts, and using contraceptives, in order to intervene in this behaviour or compensate for it. While in some segments of society the state is concerned with promoting procreation and thus with providing incentives to parenthood, in other segments of the population the state is concerned with containing and preventing procreation. In particular, certain groups, such as teenagers, unwed women, the poor, criminals and the mentally or physically ill and disabled, have been deemed (and in some instances continue to be deemed) unfit to conceive or to raise children (McWhorter, 2009).

As these cases show, sex is important at both levels of biopower, concerning as it does both the individual's use of her body and the growth and health of the population. As Foucault notes in a course lecture, 'Sexuality exists at the point where body and population meet. And so it is a matter for discipline, but also a matter for regularization [biopolitics]' (Foucault, 2003b, pp. 251–2). Making a similar point in *The History of Sexuality*, Foucault observes:

> Sex was a means of access both to the life of the body and the life of the species. It was employed as a standard for the disciplines and as a basis for regulations. This is why in the nineteenth century sexuality was sought out in the smallest details of individual existences... But one also sees it becoming the theme of political operations, economic interventions (through incitements to or curbs on procreation), and ideological campaigns for raising standards of morality and responsibility: it was put forward as an index of a society's strength, revealing of both its political energy and its biological vigor. Spread out from one pole to the other of this technology of sex was a whole series of different tactics that combined in varying proportions the object of disciplining the body and that of regulating populations.
>
> (Foucault, 1978, p. 146)

Far from being something that we have recently liberated, or are still struggling to liberate, from an archaic and repressive power, Foucault therefore argues that sex is in fact a privileged site in – and, indeed, a *product of* – the workings of modern forms of power. This is why sex became a central political concern under biopower as it never was under sovereign power. We have accepted this belief that sex is important, and thus that the sexual practices of the species, the population and our selves should be subjects of study, intervention and concern. It is the shift from sovereign power to biopower that explains why we, as a society, are surrounded by sexual images and discourses, and why we, as individuals, have come to see our identities as caught up with sex. Foucault argues that, when power was exercised through bloodshed, identity was associated with blood: one identified oneself according to one's bloodline, descent, family alliance, legitimacy of blood, blue blood, French blood (Foucault, 1978, p. 124). Now, under biopower, with power operating through the regulation of sexuality, we identify ourselves according to our sexual practices and desires.

While Foucault has shown in the first three parts of *The History of Sexuality* that power is functioning not so much to repress sex as to constitute sexualities, in parts 4 and 5 he argues that we do not tend to recognize power in its constitutive – or biopolitical and disciplinary – forms. Indeed, we tend only to recognize power when it occurs negatively, or as discursive prohibition, censorship and repression (p. 86). We therefore fail to see power *as* power when it does not come in the form of sovereign power or the law. For Foucault, this is because '[p]ower is tolerable only on condition that it mask a substantial part of itself. Its success is proportional to its ability to hide its own mechanisms' (p. 86). So far as power is successful, we are usually not aware of it. In *Discipline and Punish*, Foucault argues that disciplinary power is more efficient than sovereign power precisely because it is not expressed in the form of public laws or blatantly violent spectacles. Instead, disciplinary power is subtle, internalized and hidden; very often it does not even *seem* like power (Foucault, 1977). When we are disciplined to behave in certain ways, and have internalized this discipline, we may feel that, far from being subjected to power, we are acting of our own volition. For instance, while as children we needed to be disciplined to brush our teeth, by the time we are adults the habit of brushing our teeth has likely been internalized to such an extent that going to work or bed without brushing our teeth is uncomfortable. We then brush our teeth because we find the sensation of clean teeth pleasurable, or because we are embarrassed by the prospect of bad breath; in either case, brushing our teeth is not experienced as subjection to power but as our own volition, and the source of that volition is long since forgotten. Disciplinary power is not recognized as power because it is experienced as coming from within rather than without us, or as our own habits and desires. Ironically, it may only be when we encounter impediments to these internalized norms that we think we are experiencing power.

The example of dental hygiene is innocuous, or may even be an example of discipline as a beneficent social force; as Foucault famously observed, '[P]ower is not always bad, but it is always dangerous' (1983, p. 231). Other examples of the internalized workings of disciplinary power are more troubling, however. We may consider the ways that gender is enforced in contemporary society, for example, which Foucauldian feminists such as Sandra Bartky and Susan Bordo have described as disciplinary (Bartky, 1988; Bordo, 2004). While practices such as foot binding and laws against cross-dressing can be seen as methods through which sovereign power enforces gender, in Western societies today gender occurs much more pervasively through our disciplined habituation to *norms* of gender. Western subjects often express the view that Muslim women who wear a hijab are oppressed, for instance, whereas they see the donning of Western fashions as a demonstration of freedom and self-expression (Oliver, 2007). From a Foucauldian perspective, however, Western women's desire to wear Western feminine fashion, to bare their legs and arms, is the result of gender norms that they have internalized, and is thus just as much the result of power relations as the wearing of the hijab is for Muslim women. The norms of gender are norms that we internalize as children and that many of us come to see as natural. Once we are habituated to these norms, for many of us conforming to the gender expectations of our assigned sex feels like an innate inclination or desire. Indeed, conforming to norms of gender may be experienced as an expression of who we *are*, of who we must be allowed to be in order to be free, rather than as an effect of power. As Bartky puts it, with patriarchal expectations of femininity now operating through disciplinary power, there is no need for women to be 'marched off to electrolysis at the end of a rifle' or to dress as they do out of fear of sanctions; most women have internalized the desire for a 'normal' feminine body and appearance, as well as a cultural set of ideas about what such normalcy entails, and thus comply to gender norms of their own volition and, often, with pleasure (Bartky, 1988, p. 75). Resisting a form of power that constitutes *who we are* and produces *what we find pleasurable* is, of course, far more complicated than resisting a form of power that is exercised through force and law.

In contrast to sovereign or juridico-legal power, disciplinary power does not so much write laws and punish those who transgress them as it situates individuals in relation to norms. This does not mean that legal institutions and codes of law are disappearing. Instead, the law has been infiltrated by norms, and the courtroom has been infiltrated by medicine. Laws employ moralistic and vague terms such as 'decency' and 'outrage' and psychiatrists serve as 'expert witnesses' on these matters (Foucault, 1988c). Indeed, there has been a great deal *more* talk about laws and rights than ever before in this era when, for Foucault, law has ceased to characterize the workings of power. We have written more constitutions in these years and engaged in more 'clamoring legislative activities' than in the past, and yet this 'clamoring legislative activit[y]' is not evidence that power is still legalistic. Rather, it is one of 'the forms that made an essentially normalizing power acceptable' (Foucault, 1978, p. 144). We can demand and be granted more constitutional rights and legislative protections today than in the past precisely because the law is not primarily where power works any more.

To take an example, we can consider the 'clamoring legislative activities' around gay marriage in recent years. As is discussed further in Chapter 6, despite its radical beginnings, gay politics has come to be approached in terms of rights and laws, such as amending the constitution to refer to sexual preference or orientation. As numerous queer theorists have argued, however, what is really happening in these legislative struggles is that racially and class privileged same-sex couples are situating themselves closer to the heterosexual norm rather than affirming their transgression of that norm (Butler, 2004). Gay couples may now be granted the right to marry precisely because the very desire to marry on the part of some gay couples shows how effectively power has constituted them. Some gay couples then feel that they are transgressing social norms by getting married, and such marriages are widely celebrated as signs of social change, pacifying subjects politically, when in fact the very desire to marry arguably shows how subjected to power – to normalization – these subjects have already been. Gay couples can be granted rights, the right to be normal, precisely because their 'clamoring legislative activities' serve to mask how power is really working. Disciplinary power has worked to normalize some gay subjects to such a degree that the most subversive act they can imagine is an emulation of the white, middle-class, heterosexual status quo. Indeed, for Foucault, even identifying as 'gay' indicates one's subjection to a form of power that constitutes identities through sexual desires; demanding the right to *marry* as gay only takes this normalized identity one step further. Just as subjects imagine they are resisting power when they confess, when in fact their very desire to confess is a manner in which power has constituted them, so gay couples who imagine they are resisting power when they marry are in fact showing how thoroughly power has succeeded in constituting them as sexually normalized subjects.

Many of the workings of power today go unmarked, or are not recognized *as* power, because they function through relations with doctors, teachers, parents, social workers and psychiatrists rather than the state and law. In each case, we believe that these individuals are helping us, caring for us, educating us or healing us – as, to some extent, they may be – and thus we submit to them voluntarily and do not see this submission as an effect of power. For instance, since being 'compliant' to the instructions of doctors does not take the form of submission to law, we see this obedience to medical authority as self-care rather than an effect of power. And yet, as Foucault writes in the 'Objective' section of *The History of Sexuality*,

> To conceive of power on the basis of [sovereignty] is to conceive of it in terms of a historical form that is characteristic of our societies: the juridical monarchy. Characteristic yet transitory. For while many of its forms have persisted to the present, it has gradually been penetrated

> by quite new mechanisms of power that are probably irreducible to the
> representation of law.
>
> (Foucault, 1978, p. 89)

For Foucault, philosophical descriptions of juridico-legal or sovereign power (such as Hobbes') are 'useful for representing...[a]
power that was centered primarily around deduction and death',
but they are 'utterly incongruous with the new methods of power
whose operation is not ensured by right but by technique, not by
law but by normalization, not by punishment but by control, methods that are employed on all levels and in forms that go beyond
the state and its apparatus' (1978, p. 89). Thus Hobbes is primarily
of historical interest today; he is not useful for understanding biopower, or the ways that power now predominantly functions in the
West. Neither disciplinary power nor biopolitics is characteristi-
cally legal or juridical; although they may have infiltrated the law,
they nevertheless do not operate primarily through law codes and
the shedding of blood but, rather, through the *administering of
life* and its *normalization*. Foucault's objective, therefore, is to find
ways to theorize power that account for these new mechanisms
of power, to theorize power outside the law or to commit regicide
in political theory. As he writes, 'In political thought and analysis, we still have not cut off the head of the king' (1978, p. 89).
Foucault's aim is to rectify this. The Robespierre of political philosophy, Foucault argues that '[w]e must construct an analytics of
power that no longer takes law as a model and a code' and that
'[w]e must... conceive of sex without the law, and power without
the king' (p. 90).

METHOD: OR HOW TO THEORIZE POWER
WITHOUT THE KING

In the 'Method' section of part IV of *The History of Sexuality*,
Foucault sketches some of the main features of power, as he sees it
working in the modern West (pp. 92–102). In what follows I present and provide examples of the main features of disciplinary
power and biopower as Foucault describes them.

POWER IS EVERYWHERE

First, Foucault suggests that power is omnipresent. He writes: 'Power is everywhere; not because it embraces everything, but because it comes from everywhere' (p. 93). Everyone exercises disciplinary power – the power of enforcing social norms – and everyone exercises it over everyone else. In this sense, the shift from sovereign power to biopower is *democratic* – a rule of the people by the people – and, not coincidentally, corresponds with historical shifts from kingdoms to democracies.

A good example of the 'democratic' nature of disciplinary power is found in an article by Foucault scholar Ellen Feder. In 'Disciplining the family: the case of gender identity disorder', Feder recounts the story of a four-year-old boy named Nathan, who in 1977 was described in the psychological literature as suffering from 'confused gender identity and moderate cross-dress behavior disturbance'. Nathan verbalized the wish to be a girl, preferred to play with girls rather than boys, selected girls' clothes when playing dress-up at nursery school and displayed feminine mannerisms and voice inflections. As psychologist George Alan Rekers wrote of Nathan's case, 'His stereotypic feminine gender-role behaviors elicited comments from other children, such as "You can't be a little girl." This concerned Nathan's teachers and parents, and ultimately led to referral to treatment' (Rekers, cited in Feder, 1997, p. 195). In addition to being a psychologist and a Southern Baptist minister, Rekers is now infamous for practising 'conversion therapy' on homosexuals, testifying in court that homosexuality is sinful and that homosexuals should not be allowed to raise children, and writing books on how to raise straight children, even while hiring male prostitutes for himself. Rekers' treatment of Nathan was extensive, involving evaluation by independent clinical psychologists, the completion of 'parent-report inventories on child gender behaviors' by Nathan's mother, sessions in a clinical playroom with Nathan playing while observers watched through a one-way mirror and logged masculine and feminine behaviours, videotaped sessions with both Nathan's mother and father, the training of Nathan's mother using a 'Farrell Instruments bug-in-the-ear receiving device' to reinforce her son's masculine behaviours and discourage his feminine behaviours, the use of a wrist counter to train Nathan to 'self-regulate' or 'self-reinforce' his masculine behaviour (pressing the button whenever he engaged in masculine behaviour, with sweets as a reward for points accumulated), a 'reversal-probe session' and the introduction of observers into Nathan's nursery school (disguised as student teachers) to test the treatment's success (Feder, 1997, pp. 195–7).

As Feder notes, this was an extraordinary expenditure of energy and resources in response to what we might think were innocuous behaviours on the part of one pre-school child. She writes:

> What is striking about the conditions of Nathan's referral to Rekers is the remarkable influence the other children's judgment of Nathan's desire to play 'like a girl' has. As the case study tells it, what alarms Nathan's teachers and his parents is not Nathan's behavior as such, but rather *the other children's response to Nathan*. Teasing and name-calling, as Rekers *et al.* explain in 'Child Gender Disturbances: A Clinical Rationale for Intervention,'... 'is not only virtually certain to appear' in boys 'who reject their male role' but constitutes 'one of the manifest symptoms of child gender disturbance'... Its status as a definitive sign of pathology suggests that peer response is here imbued with a particular kind of power. While it may strike us as a truism that children's response to one another is meaningful in terms of their social and emotional development, we must wonder about the fact that the authority which would sanction Nathan's subjection to evaluation by Rekers and his team is vested in Nathan's four-year-old classmates.
>
> (Feder, 1997, pp. 199–200, emphasis in original)

What Feder is highlighting is that four-year-old children – who are not subjects we are used to considering 'powerful' – are capable of exercising a normalizing power today. It is not that these children 'have' power or are self-consciously 'using' power but, rather, that they are involved in multidirectional networks of disciplinary power, with their response determining in part what is deemed pathological and subject to medical intervention. Pre-school-age children have already internalized a socially contingent view of what 'normal' gender behaviour is, and they police the normality of their peers with serious consequences. While we might have hoped that the teachers would reprimand the nursery schoolchildren for teasing Nathan, instead they reinforced the judgement involved in this teasing and invested the children with the authority to set in action an elaborate deployment of disciplinary power that resulted in the normalization of their playmate; Nathan is reported at the end of his treatment to have 'male gender identity and no emotional disturbance' (Feder, 1997, p. 197)

POWER IS WAR

The next feature of power that Foucault describes is its bellicosity. Foucault proposes that we should think of power in terms of war rather than in terms of sovereignty, domination or law. These, Foucault argues, are the 'terminal forms power takes', though there are many other 'derivations' of power (1978, p. 92). The exercise of power involves strategies, struggles and tactics that Foucault sees as akin to military planning and battles, and so he suggests that we might 'turn the expression around, then, and say that politics is war pursued by other means' (p. 93). Foucault is referring to the statement of nineteenth-century Prussian military theorist Carl von Clausewitz, who, in his book *Vom Kriege* (*On War*), argues that 'war is the continuation of politics by other means' (Clausewitz, 1984, p. 87). While Clausewitz was observing that, when political negotiations fail, one pursues one's goals through war instead, and thus war is a natural extension of politics rather than its aggressive opposite, Foucault's inversion of Clausewitz's claim suggests that politics is inherently agonistic. This is a suggestion that has pitted him against contemporary political theorists such as Jürgen Habermas, who see politics not as a struggle for triumph but as a peaceful practice aiming at consensus or accord. Although Johanna Oksala has recently suggested that Foucault's attachment to the 'politics as war' argument was transitory (Oksala, 2011a), the idea that the workings of power, or politics, might be conceptualized as war is one that Foucault pursued in greater detail in course lectures from the period, and that explains his use of the military language (e.g. 'the deployment of sexuality') in *The History of Sexuality* and other works from this time.

POWER IS RELATIONAL

Another feature of power that Foucault describes is its relationality. Power is not something we have, possess, acquire, seize, share or lose. Rather, we are always in many shifting relations or networks of power. These are, Foucault stresses, 'non-egalitarian' relations (1978, p. 94): although no one 'has' power, some people are consistently in more privileged positions than others within these networks of power for reasons that are structural to society or institutions. Nevertheless, power relations are always moving and complex, and no one is completely powerless in them; in situations of dominance in which one individual is completely subordinated to another, Foucault argues that we are talking about violence rather than power. Foucault reiterates this point elsewhere when he writes '[t]he characteristic feature of power is that some men can more or less entirely determine other men's conduct – but never exhaustively or coercively. A man who is chained up and beaten is subject to force being exerted upon him, not power' (Foucault, 1994, p. 324). As such, situations of sheer force are contrasted by Foucault with power insofar as the latter always entails a mutual relationship with some possibility of resistance.

A controversial example of the shifting and reciprocal nature of disciplinary power relations is professor–student relations (Taylor, 2011). In contrast to Foucault's discussions of pedagogy and power in *The History of Sexuality* and elsewhere, the dominant literature on professor–student relations today does not see the university as a disciplinary institution but, rather, as what Foucault would describe as an institution of sovereign power, in which professors, like kings, have a monopoly on power and exercise it over students in a unilateral, top-down manner. A typical example may be taken from *Sexual Harassment on College Campuses: Abusing the Ivory Power*, in which Sue Rosenberg Zalk writes:

> The bottom line in the relationship between faculty member and student is POWER. The faculty member has it and the student does not. As intertwined as the faculty–student roles might be, and as much as one might exist for the other to exist, they are not equal collaborators.

The student does not negotiate – indeed, has nothing to negotiate with. There are no exceptions to this.

All the power lies with the faculty member – some of it is real, concrete, and some of it is imagined or elusive. Professors give grades, write recommendations for graduate schools, jobs, and awards and the like, and can predispose colleagues' attitudes toward students. But it goes beyond this.

Knowledge and wisdom are power. While superior knowledge, and thus presumably greater wisdom, are often ascribed to faculty members by society at large, the students' adolescent idealism exaggerates its extent.

(Zalk, 1996, pp. 85–6)

From a Foucauldian perspective, we can say that Zalk describes the power of professors as sovereign power, but that this misunderstands the kinds of power that are at work in the university, an institution in which professors are instruments of power rather than rulers. Zalk's arguments consistently describe power as something that professors have and students lack, and as working exclusively in a negative and static manner. For Foucault, however, the university is a disciplinary institution, and we should consider the ways in which desire is produced *through* these hierarchical relations, rather than being something that must be negated therein. We should, moreover, recognize that increased prohibition may backfire, being further constitutive of desire. Without denying a strong asymmetry in the hierarchical institution of the university, a contemporary Foucauldian analysis of professor–student relations might note that professors are critically scrutinized by their students all the time: students 'shop' for classes, they evaluate professors anonymously at the end of the semester, they post evaluations of professors online, they contest their grades directly to their professors and above their professors' heads. Student evaluations are significant to professors not only because they are judgements of courses in which professors have invested large amounts of time and labour but also for reasons of professional self-interest, as they strive for promotion, funding, respect from their colleagues and to keep departmental enrolment numbers high for the advantages that this accrues to the department. While professors are held accountable for their evaluations of their students (these are open to scrutiny and revision from superiors and peers), students' evaluations of their professors are anonymous and uncontestable. Professors in fact have little leeway to use their position as evaluators of student work to negotiate personal favours or to express emotional investments. Professors have to grade students reasonably fairly because, if students contest wildly inaccurate grades, this reflects badly on the professor.

It is an aspect of disciplinary institutions that, while those subjected to discipline are individuated by power, those exercising power are not individuated: professors fulfil a disciplinary function within a network of power when they grade assignments, but they are interchangeable with one another in this role; just as one prison warden may be replaced by another, so, if a student appeals a grade, another professor is interchangeable with the original professor and can regrade the assignment. As Foucault puts it in an interview, 'On power':

> I don't believe that this question of 'who exercises power?' can be resolved unless that other question 'how does it happen?' is resolved at the same time. Of course we have to show who those in charge are, we know that we have to turn, let us say, to deputies, ministers, principal private secretaries, etc., etc. But this is not the important issue, for we know perfectly well that even if we reach the point of designating exactly all those people, all those 'decision-makers,' we will still not really know why and how the decision was made, how it came to be accepted by everyone, and how it is that it hurts a particular category of person, etc.
>
> (Foucault, 1988d, pp. 103–4)

Thus, Foucault goes on to say, it is not about 'who exercises power' but about 'the strategies, the networks, the mechanisms, all those techniques by which a decision is accepted and by which that decision could not but be taken in the way it was' (p. 104). With respect to the student–professor relationship, it is not just about 'who exercises power', or the bare fact that professors make decisions about grades, but about the process through which professors are constrained to make those decisions.

POWER IS IMMANENT

Another feature of power that Foucault discusses is that power is immanent in all relationships and plays a productive role in these relationships. Thus, power does not exist only in our relations to the state, the king, the police or the law; it exists in *all* our relationships, including – as seen above – in pedagogical, sexual and romantic relationships. It will therefore not be possible to define 'good' sexual or romantic relationships as those that are free of power, and 'bad' sexual or romantic relations as those that involve power, as some radical feminists have done, for *no* relations are free of power (Brewis, 2001). As Foucault writes, 'One must not suppose there exists a certain sphere of sexuality... were it not the object of mechanisms of prohibition brought to bear by the economic or ideological requirements of power' (Foucault, 1978, p. 98).

An interesting example of the argument that power is immanent in all relationships is the significant body of literature that has developed to discuss relationships that Foucault himself never theorized: relationships between humans and domesticated animals. In 'Taming the wild profusion of existing things', Clare Palmer has provided a Foucauldian analysis of the life of a domesticated cat (Palmer, 2001). Similarly, in 'Apparatuses of animality', Stephen Thierman has written of the disciplined schedule of an urban and domesticated cat, 'involving trips to the veterinarian's office, portioned meals for weight control, and tooth brushing to ensure optimal oral hygiene', as an example of 'a power that regulates and normalizes' (Thierman, 2010). Although Foucault argues that sexuality began to be disciplined when, for instance, 'homosexuals' were understood as a 'species', we might ask: what disciplinary function does the categorization of animals into 'species' serve?

In response to a lacuna in Foucault's own work, several scholars have now drawn on Foucault's accounts of biopower and disciplinary power to describe the lives of animals, particularly in contemporary agribusiness. Richard Twine's work, for instance, provides a biopolitical analysis of livestock genetic science (Twine, 2010); Richie Nimmo has written a book-length biopolitical analysis of the British liquid milk trade (Nimmo, 2010); Lewis Holloway has offered a series of analyses of contemporary biopolitical farm practices (Holloway and Morris, 2007; Holloway *et al.*, 2009); and Dinesh Wadiwel has considered some of the ways that 'livestock' fit into a biopolitical society (Wadiwel, 2002; Taylor, 2013). In 'Cows and sovereignty: biopower and animal life', for example, Wadiwel writes:

> The key questions which relate to biopolitical life are asked here: How much life? What duration of life? What is the cost of life? How best to reproduce? What manner of death? The life of cattle (or 'livestock' as they are aptly named) is vulnerable to a politics of 'life and death', where the political question returns to life itself.
>
> (Wadiwel, 2002, p. 2)

Among his examples, Wadiwel considers the 2001 'mad cow' crisis. For Wadiwel, the slaughter that ensued from this crisis, like the unprecedented bloodshed of biopolitical states noted by Foucault, 'represents the extreme extent of this power: a power that includes the prerogative..., in the moment of crisis, to darken the skies of Europe with the ashes of the dead' (Wadiwel, 2002, p. 2). In the mad cow example we also see the ways that the lives of non-human animals are protected and destroyed according to how they are anticipated to benefit or threaten the human population. The lives of non-human animals in the food industry are managed in such a way as to be as beneficial to humans as possible (to produce the most meat, milk or eggs with the greatest efficiency at the lowest cost), while the health risks to humans associated with intensive farming are simultaneously regulated (by adding antibiotics to feed and by stunning large animals before slaughter). Like those segments of the human population that are seen as biopolitical threats or drains on the state rather than part of the society that the biopolitical state is mandated to foster, the lives of non-human animals are considered not for their own sake but only in terms of how they may benefit or endanger those humans about whom the state is concerned.

POWER COMES FROM BELOW

Foucault then argues that power comes from below and 'traverses' society, despite the fact that we normally imagine power coming from above and moving exclusively in a top-down direction (1978, p. 94). Consequently, we miss much of how power works when we focus on politicians and laws, without seeing how our peers, lovers, students, neighbours and even children are normalizing us. We may think again of how professors are disciplined from 'below' by student evaluations, or of Feder's discussion of the manners in which nursery schoolchildren normalize their peers in ways that are perceived to require responses from those 'above' them, such as teachers, parents and health professionals (Feder, 1997). Feder also provides an insightful analysis of lateral power relations in her book *Family Bonds: Genealogies of Race and Gender* (Feder, 2007). Here she describes the ways in which disciplinary power is exercised both on and within the family. Children internalize an awareness that they are under the surveillance of their parents, asking 'What would my parents think?', and parents are conscious of their surveillance by neighbours, asking 'What will the neighbours think?' (Feder, 2007, pp. 15, 41). Children conform to social norms and the expectations of their parents, and parents to the gazes of their neighbours, as well as to those of teachers, doctors, classmates and the parents of classmates, whom they monitor in turn. Indeed, parents discipline their children because they are concerned with what the neighbours will think, and children internalize this concern, learning to self-monitor their behaviour to spare their parents shame. Because neighbours are equals rather than superiors, this is an instance in which we can see power working laterally and reciprocally rather than in a top-down and unidirectional manner.

Significantly, Foucault's argument that power comes from below, is democratic and traverses society or moves laterally is not meant to deny that some people are more oppressed than others, or that there are what he calls 'major dominations'. Foucault describes power as having 'serial arrangements and convergences of the force relations'; he explains 'major dominations' as 'the hegemonic effects that are sustained by all these confrontations'

(1978, p. 94). One example of a 'major domination' is the subjection of women to men within a patriarchal society, though we must qualify this by acknowledging other axes of oppression, such as class and race, which result in *some* women exercising privilege in non-egalitarian relations with *some* men. Foucault's point, however, is that the 'major domination' that we call patriarchy does not function in a top-down manner either, but is relayed through countless relations across society that enforce gender roles and norms, including parent–child, teacher–student, doctor–patient, neighbour, friend and partner relations. A woman may find that familial expectations (including the opinions and desires of her children, or her children's peers), 'expert advice' from health practitioners, the surveillance of neighbours, the opinions of friends, and the desires of her romantic partners all converge to enforce norms of femininity that perpetuate her subordinate status, even when gender equality is enshrined in the law and no 'ruler' is obliging her to be either feminine or subordinate in her relations with men.

POWER RELATIONS ARE INTENTIONAL AND NON-SUBJECTIVE

Foucault then notes that power relations are both intentional and non-subjective (1978, pp. 94–5). This means that, although there are very often self-conscious calculations and strategies involved in power relations, and people are often quite aware of what they are trying to do in these machinations, there is no mastermind who sees the bigger picture. For instance, psychiatrists and doctors, educators and nurses all see themselves doing what they do in order to help people, or they engage in research for the sake of knowledge and their own career trajectories, unaware of the spiralling power effects of their work. As Foucault writes elsewhere: 'People know what they do; they frequently know why they do what they do; but what they don't know is what what they do does' (cited in Dreyfus and Rabinow, 1982, p. 187). The perverse implantation is an example of this. To return to the gender example above, when we compliment a woman for her appearance or dress – which very often means that we compliment her for conforming successfully to the norms of her assigned sex, or to femininity – we may simply be expressing a genuinely felt appreciation and we may be intending to make her happy. We may not be aware that we are exercising power in making this compliment, or that our words will have a power effect at all. Nevertheless, one effect of our speech act is that this woman's femininity is reinforced, for she receives approbation when she invests in femininity and suffers a deprivation of that approbation when she puts less effort into conforming to gender norms. Although, in uttering our compliment, we merely intend to express our admiration and to please the woman, an unintended effect of our words is that we have participated in a normalizing form of power. That we find certain gendered appearances rather than others pleasing is itself the result of gender norms that precede and constitute us.

In *Bodies and Pleasures: Foucault and the Politics of Sexual Normalization*, Ladelle McWhorter describes the constant surveillance to which she was submitted as a queer child and adolescent, much of which came not from authority figures but from strangers and peers. She writes,

> For most of my life I had been watched almost constantly for any signs of sexual deviance – which might include acts or expressions of desire but might also include almost anything from the length of my stride to the pitch of my voice. This watching went on everywhere, all the time, and was performed by everyone, even strangers – many of whom did not hesitate to offer unsolicited comments. My peers were as conscientious in their observations as our superiors, who coached and encouraged them. At the same time, however, I knew that this ubiquitous network of surveillance was not the product of a conspiracy, nor was it aimed particularly at me. We were all being scanned constantly for information about our sexuality; we were all constantly scanning ourselves. And nobody in particular was in charge of the whole enterprise.

> (McWhorter, 1999, p. 24)

In this description, we see what Foucault means by power relations being both intentional and non-subjective. The strangers, peers, teachers, neighbours, doctors, nurses, social workers and parents who all scrutinized McWhorter's every move, and interfered when any of those moves seemed strange or 'queer', knew what they were doing and in some sense did what they did intentionally: they were looking out for signs that McWhorter was straying from the norms of heterosexual femininity, and they were trying to correct and prevent her from straying in these ways. They did this for what they thought of as 'her own good'. Nonetheless, they did so without knowing, or understanding, how certain norms had come to seem 'good' to them, how biopower functions or what role they were playing within the biopoliticization of human life.

POWER PRODUCES RESISTANCE

Finally, and most enigmatically, Foucault argues that resistance is another feature of power. As he famously writes, 'Where there is power, there is resistance, and yet… this resistance is never in a position of exteriority in relation to power' (1978, p. 95). That Foucault invokes resistance as a feature of power in *The History of Sexuality* is significant, as his previous books, including *Discipline and Punish*, did no such thing. Up until this point, Foucault had depicted a severely constructivist view of subjectivity in which a role for agency and responsibility is difficult to imagine. Although Foucault's statement that '[w]here there is power, there is resistance' is thus enticing and often cited, it remains brief and unillustrated; unfortunately, Foucault provides no examples of resistance in *The History of Sexuality* that could help explain his point. Although McWhorter writes '*What* is to be resisted, Foucault's *History of Sexuality* implies, is sexual identification', *how* Foucault envisages this resistance – or, indeed, what exactly Foucault *means* by resistance – remains unclear and subject to debate (McWhorter, 1999, p. 100).

One thing that can be noted, however, is that Foucault describes resistance in this famous phrase without mentioning agents. Agents, or people, are not the subjects of this sentence; rather, *power* is simply asserted as a presence, and people seem to be moved by this power–resistance dyad rather than moving it. Put otherwise, Foucault describes resistance as an outcome of power that happens to people rather than as something that people engage in. Resistance is something inevitable or automatic: it is not that we may or may not *choose* to resist power but, rather, that resistance will always arise *wherever* there is power, and it will do so whether we *want* to resist or not. Resistance may even be something our bodies do against our wills, an inevitable *effect* of power rather than an assertion of agency. Moreover, because this resistance is reactionary, Foucault is clear that it never sets the individual who is resisting apart from power.

Such is the picture that Foucault paints in two of his most sustained descriptions of resistance in his course lectures from this period: in *Psychiatric Power*, Foucault writes of hysteria as a kind of involuntary resistance to doctors on the part of intensely medicalized women; and, in *Abnormal*, he writes of demonic 'possession' as an involuntary 'resistance effect' to confession on the part of religious women (Foucault, 2003a; 2006b). In neither the case of hysteria nor that of possession was the resistance intentional, and in neither case did the resistance liberate the resistors from their hospitals or convent cells. Very arguably, in both cases resistance harmed the women whose bodies were resisting, or they were worse off as a result of it, since even more draconian forms of control were the result. For Foucault, the phenomena of hysteria and possession were nevertheless resistance, in that they entailed rebellions of the body that defied the wills of those who would dominate them. The phenomena of possession and hysteria were both passive and feminine; at the same time, both threw significant wrenches into the operations of power. If these examples are representative for Foucault, it may be that he saw resistance as an unpredictable and involuntary result of power on the body that arose in the absence of agency, and thus that he theorized resistance without fundamentally altering the vision of human beings as devoid of agency that is at least suggested in *Discipline and Punish*.

Another clue to how Foucault sees resistance working in *The History of Sexuality* arises closer to the end of the volume, when he writes, equally famously and enigmatically, that 'the rallying point for the counter-attack against the deployment of sexuality ought not to be sex-desire, but bodies and pleasures' (1978, p. 157). Once again Foucault appears to be talking about how we might resist power, and the deployment of sexuality in particular; after all, he is describing how we might *strike back* against this power that does not so much dominate as constitute us. Once again, however, the passage is cryptic, and has given rise to both disagreement and perplexity on the part of Foucault scholars. While the problem with thinking we might resist power through assertions of sex-desire is fairly clear at this stage in the volume (this is what the sexual liberation movement tried to do, and Foucault has shown that this movement inadvertently extended rather than resisted the deployment of sexuality), how 'bodies and pleasures' are *distinct* from 'sex-desire', and how we might use them as a 'rallying point' for a 'counter-attack' against the deployment of sexuality, are less obvious. Indeed, more than one scholar, frustrated with this passage, has argued that Foucault offers limited resources for theorizing the kind of resistance that most political theorists and activists seek (McNay, 1992), or that his discussion of resistance appears to entail a naïve slip back to the idea of a pre-discursive or 'wild' body (Butler, 1999). In *The Psychic Life of Power*, Judith Butler argues that resistance, for Foucault, occurs either when subjectification exceeds or has effects that undermine its own normalizing goals: 'Thus resistance appears as the effect of power, as part of power, its self-subversion' (Butler, 1997, p. 93). Resistance is often an effect of an error in power's application, rather than a self-conscious rising up on the part of the subjects to whom it is applied. It therefore appears that, for Foucault, resistance is something that happens in bodies when there are gaps or contradictions in power, or it is an unpredictable result of the excesses of power on the body.

Although she is less quick to critique Foucault than some other scholars, philosopher Elizabeth Grosz also puzzles over his counter-attack proposal, asking:

> Is it that bodies and pleasures are somehow outside the deployment of sexuality? Or are they neuralgic points within the deployment of sexuality that may be strategically useful in any challenge to the current nexus of desire–knowledge–power? Why are bodies and pleasures a source of subversion in a way that sex and desire are not?
>
> (Grosz, 1994, pp. 155–6)

For her part, McWhorter, who has authored a book titled *Bodies and Pleasures*, describes her own confusion over what, precisely, the terms in her title mean for Foucault. As she writes:

> Foucault had insisted: 'The rallying point for the counterattack against the deployment of sexuality ought not to be sex-desire, but bodies and pleasures.' And that was exactly what I had been doing, wasn't it? I had been trying to refuse, ignore, de-center, contest, and even attack the notion of sex-desire as the founding truth of a human life, and at the same time I had been trying... to maintain a genuine connection to my bodily well-being and to my homosexual pleasures. Wasn't that right? Didn't I have it right? Well? Didn't I?
>
> Maybe not.
>
> I had just assumed that I more or less knew what the terms in that vague little sentence really meant.
>
> (McWhorter, 1999, p. 107)

As McWhorter explains, she had assumed that what Foucault meant was that we should refuse to identify with sexual labels, such as 'homosexual', even while affirming our pleasures and bodies, including bodily pleasures with people of the same sex. As she had discovered, however, it is nearly impossible today to live a life of same-sex pleasures while refusing the label 'homosexual', or while refusing to accept any sexual identity at all. Having tried to resist a sexual identity for years, McWhorter describes being defeated and finally 'confessing', or 'coming out'. Moreover, McWhorter noticed that Foucault referred to himself as a 'homosexual' on numerous occasions, all of which makes her think that resisting sex-desire while launching a counter-attack from bodies and pleasures must mean something other than what she had assumed. Ultimately, McWhorter argues that resistance and counter-attack may not be the same thing, and that it may only be once we have forgone resistance – or accepted our socially constituted sexual identities – that we are in a position to launch a counter-attack, at which point new forms of resistance become possible. Perhaps it is only by first accepting our subjection to power that we can effectively resist that power. After all, as Foucault says, there is no outside to power, and so perhaps our counter-attack *against* power can take place only once we have accepted our subjection *to* power, or the fact that we have already been constituted as sexual subjects.

As an example, we can return to Foucault's discussion of a 'reverse discourse' in *The History of Sexuality*. As Foucault's discussion of 'reverse discourse' suggests, one way that subjects can resist the medicalization of their sexuality is by first internalizing or identifying with the medical label that doctors have given them: it was necessary to first *be* a homosexual, in other words, in order to critique the pathologization of homosexuality. One had to initially accept that one *was* this medically constituted thing called 'homosexual' before one could say: 'Alright, but this identity does not make me sick.' It may also be that it was only by accepting the identity of homosexual that a political movement could be formed around that identity, or that people who so identified could form a community and coalition to resist police brutality, anti-gay acts of violence and social stigma. Although this involves an initial submission to power – accepting the sexual label that the deployment of sexuality imposes – ultimately it allows one to fight back against power in a way that one could not have done otherwise, and to do so in ways that subvert the intentions of how power was originally wielded. For instance, as noted in the previous chapter, when doctors labelled individuals as 'homosexual' in the nineteenth century, their intention was not to have those subjects accept that label and redeploy it as an identity position about which homosexuals could be proud, around which they could form neighbourhoods, establish bars, start their own Olympics, repeal sodomy laws and, eventually, insist on the removal of that label from the *Diagnostic and Statistical Manual of Mental Disorders* of the American Psychiatric Association.

NOTE

1 For a Foucauldian study of how biopower and discipline control the care of one's body, see Bartky (1988); for a study of how disciplinary power controls diet, see Bordo (2004) and Heyes (2006); for a Foucauldian study of how biopower controls housing choices and opportunities and the raising and education of children, see Feder (1997; 2007); for an analysis of the disciplining of speech, see St. Pierre (2012).

SUGGESTIONS FOR FURTHER READING

Campbell, Timothy. 2013. *Biopolitics: A Reader*. Durham, NC: Duke University Press.

Cisney, Vernon, and Nicolae Morar (eds.). 2015. *Biopower: Foucault and Beyond*. Chicago: University of Chicago Press.

Faubion, James D. (ed.). 1994. *Essential Works of Foucault*, vol. 3, *Power*. New York: New Press.

Foucault, Michel. 1980. *Power/Knowledge: Selected Interviews and Other Writings*. New York: Pantheon.

Golder, Ben (ed.). 2013. *Re-Reading Foucault: On Law, Power and Rights*. Abingdon, UK: Routledge.

Golder, Ben, and Peter Fitzpatrick. 2009. *Foucault's Law*. Abingdon UK: Routledge.

Lemke, Thomas. 2011. *Biopower: An Advanced Introduction*. New York: New York University Press.

Rose, Nikolas. 2006. *The Politics of Life Itself: Biomedicine, Power, and Subjectivity in the Twenty-First Century*. Princeton, NJ: Princeton University Press.

3

WOMEN, CHILDREN, COUPLES AND 'PERVERTS'

DENATURALIZING SEX

In the 'Domain' section of part IV of *The History of Sexuality*, Foucault describes what he envisaged to be the topics of analysis for the remaining volumes of *The History of Sexuality*. These were: '1. A hysterization of women's bodies... 2. A pedagogization of children's sex... 3. A socialization of procreative behavior... [and] 4. A psychiatrization of perverse pleasure' (Foucault, 1978, p. 102). The original French edition of volume 1 provided the projected titles for five more volumes of the series. These were: *La chair et le corps* (*The Body and the Flesh*), *La croissade des enfants* (*The Children's Crusade*), *La femme, la mère, l'hystérique* (*The Woman, the Mother, the Hysteric*), *Les pervers* (*Perverts*) and *Population et races* (*Population and Races*) (Macey, 1993, p. 354). In 1976, Foucault thus imagined writing five additional volumes of *The History of Sexuality*, four of which would have examined one of the figures corresponding to these 'four great strategic unities': the masturbating child, the hysterical woman, the sexual 'pervert' and the procreative couple that was responsible for reproducing the population and the race (Foucault, 1978, p. 102). Had Foucault pursued this plan, with the exception of *La chair et le corps*, he would have maintained a historical focus on the late eighteenth, nineteenth and early twentieth centuries, as in volume 1 of *The History of Sexuality* and in all his earlier works. As we now know, Foucault would never write the books he anticipated in volume 1. Instead, and to the regret of many Foucault scholars, he would depart from the historical period in which he had developed an expertise in order to write volumes 2 and 3 of *The History of Sexuality* on sexual ethics in ancient Greece and Rome; volume 4 – which was drafted at the time of Foucault's death but has never been published – focuses on early Christianity.

What did Foucault intend to demonstrate in these never-to-be-written volumes with respect to the hystericized woman, the masturbating child, the sexualized 'pervert' and the procreative couple? While we are given only a glimpse of what Foucault was thinking about these figures in the 'Domain' section of *The History of Sexuality*, by looking at what he says about them in other parts of the volume, and in his course lectures from the same period, we can construct at least a sense of what the arguments of these books would have entailed. In broad terms, Foucault's plan for these volumes was to provide concrete examples of the argument that he was making theoretically in the first volume, which is that sexuality – and the sexuality of each of these figures in particular – is a 'historical construct' *produced by* rather than subjected to modern forms of power (1978, p. 105). Indeed, although Foucault is widely known as a 'social constructivist', and the idea that sexuality is 'socially constructed' is perhaps the most influential argument in *The History of Sexuality*, the opening pages of the 'Domain' section are one of the few places in which he uses this terminology explicitly. Indeed, in a 1982 interview, Foucault surprisingly refuses to take a position on whether sexuality is the result of an 'innate predisposition' versus 'social conditioning', simply stating: 'On this question I have absolutely nothing to say. "No comment"' (Foucault, 1989b, p. 323). In the 'Domain' section of *The History of Sexuality*, however, he writes of a 'production of sexuality' and states that '[s]exuality… is the name that can be given to a historical construct' (1978, p. 105). This is in opposition to the view of sexuality that Foucault refutes at the outset of this section, insisting that '[s]exuality must not be described as a stubborn drive' (p. 103).

In rejecting the view of sexuality as a drive, as in his rejection of the 'repressive hypothesis', Foucault is setting himself in opposition both to psychoanalytic theory and to a 'popular' view of sex. Freud describes sexuality as a biological drive (*Trieb*) that conflicts in many ways with the requirements of society or civilization. For Freud, our sexual instincts are, for instance, polymorphously perverse, bisexual, sadistic and incestuous, while the requirements of civilization are that our sex lives be reproductive, genital, heterosexual, non-violent and exogamous or non-incestuous. For Freud, this means that society necessarily exercises a repressive power over our primordial sexual urges, but never fully successfully, and not without psychic repercussions.

More generally, the view of sexuality as a natural drive is pervasive. We may think, for instance, of Gay Liberation arguments that homosexuals are 'born that way'. The instinctual drive view of sexuality (and especially of male sexuality) is also seen in contemporary interviews with male clients of sex workers (MacInnes and Nason, 2013; Sanders, 2008; Jordan, 1997). Clients frequently compare their need for sex to their need for food. Clients state that their sexual urges – not only for sex but for sexual variety – are 'hard-wired', biological and innate, since males of the species are genetically programmed to spread their seed. Clients thus conclude that no laws will ever prevent men from buying sex, because they were determined to do so in the primordial slime. This, we are told, is why sex work is the 'oldest profession'. Society, or power, on this popular view, is something that tries to stop sexuality – and does so through the repressive force of law, such as laws criminalizing sex work and the purchasing of sex – but will always fail in its task, because it is up against something greater than itself: nature.

The primordial slime theory does nothing, however, to explain the huge variance in how many men have sex with prostitutes across cultures. Historical and sociological studies show that prostitution has not existed in every culture and in every historical period and it has existed in very different forms in different cultures and different eras. Currently we see a vast difference in how many men go to sex workers in some countries versus others; for instance, approximately 6 per cent of men in Canada and 14 per cent of Scandinavian men hire sex workers but about 75 per cent of men in Thailand hire sex workers. Clearly, if this were just the result of a biological drive, we would see similar rates of purchasing sex across cultures. The fact that it is almost exclusively men who buy sex, and that men in some cultures buy it much more frequently than men in other cultures, indicates that whether or not one buys sex has to do with social factors such as gender and cultural norms around sexuality.

Against the primordial slime theory of sexuality, Foucault insists that sexuality is *not* a primitive instinct that society is perpetually and more or less vainly attempting to hold back. On the contrary, sexuality is what power produces. As he writes, sexuality is

> an especially dense transfer point for relations of power: between men and women, young people and old people, parents and offspring, teachers and students, priests and laity, an administration and a population. Sexuality is not the most intractable element in power relations, but rather one of those endowed with the greatest instrumentality: useful for the greatest number of maneuvers and capable of serving as a point of support, as a linchpin, for the most varied strategies.
>
> (Foucault, 1978, p. 103)

The sustained cases through which Foucault thought he would demonstrate this thesis were the sexuality of women, children, procreative couples and 'perverse' adults. Importantly, Foucault notes that the sexualization of each of these figures has been constituted either in or through the institution of the family. Foucault emphasizes throughout the 'Domain' section that it was crucial for biopower to infiltrate the family in order to be effective in its goals, and he anticipated paying considerable attention to the family in the volumes to follow. As he writes:

> The family was the crystal in the deployment of sexuality: it seemed to be the source of a sexuality which it actually only reflected and diffracted. By virtue of its permeability, and through that process of reflections to the outside, it became one of the most valuable tactical components of the deployment.
>
> (Foucault, 1978, p. 111)

Although Foucault would never write the volumes in which the family was to be at stake, he discusses this institution at length in *The History of Sexuality* and in his course lectures from the same period. In the following section, I piece together some fragments of Foucault's analysis of the family from these sources.

DOMAIN: THE FAMILY

Foucault argues that, historically, the family was an institution of sovereign power, with patriarchal heads of households able to do with their wives, slaves and children as they willed. In part V of *The History of Sexuality* Foucault describes the ancient Roman *familia* as the pure example of sovereign power (1978, p. 135). The question, for Foucault, which he revisited continually between 1974 and 1976, was the extent to which the modern family has *remained* an institution of sovereign power and the extent to which it has been transformed by biopower. In *Discipline and Punish*, Foucault notes that 'one day we shall show how intra-familial relations, essentially in the parents–children cell, have become "disciplined," absorbing since the classical age external schemata, first educational and then military, then medical, psychiatric, psychological' (Foucault, 1977, pp. 215–16). The family has been disciplined, Foucault acknowledges at this point, but these mechanisms are deemed 'external' to the type of power by which it is fundamentally characterized. Similarly, in *Psychiatric Power*, Foucault argues that the family is and remains a sovereign institution. He writes, '[I]t seems to me that the family is a sort of cell within which the power exercised is not, as one usually says, disciplinary, but rather of the same type as the power of sovereignty' (Foucault, 2006b, p. 79). Ironically, although Foucault so often argues that we theorize power as sovereign when it is in fact disciplinary, in the case of the family he initially makes the reverse claim: whereas we think of the family as disciplinary, it is actually sovereign (p. 80). Insofar as the family disciplines children, these practices have merely been 'grafted onto' the institution, and the family could and often does function without them: 'Supervision is not constitutive of but supplementary to the family, whereas permanent supervision is absolutely constitutive of disciplinary systems' (p. 80).

Sovereign power, Foucault explains, is grounded either in blood-right or blood-conquest (p. 43). With sovereign power there is always a 'founding precedence' situated in the past, such as a battle or a royal birth, that justifies the sovereign's rule. Sovereign power regularly reaffirms its authority through rituals that refer back to this original event of bloodshed or blood-right. Additionally, under sovereign power, individuality is located at the top, in the body of the sovereign, whereas those submitted to sovereign power are not individuated. In contrast, disciplinary power is future-oriented, replacing backward-looking rituals with graduated exercises aimed at an optimal future state (p. 47). Discipline is justified by the perceived desirability of the disciplined state that its practices bring about: the well-trained soldier, the high-achieving student, the orderly ward, the productive workshop. Discipline is thus forward-looking, in opposition to sovereign power. In disciplinary institutions, power is de-individualized – one warden could be replaced by another warden or by a surveillance camera – whereas those submitted to discipline are individualized (p. 54). According to these criteria, Foucault initially thought that even the modern family could be situated as a sovereign institution.

In support of this view, the authority of parents over their children is normally one of blood-right. The results of DNA tests make a difference with respect to what power certain people can exercise over other people. Specific parents have authority over specific children because their own blood runs in their veins. Parents may monitor their children, they may keep them prisoners in their homes, they may discipline them and keep them on a strict timetable, but they have the authority to do so because of a blood-right that is intimately known, and not as a consequence of the anonymous workings of disciplinary power. Disciplinary practices thus supplement the family but do not constitute it: a family that does not discipline its children is still a family. Similarly, marriage was traditionally understood as a conquest involving bloodshed (the breaking of the hymen), and the community accepted this alliance only once the woman's blood was seen. Blood, then, has historically been as important to the husband–wife axis as to the parent–child axis of the family, though it is blood in the form of bloodshed rather than birth or descent, and this manner of viewing marriage is clearly more outdated in the West than the similarly blood-based view of parenthood.

Also situating it on the side of sovereign power, the celebration of backward-looking rituals, such as birthdays and wedding anniversaries, regularly reminds the family's members of its authority; these rituals recall foundational moments of bloodshed and birth. As Foucault writes, 'It is this reference to the earlier act, to the status conferred once and for all [by marriage or birth], which gives the family its solidity' (2006b, p. 80). The family, like sovereign institutions more generally, aims to be solid and static, to reproduce itself or to stay the same, in contrast to the ever-expanding, creative, annexing and innovative institutions of disciplinary power (Foucault, 1978, p. 107).

More contentiously, Foucault argues in *Psychiatric Power* that fathers are individuated in the family, like the head of the Leviathan, in a way that no other family members are. Foucault asks rhetorically, 'What do we see in the family if not a function of maximum individualization on the side of the person who exercises power, that is to say, on the father's side?' (2006b, p. 80). The power of patriarchs over their family members also lacks the anonymity of power in the panoptic system. Put otherwise, fathers are not interchangeable in the way that disciplinary figures such as prison wardens, doctors and teachers are.

In *Psychiatric Power*, Foucault thus argues that, despite the ways in which the family has been invaded by new technologies of power in the modern era, the sovereign power of the family continues to play a crucial collaborative role within a disciplinary society. For one thing, the family's sovereign power is essential for inserting family members into disciplinary institutions. The family insists that its children go to school, that its sons do military service and that its members go to work each day. When children and spouses fail to do these things, it is often the family that hands them over to disciplinary institutions, consigning them to asylums or taking them to therapy. This collaboration with the disciplinary institutions is not a one-sided relation or mere evidence that the family has been co-opted by discipline. On the contrary, families turn their members over to disciplinary institutions because the favour is reciprocated: the disciplinary institutions return children and spouses after having transformed them into familialized subjects, individuals who will submit to the family and its goals. For Foucault, the morality that passes as psychiatric cure prescribes marriage and parenthood against drunkenness, promiscuity, illegality, disorder, negligence and laziness – all behaviours that undermine the family's goals. For Foucault, the sovereign institution of the family and the very different disciplinary institutions with which it interacts are thus in a series of symbiotic relations today.

Against his own arguments for the sovereignty of familial power in *Psychiatric Power*, by the time he wrote *The History of Sexuality* Foucault had realized that, at least in recent decades in the West, the family does not justify its power *exclusively* through backward-looking rituals but *also* through its ability to produce well-disciplined subjects. The family accomplishes this production through graduated exercises, often involving a strict timetable (meal times, school hours, homework, scheduled extra-curricular activities, bedtimes), that aim at a future optimal state: the production of healthy, 'normal' adults. A family that fails to produce well-disciplined and 'normal' subjects may lose its authority over its members through the interventions of state and disciplinary agents. In the modern family, the power of the father has moreover been greatly diminished. The father's sovereign power to punish corporeally has virtually disappeared in Western societies, and, if it is exercised, may also lead to interventions by disciplinary institutions or the state seizure of children. Increasingly forbidden to punish corporeally, the family resorts to techniques such as isolation and privation, 'grounding', 'time-out' and the withdrawals of privileges and freedoms, thus more closely reproducing the punitive strategies of the prison than those of Renaissance kings.

The sovereign power of fathers and husbands over the sexuality of their children and wives is also subject to disciplinary interventions. In *The History of Sexuality*, Foucault discusses the removal of children from families suspected of incest (1978, pp. 129–30). Moreover, as Foucault realized by the time he wrote *The History of Sexuality*, mothers are now at least as individuated within the family as fathers. If we return to the case of Nathan discussed in Chapter 2, for instance, Feder notes that Nathan's mother was far more individuated in the case study than his father: although the father quickly disappears from the treatment programme, Rekers' team recognized that, to successfully normalize Nathan, his mother's efforts would need to be co-opted. Finally, even the most indisputable reason for viewing the family as sovereign – the significance of blood – is being diminished under the pressures of reproductive technologies and new familial forms.

In contrast to *Psychiatric Power*, and more in keeping with these modern trends in familial power, in Foucault's lectures from the following year, *Abnormal*, he argues that a 'new' kind of family was 'born' in the nineteenth century, and has 'replaced' the older, sovereign family. The new family is a medicalized, panoptic and normalizing entity, and mothers as well as fathers function as doctors within it – or, to be exact, as the instruments of doctors, therapists and biopolitical state interests. Practices of normalization are described as 'constituting' the newly born family rather than being merely 'grafted' onto an older institution. In these lectures, Foucault contrasts the kind of family that existed up until the mid-eighteenth century, at least among the upper classes, with the family that has 'replaced' it. He writes:

> Until the middle of the eighteenth century the aristocratic or bourgeois family... was above all a sort of relational system. It was a bundle of relations of ancestry, descent, collateral relations, cousinhood, primogeniture, and alliances corresponding to schemas for the transmission of kinship and the division of goods and social status. Sexual prohibitions effectively focused on these kinds of relations.
>
> (Foucault, 2003a, p. 248)

In contrast to this traditional family, we now have the modern family, or the biopolitical family cell:

> What is now being constituted is a sort of restricted, close-knit, sub-stantial, compact, corporeal, and affective family core: the cell family in place of the relational family; the cell family with its corporeal, affective, and sexual space entirely saturated by direct parent–child relationships.
>
> (Foucault, 2003a, p. 248)

Whereas the sovereign family forbade incest (such as marriage between first cousins), Foucault argues that the modern family is produced by 'incestuous' parent–child sexuality. One of the ways that the family produces 'incestuous' desire is through the parental monitoring of children's sexuality. In the nineteenth century this occurred through a war waged by parents – at the behest of doctors – against masturbation. This war required constant attentiveness to one's children, a smelling of sheets and hands, an alertness to erections, an examination of undergarments, a surveillance of children as they washed, went to bed, woke up and slept, and even a binding of bodies and a sharing of beds.

Although Foucault claims in *Psychiatric Power* that nothing about the family resembles the strategies of disciplinary institutions, by the time of the 1976 *Abnormal* lectures he describes parental monitoring of children's sexuality in precisely these terms. First, children are to be isolated: there was 'essentially a new organization, a new physics of family space: the elimination of all intermediaries and the suppression, if possible, of domestics, or at least a very close supervision of domestics, the ideal solution being the infant alone in a sexually aseptic family space' (2003a, p. 245). Second, parents are to engage in surveillance: 'the family space must be a space of continual surveillance... Parents must keep a lookout all around their children, over their clothes and bodies. The child's body must be the object of their permanent attention' (p. 245). The parents' isolation with and attentiveness to children is described as a kind of corporeal envelopment, an absorption into their own bodies.

Of this 'incestuous' parent–child relation Foucault writes that, '[o]f course, the direct parent–child contact so urgently prescribed in this familial cell gives absolute power to parents over their children', and yet he also argues that parental power is a mere 'fiction', since it is in fact subservient to medical power (pp. 249–50). Foucault stresses that this does not mean that parents have taken on the disciplinary power of doctors, but that they defer to and extend it: 'This also means that their control is subordinate, that it must be open to medical and hygienic intervention, and that they must call upon the external and scientific authority of the doctor at the first warning signs' (p. 250). Foucault describes a scenario in which parents have the authority to decide whether their children will receive medical treatment for their 'abnormal' conditions, but the decisions they make are thoroughly informed by the ways in which they have internalized medical norms: 'All immediate power over the child's body… is given to this medicalized family that is, however, controlled externally by medical knowledge and techniques' (p. 254).

Foucault traces the emergence of this new family to biopolitics. Although the worries about masturbation were a medically constructed fiction, the medical establishment used this crusade to get parents to pay attention to their children, and this, in the age of emerging biopower, in order *to keep them alive*. Doctors and the state wanted parents to pay attention to their children not because masturbation was actually lethal but because parental attentiveness to their children's activities would lower childhood fatalities *from other causes* (p. 255). As Foucault writes, 'In my view, the sexuality of children concerns parents more than children' (p. 258). Foucault is perhaps drawing on histories of childhood that indicate a relative lack of parental interest in their children up until the modern period (Ariès, 1988). Some historians have argued that pre-modern parents did not bond with their children because, given infant mortality rates of the time, they half expected them to die. In a sort of vicious circle, this lack of parent–child bond contributed to the high mortality rates that inhibited parents from forging affective bonds with their children in the first place (Cunningham, 2005; 2006; Duncan, 1973; James,

1997). It was lower mortality rates in the modern era, brought about by a number of factors (fewer famines, the end of the plague, maternal nursing replacing wet-nursing, improved hygiene), that finally allowed parents to invest emotionally in their children, and this new investment contributed in turn to lower mortality rates. Foucault's argument is that part of the new interest of parents in children was sexual, and that this libidinal investment was cultivated by doctors. While the eighteenth- and nineteenth-century medical crusade to urge mothers to breastfeed their children is well documented in studies of childhood, Foucault describes a contemporary crusade on the part of the same doctors, one that also targeted middle-class mothers. Like the crusade against wet-nursing, the crusade against masturbation led to the expulsion of 'intermediaries' and cultivated a more intimate parent–child bond, contributing to the formation of the bourgeois, cellular or nuclear family.

In *The History of Sexuality*, first published the year after he delivered the *Abnormal* lectures, Foucault once more describes the disciplining and biopoliticization of the family in the modern era in some detail, observing the manners in which the nineteenth-century family was steeped in sexuality. According to Foucault, the three great axes of biopower – pedagogy, medicine and demography – target the three main units within the family respectively: children, women and the reproductive couple. Pedagogy waged war on the onanistic practices of children; medicine 'saturated' the feminine or maternal body with sexuality; and demography took up the regulation of the population, monitoring births and birth control practices (Foucault, 1978, pp. 104–5). The fourth domain of the deployment of sexuality, the taxonomization of perversions, is, Foucault acknowledges, more marginally a familial matter, but he discusses the manners in which families collaborated with doctors in this regard. Indeed, Foucault observes that families *sought out* psychiatrists to help them with their sexually abnormal members, only to be told by these doctors that *they* were the problem, the root of perversion, from whom their abnormal family members needed to be sequestered in order to be cured. As he writes:

Then these new personages made their appearance: the nervous woman, the frigid wife, the indifferent mother – or worse, the mother beset by murderous obsessions – the impotent, sadistic, perverse husband, the hysterical or neurasthenic girl, the precocious and already exhausted child, and the young homosexual who rejects marriage or neglects his wife... Then a pressing demand emanated from the family: a plea for help in reconciling these unfortunate conflicts between sexuality and alliance; and caught in the grip of this deployment of sexuality which had invested it from without, contributing to its solidification into its modern form, the family broadcast the long complaint of its sexual suffering to doctors, educators, psychiatrists, priests, and pastors, to all the 'experts' who would listen. It was as if it had suddenly discovered the dreadful secret of what had always been hinted at and inculcated in it: the family...was the germ of all the misfortunes of sex. And lo and behold, from the mid-nineteenth century onward, the family engaged in searching out the slightest traces of sexuality in its midst, wrenching from itself the most difficult confessions, soliciting an audience with everyone who might know something about the matter, and opening itself unreservedly to endless examination.

(Foucault, 1978, pp. 110–11)

Foucault writes that families, 'burdened down as they were with this sexuality that saturated them, appealed for mediation and treatment' from doctors and psychiatrists, who blamed the family for their patients' ills but did at least return these patients as 'individuals who were sexually compatible with the family system' (p. 112). Once again we can recall four-year-old Nathan, whose gender dysphoria was blamed on his mother, but whom Rekers returned to his family with 'male gender identity and no emotional disturbance', and hence as a more likely candidate for heterosexual marriage and fatherhood than he had been beforehand.

By the time he wrote *The History of Sexuality*, Foucault thus seems to have shifted his position on familial power from the one he had taken in *Discipline and Punish* and *Psychiatric Power*. In these slightly earlier works, Foucault describes the traditional, patriarchal and extended family as an institution of sovereign power, in which the patriarchal head of the household is the 'king of his castle'. Like a sovereign ruling his kingdom, the patriarch lays down the law and punishes those who transgress it, often through physical violence, and he is himself above the law. In 1974 and 1975, when he gave the *Psychiatric Power* lectures and published *Discipline and Punish*, although Foucault acknowledged that disciplinary tactics had been 'grafted' onto the traditional family, he did not think that the family had been fundamentally altered by these graftings. In contrast, in both *Abnormal* and *The History of Sexuality*, presented and published in 1975 and 1976, Foucault argues that the family had been radically transformed in the course of the nineteenth and twentieth centuries. In *The History of Sexuality* and *Abnormal*, Foucault is concerned with describing the specifically *modern* family, one that is both the target and product of biopower.

The modern family is very different from the traditional family: it is a nuclear family composed not of extended relations and many generations but of two axes – the parent–child axis and the husband–wife axis. We now have small, two-generation families and parental power rather than patriarchal power. This means that mothers and wives play a significant role in familial power, much like fathers and husbands. The family has diminished in size, and, because it is a privileged site for the deployment of sexuality, it has become 'incestuous' rather than a site of sexual repression. Again, Foucault is arguing against a sovereign view of power in which power, in the form of the law, says 'No' to incest. On the contrary, by targeting the family as a site for the deployment of sexuality, the workings of power have sexualized the family.

At the same time, in *The History of Sexuality* Foucault takes a more moderate view of the family than he does in *Abnormal*, declining to see it as entirely new or exclusively biopolitical. Instead, he contrasts the biopolitical deployment of sexuality with the sovereign deployment of alliance, which characterized the traditional family and, Foucault argues in this work, has not yet disappeared. Foucault thus contends that the family today is characterized by the remnants of a sovereign deployment of alliance *as well as* the biopolitical deployment of sexuality. He writes:

> It is not exact to say that the deployment of sexuality supplanted the deployment of alliance. One can imagine that one day it will have

replaced it. But as things stand at present, while it does tend to cover up the deployment of alliance, it has neither obliterated the latter nor rendered it useless.

(Foucault, 1978, p. 107)

This deployment of alliance is characteristic of sovereign power, as it may be contrasted, 'term for term', with biopower (pp. 106–9). The traditional deployment of alliance is a static system of prohibitions, in contrast to the modern deployment of sexuality, which is mobile, polymorphous and contingent in its techniques, continually expanding its areas and forms of control. The deployment of alliance is repressive, whereas the deployment of sexuality is productive. In part V of *The History of Sexuality*, the sovereign symbolics of alliance and blood are contrasted with the biopolitical analytics of sex. 'Systems of alliance' are called 'the political form of the sovereign', in which, as in the family, 'the value of descent lines were predominant' (p. 147). Insofar as Foucault is arguing in *The History of Sexuality* that the modern family is the site of both a deployment of alliance and a deployment of sexuality, he is characterizing it as an institution of both sovereign power and biopower. Indeed, Foucault argues that the analytics of sex and the symbolics of blood and alliance, though 'two very distinct regimes of power', are characterized by 'overlappings, interactions, and echoes', and the family and marriage are two sites of interaction between these forms of power (p. 149). Put simply, sovereign power is about blood, biopower is about sex, and today the family is about both. Historically, this was not the case: until recently the family was almost exclusively preoccupied by blood, and its relation to sex was primarily one of prohibition. Today, however, the sexualization of the family is so intense that it almost masks the underlying significance of blood.

As is apparent, Foucault continually and somewhat confusingly shifted his account of the family between 1974 and 1976, initially viewing the family as a bastion of sovereign power onto which disciplinary mechanisms had merely been 'grafted'; then arguing that the sovereign family had been entirely 'replaced' by the modern, biopolitical family; and, finally, taking an in-between position in which the family maintains elements of both sovereign and disciplinary power, though the latter is increasingly eclipsing the former. What is clear from his repeated attempts to grapple with the domestic sphere in the years that he was theorizing disciplinary power and biopower is that Foucault saw the family as a crucial stake for the emergence of biopower in the nineteenth and twentieth centuries, and an institution that it was thus politically essential to understand. Because the family is the privileged locus of at least three of the four major strategies in the deployment of sexuality, it is described by Foucault as the target par excellence of biopower (p. 108).

In the following sections, I consider what Foucault has written about 'the four great strategic unities' for the deployment of sexuality as these were situated in or through the family: women, children, the reproductive couple and those diagnosed with 'perversions'. Although Foucault did not ultimately write a volume on each of these unities, I unpack what he did write about each of them in *The History of Sexuality*, supplementing this picture with relevant readings from his contemporary course lectures.

WOMEN

Foucault consistently makes the point in *The History of Sexuality* that, when biopower targets a type of individual or relationship, what happens is not that the innate sexuality of that individual or relationship is repressed but that the individual or relationship is sexualized in unprecedented ways. Again, biopower does not so much censor pre-existing sexualities as it constitutes new sexualities and new forms of sexualization. In just one of many examples of this sexualization phenomenon in *The History of Sexuality*, Foucault argues that, when biopower targeted women's bodies, it did not so much repress their innate sexual drives as it permeated them with sex, *constituting* female sexuality in new ways, including hysterical forms of sexuality. It should come as no surprise that biopower *would* target women's bodies, since the reproduction of the population takes place through those bodies. It is of clear biopolitical importance to the state to control women's bodies in order to manage the form their fertility takes, ensuring that the population grows, or does not grow, in particular ways. Women, therefore, became 'saturated with sexuality' under biopower. The highly gendered nineteenth- and twentieth-century phenomenon of hysteria, Foucault suggests, is one way that women's bodies responded to this saturation.

In arguing that women's bodies are 'saturated with sexuality' (while making no similar claim about men's bodies as a general class), Foucault makes a point that feminist scholars had made before him and have made since, which is that women's bodies have been particularly sexualized and (consequently) particularly medicalized in the modern era. Indeed, we may recall from Chapter 1 that Virginia Woolf wrote of the proliferation of scientific discourses on 'sex – women, that is to say'. As Woolf's terse phrase makes clear, the 'problem' of 'sex' very often simply meant the 'problem' of 'women'. In this way, Woolf draws attention to the fact that the sexualized human being, the human being about whom most of the writings of the sexual sciences were in fact concerned, was female. On the first page of *The Second Sex*, Simone de Beauvoir similarly writes: 'But first, what is a woman? "*Tota mulier in utero*: she is a womb," some say' (Beauvoir, 2010, p. 3). Like Woolf, de Beauvoir is noting that women are reduced (by male writers) to their sex, and moreover that their sex is reduced to their wombs or reproductive functions. No one was saying: 'What is a woman? She is a clitoris.' Woman's *reproductive* role has been equated with her sexuality, and her sexuality, in turn, was assumed to determine her destiny. Freud would write that women's struggles for equality were in vain since 'anatomy is destiny' (Freud, 1976, p. 320), and, of all her organs, woman's anatomy was equated with her uterus. As Foucault writes a bit later in *The History of Sexuality*:

> Thus, in the process of [the] hysterization of women, 'sex' was defined in three ways: as that which belongs in common to men and women; as that which belongs, par excellence, to men, and hence is lacking in women; but at the same time, *as that which by itself constitutes woman's body, ordering it wholly in terms of the functions of reproduction and keeping it in constant agitation through the effects of that very function*.
>
> (Foucault, 1978, p. 153, emphasis in original)

Woman, according to Freud and to the medical experts of both Woolf's and Beauvoir's times, was determined by the womb's anxious drive to fill itself, and hence fated to heterosexuality and a reproductive role in life. Women were, in other words, destined to be sex objects for men and to be mothers. Even women who rejected marriage and motherhood found themselves recuperated by this story of a womb-driven heterosexuality, for their rejection of traditional roles demonstrated not other aspirations beyond reproductive (hetero-)sexuality but penis envy and frigidity, or mere heterosexuality gone awry. In this way, women's bodies were, in Foucault's words, 'thoroughly saturated with sexuality' in the nineteenth and twentieth centuries, which meant not just that they were seen and produced primarily as objects of sexual pleasure for men but also that they were utterly medicalized.

Since the Greek word for uterus is *hystera* (υστέρα), Foucault's use of the phrase 'a hysterization of women's bodies' could simply refer to the reduction of women to their wombs. Beyond this, however, Foucault is referring to the medicalized phenomenon of hysteria, which was originally attributed to a 'wandering womb' (Corbin, 1990, p. 625). In his 1974 lectures at the Collège de France, *Psychiatric Power*, Foucault discusses hysteria as an unintended by-product of the medicalization of women's bodies. As discussed in the previous chapter, Foucault interprets hysteria as an effect of power on women's bodies, or a way in which women's bodies involuntarily resisted their hypersexualization and subjection to medical power. Although women could not free themselves from the patriarchal and medical control of their bodies, they could resist it through the symptoms of hysteria, which often made them incapable of performing their roles as wives and mothers. In states of psychosomatic paralysis, pain, delusions and fits, hysterical women could not manage their households, raise their children or be sexually available to their husbands, and many spent years bedridden or in asylums. The continually shifting, medically baffling symptoms of hysteria seriously undermined medical power's claims to knowledge and cure, and so, even if these symptoms did little to liberate women from a patriarchal medical power's grip, they did constitute a form of resistance: through these symptoms, thousands of women evaded their roles as wives, mothers and pawns of power. For this reason, Foucault writes in *Psychiatric Power* of 'the hysterics, those famous, dear hysterics', as a 'front of resistance' to disciplinary power (2006b, p. 253).

CHILDREN

As Foucault writes, children represent a 'precious and perilous, dangerous and endangered sexual potential' to biopower (1978, p. 104). As a result, 'precocious sexuality was presented from the eighteenth century to the end of the nineteenth as an epidemic menace that risked compromising not only the future health of adults but the future of the entire society and species' (p. 146). It is clear that a kind of power that aims to manage the population will need to control the form that the sexuality of the next generation takes. If the sexuality of children were to be allowed to go astray, this would pose an inestimable danger to the future of the biopolitical state. As Ann Laura Stoler observes, '[B]y the mid-nineteenth century, the notion in Europe that "the nation comes from the nursery," that "the history of nations is determined not on the battlefield but in the nursery" was heard again and again' (Stoler, 1995, p. 163). The problem for biopower is that children tend to be under the control of their families, and of parents in particular, with only a minority of children being wards of the state. The need to control the sexuality of children thus put biopower in conflict with the institution of the family. In order to control the sexuality of children, society needed to be transformed so that disciplinary figures such as doctors and teachers could intervene in children's sexuality rather than leaving this 'precious... potential' to the whims of parents. To some extent this required seizing children from the grasp of their parents, by placing unprecedented numbers of children in state-run institutions, and by allowing doctor's orders to trump the wishes of parents in some cases. Even more significantly, however, it required transforming parents so that they would reliably serve the interests of the biopolitical state. The struggle over the bodies of children and what Foucault calls 'the pedagogization' of their sex resulted in centuries-long struggles between parents and the state, and between parents and disciplinary figures. To this day the war is not won. Should parents or doctors have the ultimate authority to decide if a child in medical crisis should have a blood transfusion? Who should decide if a child is taught about evolution or sexuality in school, and what should be said? These are battles that continue today, in which a sovereign blood-right still occasionally holds sway over the perceived interests of children and the state.

In the 'Domain' section of *The History of Sexuality* Foucault flags the importance of the medical battle against childhood masturbation in allowing a disciplinary and biopolitical penetration of the family. To take but one example of this battle, in his 1886 *magnum opus*, *Psychopathia Sexualis*, Richard von Krafft-Ebing warns readers that childhood masturbation could lead to homosexuality:

> Nothing is so prone to contaminate – under certain circumstances, even to exhaust – the source of all noble and ideal sentiments, which arise of themselves from a normally developing sexual instinct, as the practice of masturbation in early years. It despoils the unfolding bud of perfume and beauty, and leaves behind only the coarse, animal desire for sexual satisfaction. If an individual, spoiled in this manner, reaches an age of maturity, there is wanting in him that aesthetic, ideal, pure, and free impulse which draws one toward the opposite sex. Thus the glow of sensual sensibility wanes, and the inclination toward the opposite sex becomes weakened. This defect influences the morals, character, fancy, feeling, and instinct of the youthful masturbator, male or female, in an unfavorable way, and, under certain circumstances, allows the desire for the opposite sex to sink to *nil*; so that masturbation is preferred to the natural mode of satisfaction.
>
> (Krafft-Ebing, 1894, p. 188, emphasis in original)

It was, in part, by arguing that childhood masturbation was dangerous that a medicalization of the family occurred, and the domestic sphere was transformed from 'a man's castle' to a clinic. As was also discussed above, Foucault argues that, although these measures may have been taken out of a proclaimed (and, in some cases, genuine) desire to protect children from the dangers of sex, the result was a sexualization of the family and children: in waging combat against masturbation, familial relations were rendered 'incestuous'.

What Foucault means by 'incest' – which he himself puts in scare quotes at at least one point – is unclear. Foucault's use of this term may not mean that he thought there had been an increased frequency of genital acts between parents and children since the biopoliticization of the family, nor that there is more sexual abuse of children today than existed historically. Because it is mothers rather than fathers who were particularly recruited into the role of monitoring children's bodies, Foucault's argument would predict that most incest is perpetrated by mothers, and would target boys and girls equally. If by 'incest' we mean genital contact and sexual abuse, however, this does not seem to be the case. On the contrary, it appears to be fathers and other male relatives far more frequently than mothers and women who engage in genital sexual acts with children, and girls who are the primary victims of incest (Bell, 1993). Since Foucault probably knew this, we can assume that his use of the term 'incestuous' at times refers less to genital acts than to the production of close-knit relations and intimate, possessive family bonds. He writes of 'the affective intensification of the family space', which may be loosely characterized as erotic, even if it does not involve sexual abuse, genital contact or genital pleasure (Foucault, 1978, p. 109). In *Abnormal*, Foucault describes this 'incest' as 'epistemophilic', suggesting that it entailed first and foremost a desire to *know* about children's sex, rather than a desire to *have* sex with children (2003a, p. 249). Foucault thus appears to describe the modern, nuclear family as 'incestuous' as a shorthand and hyperbolic way of describing the power/knowledge relations involved in the modern family's escalated intimacy, affectivity and libidinal investments, all of which, unlike genital acts of incest, may in fact be more prevalent in mother–child relations than in father–child relations, even today.

As in the case of women, Foucault argues that children have been sexualized as a result of the biopolitical investment in their sex. Even if the purpose in monitoring children's bodies was to protect them from sex, to shield them from premature sexual knowledge and contact, and to preserve childhood as a period of 'innocence', Foucault argues that the outcome has backfired, steeping children in sex. We can consider the current perception of paedophilia as an example. Although we know that most sexual abuse occurs in the home, the persistent conception of paedophiles as strangers lurking at the outskirts of playgrounds and school yards has resulted in practices of viewing children through what law professor Amy Adler calls 'the pedophilic gaze' (Adler, 2001, p. 256). We are now ever-vigilant to the threat that someone might perceive our children in sexual ways, and are on the lookout for 'stranger danger' in order to intervene. This has sexualized children, however; we now see them constantly as potential sexual prey through the lens of a dangerous other's imagined desire. Certain adults have also been sexualized in the process: a man sitting in a park where children play, a neighbour walking his dog who stops to talk to a child, a mother who photographs her child naked; each of these figures has been imbued with a suspicious, perverse sexuality that they would not have had previously. Although parents and adults generally have become alert to 'stranger danger' whenever children are around in order to protect them from this threat, their very alertness obliges them to constantly think about children as sexual objects, and arguably contributes to the production of the very desires it aims to combat.

Far from protecting the sexual innocence of childhood, in fact, this vigilance has made previously innocent images and behaviours sexual (Levine, 2002). Films and photos showing naked children once signified as natural and innocent, but now appear to us as pornographic and perverted. Family photographs and artwork showing naked children have repeatedly been interpreted as child pornography in recent years, to the astonishment of the photographers and artists, but in ways that have changed how we see. Now these images *do* appear pornographic, or *are* pornographic, because we have been taught to see them in this way. By censoring these images *as* pornographic, however, we force people who might not otherwise have done so to see children sexually. Arguably, and although this was not the intent, children are sexualized rather than protected from sex in the process of these shifts.

COUPLES

The third way that Foucault describes sexuality being deployed in the course of the nineteenth and twentieth centuries is through '[a] socialization of procreative behavior' (1978, p. 104). Although in earlier centuries procreation had been seen as the only morally acceptable reason to have sex, abstinence or life-long virginity were equally good options (if not better ones) from this moral perspective. The sinfulness of non-procreative sex did not make procreation a *social* obligation, however; it just meant that, *if* you were going to have sex, it had better be legitimate babies that were on your mind. While couples might have felt a familial responsibility to procreate prior to the biopolitical era – to produce heirs and ensure the survival of the familial line – they would not have felt a duty to have children for the sake of *society*. For the last few centuries, in contrast, reproduction, at least for some segments of the population, has been seen as a *social* good and even a patriotic duty, and society is assumed to have debts of gratitude towards those well-behaved citizens who pass on their 'worthy' genes. For example, the Canadian Family Allowance Act that was passed after World War II provided 'baby bonuses' for couples who reproduced. Significantly, however, these bonuses were taken away if the parents did not send their children to school. The idea seemed to be that we *ought* to give genetically fit procreative couples tax breaks, paid leave from work, subsidized day care and other compensations, but only so long as they are ceding their children to the state. Well-behaved procreative couples deserve 'bonuses' or rewards since, presumably, they altruistically bore children for the sake of the nation.

Importantly, however, this set of assumptions holds true only for privileged (primarily white, middle-class, able-bodied, cognitively normal, mentally 'fit') members of society whose genes are deemed advantageous to pass on; for other segments of society – those deemed 'unfit' to reproduce – procreation has been seen as an offence against society, resulting in children who are a burden to the state and taxpayers. As Foucault writes,

[T]he analysis of heredity was placing sex (sexual relations, venereal diseases, matrimonial alliances, perversions) in a position of

> 'biological responsibility' with regard to the species: not only could sex be affected by its own diseases, it could also, if it was not controlled, transmit diseases or create others that would afflict future generations. Thus it appeared to be the source of an entire capital for the species to draw from.
>
> (Foucault, 1978, p. 118)

Studies of heredity and genetic counselling were undertaken, and, while for some individuals procreation was seen as a social responsibility, with one's sexuality viewed as 'capital' belonging to the species or the state, for others (those who might pass on diseases or disabilities) it was seen as irresponsible to procreate.

Regardless of whether one's prospective children were deemed boons or burdens to society, by the nineteenth century procreation had come to be viewed as a *social* concern rather than a personal choice or familial duty. This is because the modern state has recognized a need both to increase and genetically 'improve' its population. Healthy and 'fit' babies need to be born to ensure that the nation has a strong workforce and military, while the number of children who are considered a drain on state coffers needs to be decreased. The patriotic duty of those deemed 'fit' to procreate was perhaps most acutely felt following the world wars, when middle-class women were expected to withdraw from the workforce and retreat to the suburbs, marry if they were not married already and have multiple children. In this way, eugenically valuable women were expected not only to make way for returning soldiers who wanted these women's jobs (and wanted those women as (house-)wives) but also to replenish the depleted, post-war population. Eugenically 'fit' women who declined to have babies – who wished to pursue studies or careers instead – were chastised for their 'race-destroying' selfishness. By and large, however, genetically 'fit' couples rose to the patriotic call, producing what is called the 'baby boomer' generation, while in the same years thousands of individuals deemed genetically 'unfit' were sterilized against their will or prevented from reproducing through sex-segregated institutionalization

(Bruinius, 2007; Davis, 1983; Harris-Zsovan, 2010; Grekul, 2011).

In addition to producing an ideology of procreation as a national duty and providing social and financial incentives for genetically 'valuable' couples to marry and procreate, the biopolitical state has funded considerable sexological research on heterosexual sex with the explicit objective of keeping these 'fit' procreative couples married and reproducing. Janice Irvine observes that sexology has been 'a profession committed to rehabilitating [heterosexual] marriages through better sex' (Irvine, 2005, p. 117). Intervening in the 'crisis in marriage' that threatens 'the family' has been the fundamental justification for sexological research since Alfred Kinsey (Kinsey *et al.*, 1948; 1953), and has been crucial for securing research funding and institutional support for this field. As McWhorter writes:

> The bourgeois family, Foucault tells us, was and is a thoroughly sexualized institution. At its foundation lies not a tradition or a territory, as in previous versions of the concept of 'family,' but a single sexual relationship, the intercourse of husband and wife. By the 1920s, therefore, the work of eugenicists intersected with that of sexologists and formed mutually reinforcing networks of knowledge and normalizing disciplinary authority. That single, crucial sexual relationship not only had to be safeguarded; it also had to be good.
>
> It had to be good in two ways. It had to be physically and emotionally satisfying... And it had to be morally acceptable, despite the fact that making it physically satisfying to both parties over the long term necessarily involved indulgence and even at times glorification of the carnal.
>
> (McWhorter, 2009, p. 258)

As McWhorter goes on to note, 'Sexologists had been working on making sexual pleasure morally acceptable for a long time already' (p. 258).

Although this may seem to imply that sexologists are left-wing sexual liberators, Foucauldian and feminist scholars alike have demonstrated that the objectives of sexologists in making sex 'good' was and continues to be the socially conservative task of keeping marriages intact. As McWhorter explains,

> Cultivating [sexuality] was especially important in light of the fact that eugenic marriage and child rearing required a great deal of sacrifice, especially on the part of women. Feminists had been complaining about the institution of marriage at least since Mary Wollstonecraft. Although things had changed somewhat since Wollstonecraft's time (1759–97), women who married still gave up many of their property rights, their right to choose their domicile, and to a significant extent their right to self defense. (A certain amount of wife-beating was a husband's prerogative well into the twentieth century.) In addition, childbearing could be mortally dangerous [indeed this is what killed Mary Wollstonecraft], and multiple pregnancies (an inevitability for most women without access to contraception) were debilitating. If there were no rewards to offset the sacrifices and risks, why would superior women, who were increasingly well educated and able to support themselves in a rising industrial economy, choose to become wives and mothers? Sexologists had the answer eugenicists sought: orgasm.
>
> Motherhood would be praised to the heavens, but the lure that would keep those eugenically valuable females in the baby-making trenches of the marriage bed year after year was good sex. Sexologists like Theodore van de Velde and Helene Wright offered help. In 1928, even though in many states oral sex was a criminal act, van de Velde recommended that men lubricate their wives' vaginas by means of the 'genital kiss,' that is, 'by gentle and soothing caresses with lips and tongue.' Wright's *The Sex Factor in Marriage* (1930) advises men to learn their wives' rhythms and lovingly attend to their clitorises. In fact, marriage manuals from the 1920s into the 1940s were full of advice to men about patience, clitoral stimulation, and foreplay. Very often the advice was laced with the repeated warning that the husband who failed to satisfy his wife sexually would likely lose her.
>
> (McWhorter, 2009, pp. 259–60)

So keen were sexologists to find ways to keep wives happy in the marriage bed that some even turned to lesbians for help. As McWhorter observes, 'Near the conclusion of New York's

Committee for the Study of Sex Variants report, George Henry writes, "Much can be learned from the study of the affectionate relations of sex variants which might contribute to the success of heterosexual unions"' (p. 261). Although, as McWhorter acknowledges, '[i]t may seem strange that eugenicists as far back as the 1920s would be pro-sex, especially pro-clitoral orgasm', and open to sex education from lesbians, what accounts for this sex positivity is their recognition that

> as women gained... rights, it was necessary to find ways to keep them from putting off marriage too long or eschewing it altogether. They had to be enticed. And they had to be kept happy once they were wed. Only so could the generative process reach its completion in the production of sexually mature, well-adjusted offspring ready to pair off and pass on those superior genes.
>
> (McWhorter, 2009, p. 261)

Although women could once have been expected to marry, and to remain married, because they had few or no alternatives, as the twentieth century progressed sexologists realized that women now needed to be lured into marriage, and kept sexually satisfied enough to remain there. While Freud still thought that women's uteruses could be relied on to keep them in the 'baby-making trenches' of the marriage bed, sexologists who followed him realized that attention needed to be shifted to the clitoris, if only to keep those eugenically fit uteruses filled. This illustrates Foucault's point that increased discourses around sexuality, however sexpositive they may seem, do not necessarily mean that an oppressed sexuality is being liberated from power; on the contrary, these discourses may be bent on keeping subjects trapped in their traditional roles of service to the family and the state.

'PERVERTS'

Finally, the fourth manner in which Foucault discusses sexuality being deployed in the nineteenth and twentieth centuries is through a psychiatrization of perverse pleasures. As he writes, beginning in the nineteenth century 'a clinical analysis was made of all the forms of anomalies by which [the sexual instinct] could be afflicted; it was assigned a role of normalization or pathologization with respect to all behavior; and finally, a corrective technology was sought for these anomalies' (1978, p. 105). Rather than simply condemning all extra-marital and non-procreative forms of sexual activity as sin, the sexual sciences scrupulously taxonomized the 'abnormal' forms that sexuality could take and devised treatment protocols to normalize them when possible. Importantly, when non-procreative and extra-marital sex was simply perceived as sinful, it was thought that *anyone* could be tempted to engage in these acts. That one engaged in them or did not merely demonstrated one's virtue or lack thereof, not that one had a particular type of sexuality. A person who ceded to carnal temptation and raped a woman was not very different from a person who gave in to a similarly carnal temptation and masturbated or had sex with a calf, a corpse or a close relative. In each case, one had engaged in an immoral carnal act, but this did not make one a particular kind of person (Foucault, 1978, p. 118). While some acts (masturbation, sex with non-human animals, sex with people of the same sex) were considered worse than others (rape, adultery) because they violated laws of nature and not just laws of civil society, engagement in these acts meant only that one had surrendered to carnal temptation in a particularly egregious way; it did not make one a particular *type* of person. Whether one had sex with a sheep or one's cousin, what had occurred was a *moral* failure and often a crime, but not the manifestation of an illness. In contrast, in works such as Heinrich Kaan's 1844 *Psychopathia Sexualis* and Krafft-Ebing's 1886 *Psychopathia Sexualis: A Medico-Legal Study*, sexually aberrant acts came to be attributed to 'constitutive anomalies, acquired derivations, infirmities, or pathological processes' (Foucault, 1978, p. 117).

To some degree the medicalization of sexual 'perversion' could morally and legally exculpate sex 'deviants': their behaviour implied not that they were immoral or criminal but that they were ill. Krafft-Ebing firmly situates sexual perversion in the domain of 'Medicine' rather than 'Morality' in the preface to *Psychopathia Sexualis*. As he writes:

The purpose of this treatise is a description of the pathological manifestations of the sexual life and an attempt to refer them to their
underlying conditions... The importance of the subject for the welfare
of society, especially forensically, demands, however, that it should be
examined scientifically... Even at the present time, in the domain of
sexual criminality, the most erroneous opinions are expressed and the
most unjust sentences pronounced, influencing laws and public opinion... It is the sad province of Medicine, and especially of Psychology,
to constantly regard the reverse side of life, – human weakness and
misery.

Perhaps in this difficult calling some consolation may be gained,
and extended to the moralist, if it be possible to refer to morbid conditions much that offends ethical and aesthetic feeling. Thus Medicine
undertakes to save the honor of mankind before the Court of Morality,
and individuals from judges and their fellow-men.

(Krafft-Ebing, 1894, pp. iv–v)

For Krafft-Ebing, sexual perversions were afflictions, akin to
tuberculosis or smallpox, that should be seen as part of the 'misery' of human life; to punish the ill was not justice but to heap
misery on misery. Sexual perversions, like other medical afflictions, required treatment or quarantine rather than punishment,
Krafft-Ebing argues, and, just as doctors distinguish between
many kinds of cancers in order to develop targeted cures, so they
must distinguish between different sexual perversions in order to
best treat or contain them.

While the medicalization of sexual deviance is in some sense
more compassionate than the juridico-legal, moral and 'aesthetic'
judgements it aimed to replace, as seen in the case of Charles Jouy,
the consequences for those deemed sexually 'sick' could be dire.
Although the sexually abnormal might be morally and legally
innocent, psychiatrists such as Kaan and Krafft-Ebing still viewed
them as dangerous to society, in large part because their deviance
was considered congenital. In his chapter on 'homo-sexuality', for
instance, Krafft-Ebing writes:

In this case, the cause is to be sought only in an anomaly of central conditions, – in an abnormal psycho-sexual constitution. This

constitution, as far as its anatomical and functional foundation is concerned, is absolutely unknown. Since, in almost all such cases, the individual subject to the perverse sexual instinct displays a neuropathic predisposition in several directions, and the latter may be brought into relation with <u>hereditary degenerate conditions</u>, this anomaly of psycho-sexual feeling may be called, clinically, a functional sign of <u>degeneration</u>. This perverse sexuality appears spontaneously, without external cause, with the development of sexual life, as an individual manifestation of an abnormal form of the vita sexualis, and then has the force of a *congenital* phenomenon; or it develops upon a sexuality the beginning of which was normal, as a result of very definite injurious influences, and thus appears as an *acquired* anomaly. Upon what this enigmatical phenomenon of acquired homo-sexual instinct depends is still inexplicable, and only a matter of hypothesis. Careful examination of the so-called acquired cases makes it probable that the predisposition also present here consists of a latent homo-sexuality, or, at least, bi-sexuality, which, for its manifestation, requires the influence of accidental exciting causes to rouse it from its slumber.

(Krafft-Ebing, 1894, p. 187, italics in original, emphasis added by author)

In accounting for the causes of same-sex desire, Krafft-Ebing refers repeatedly to a theory of 'degenerescence'. The theory of degenerescence was a theory of inverse evolution that was influential from the 1850s until the middle of the twentieth century. In the 1850s a French doctor named Benedict Morel argued that the human species had ceased evolving and was now degenerating, or moving backwards in terms of evolution. Following Darwin, scientists argued that humankind's nature and development were not fixed but could evolve, or, just as easily, deteriorate, with humans becoming weaker, sicker, less intelligent and less moral over time. Eugenicists voiced concerns that urban populations, and the populations of certain countries in particular, were degenerating. Some even worried that humans might be overtaken by better-adapted species, or that, if humans degenerated in one part of the world, such as Europe, they might be conquered by more evolved people of another race or nation. Pierre Boulle's 1963 novel *La planète de singes* – which inspired the 1968 Hollywood film *Planet of the Apes*, and all its spin-offs – imagines a future in which the human species has degenerated, lost its ability to use language and returned to the jungle. Earth is now dominated by other species of primates who evolved to use language and tools while the human species regressed. Speaking gorillas are depicted hunting and enslaving humans, while chimpanzee and orang-utan primatologists study the inferior primate species that is 'man'. Because the humans starring in *Planet of the Apes* are white, while the primates who are oppressing them are black and brown animals of Africa and Asia, these films reflect the eugenicist worry that non-European races could eventually evolve into ascendency over the white race (Haraway, 1989; Jahme, 2000). Nineteenth- and twentieth-century eugenicists discussed whether humans (and Europeans in particular) were still evolving or if they were now on the decline as the result of various factors, including urbanization and unhealthy lifestyles. Homosexuality was frequently taken as an example of such an unhealthy urban lifestyle, and eugenicists speculated that there was more homosexuality than previously. If this was true, it was taken to indicate that the species (or race) was becoming less adapted to survive: if humans (or Europeans) were less inclined to form procreative unions, this boded badly for the species (or for Europe).

For nineteenth- and early twentieth-century eugenicists, one way that the species or race could degenerate would be if acquired characteristics such as drug addiction, sexual perversion or criminality could be passed on to or otherwise impact offspring. One generation might opt for these unhealthy or immoral lifestyles as the result of urbanization, but the next generation could simply inherit or be banefully impacted by them, and the race would degenerate as a result of the immorality of one generation. Eugenicists thus argued that 'unfit' people such as 'perverts', criminals and alcoholics be sterilized so that they would not contribute to the degeneration of the human species, or of the white race in particular. Krafft-Ebing is taking a position within these debates, arguing that homosexuality is indicative of degeneration, and is a heritable trait. He locates homosexuality in the constitution or anatomy of the individual, even if he acknowledges that the anatomical cause has not yet been discovered. Krafft-Ebing argues that even in seemingly 'acquired' cases of homosexuality – cases that occur later in life, coexist with heterosexual behaviour and thus appear to be chosen – homosexuality is still congenital, with a latent homosexual 'predisposition' having been triggered by some 'very definite injurious influences'.

While the argument that homosexuals are 'born that way' is often assumed to have liberatory potential, the conclusion that Krafft-Ebing and other sexual scientists draw from this position shows that it could in fact work in the opposite manner. They argue that if homosexuality is congenital then homosexuals are dangerous to society for at least two reasons: (1) they can pass on their degenerate genes should they reproduce; and (2) they can instigate precisely the kind of events that activate latent homosexuality in the so-called 'acquired' cases, thus increasing the numbers of their kind. It is encounters with other homosexuals that are the 'very definite injurious influences' to which Krafft-Ebing refers. If homosexuals are left at liberty they will recruit other homosexuals, Krafft-Ebing fears, and, since they may occasionally still have intercourse with people of the opposite sex, they will contaminate the gene pool.

As Foucault notes, the theory of sexual perversion as hereditary and indicative of degenerescence did not simply suggest that homosexuals would pass on their own traits or give birth to more homosexuals but that people with degenerate genes of any kind would spawn children with degenerate genes of all other kinds. As Foucault writes, '[L]ook into the genealogy of an exhibitionist or a homosexual: you will find a hemiplegic ancestor, a phthisic parent, or an uncle afflicted with senile dementia… [A] sexual perversion resulted in the depletion of one's line of descent – rickets in children, the sterility of future generations' (1978, p. 118). For sexual scientists such as Krafft-Ebing, everything could be blamed on just one sign of abnormality or degeneration, much as masturbation could be blamed for homosexuality. For these early sexologists, deviants such as 'homo-sexuals' could not be cured and thus needed to be incapacitated – not in prisons, since they were morally innocent, but, like Charles Jouy, in hospitals, where they would spend the rest of their days.

PERIODIZATION

In the 'Periodization' section of *The History of Sexuality*, Foucault argues that the most important moments in the recent history of sexuality in the West are *not*, as is commonly assumed,

1   a seventeenth-century repression of sexuality, and
2   a twentieth-century sexual liberation movement.

Indeed, Foucault has hoped by this point to cast into doubt the 'hypothesis' that a repression of sexuality occurred at all, and has argued that the sexual liberation movement of the 1960s and 1970s did not so much resist sexual repression as it assisted in the biopolitical deployment of sexuality. Rather than a history of repression and liberation, Foucault suggests that the most important moments in the history of Western sexuality are:

1   the sixteenth-century mandating of sexual confession, and
2   the nineteenth-century development of 'medical technologies of sex' (1978, p. 119).

The sixteenth-century technologies of religious confession were discussed in Chapter 1, while the nineteenth-century development of 'medical technologies of sex' – including secular forms of sexual confession, the science of heredity, the psychiatrization of sexuality, and eugenics – have been discussed at length in this and the previous two chapters.

It is with respect to Freud's rejection of the theory of 'perversion–heredity–degenerescence', and thus his resistance to eugenics, that Foucault has a few words of praise for psychoanalysis in the 'Periodization' section that concludes part IV of *The History of Sexuality*. As he writes,

> It is very well to look back from our vantage point and remark upon the normalizing impulse in Freud; one can go on to denounce the role played for many years by the psychoanalytic institution; but the fact remains that in the great family of technologies of sex, which goes so far back into the history of the Christian West, of all those institutions that set out in the nineteenth century to medicalize sex, it was the one that, up to the decade of the forties, rigorously opposed the political and institutional effects of the perversion–heredity–degenerescence system.
>
> (Foucault, 1978, p. 119)

Although Freud considered homosexuality to be an 'aberration' or 'perversion', and although he made half-hearted efforts to 'cure' some homosexuals, when compared to the sexual scientists who preceded him, Freud's position on homosexuality was almost open-minded. In 'The sexual aberrations', an early essay in the *Three Essays on the Theory of Sexuality*, Freud argues that sexuality could be aberrant either in its object or its aim; in the case of an aberrant object, one desires an object with which one cannot procreate (Freud, 2011). This could be a person of the same sex, in the case of 'inversion'; a child, in the case of 'paedophilia'; a non-human animal, in the case of 'zoophilia'; a foot, in the case of 'foot fetishism'; or a dead body, in the case of 'necrophilia'. An aberrant sexual aim is when one's desire aims at anything other than the procreative act; thus manual and oral sex are aberrant if they are taken as ends in themselves, as opposed to when they are undertaken as part of what Freud calls 'fore-pleasure' ('foreplay'). In the first part of 'The sexual aberrations', Freud focuses on 'inversion', or homosexuality, and argues that there are three types of inverts: 'absolute inverts', who only ever desire people of their own sex and whose preference is present from a very early age; 'amphigenic inverts' or 'psychosexual hermaphrodites' (bisexuals); and 'contingent inverts', who are heterosexual under normal conditions but are capable of taking pleasure with someone of the same sex under certain conditions, such as in sex-segregated institutions or following negative heterosexual experiences. Whatever kind of 'invert' we are speaking of, however, Freud argues that 'degenerescence' is not at issue. Indeed, Freud cautions against speaking indiscriminately about 'degeneration', and, while he did not reject the term entirely, he insisted that it was overused.

Freud argues that the term 'degenerate' should be used only in cases in which individuals had deviated from the normal in multiple ways, and were consequently impaired in their ability to function or survive. He then argues that, while 'inverts' may deviate from the normal in one way (by making a less common choice of sexual object), this norm is in itself culturally contingent; Freud notes that, in ancient Greece, men making homosexual object choices would not have deviated from the normal. Freud then argues that, even within modern society, in which homosexuality is statistically abnormal, homosexuals do not qualify as degenerate since they deviate from the norm in only one way and may otherwise be normal. Moreover, Freud argues that homosexuals do not qualify as degenerate since they are not impaired in their ability to function or survive as a result of their choice of sexual object. In fact, Freud notes that many 'inverts' are highly cultivated and distinguished intellectuals.

Freud also rejects the theory of degenerescence in the case of homosexuality because he disagrees with Krafft-Ebing that homosexuality is necessarily congenital or innate. Freud notes that it is only the first group of 'absolute inverts' that we might consider to be innately homosexual. The second two groups, and especially the third (contingent inverts), put into doubt the idea that inversion is innate. Moreover, Freud says that, even in the case of absolute inverts, there is often some event in childhood that produced the tendency towards homosexuality in the person. Freud also argues that external factors play a role, which would not be true if homosexuality were innate. He even observes that inversion can be removed by hypnosis, which would be unbelievable if it were an innate characteristic. Freud observes that some of the 'external circumstances' – such as detention in prison – that lead to inversion in some do not lead to inversion in others, which leads him to suspect that it is not an absolute choice between 'innate' or 'acquired' but some combination of the two.

Although we might deplore Freud's situating of homosexuality as an aberration at all, Foucault applauds him for at least rejecting the theory of degenerescence. Freud's resistance to the theory of degenerescence may have been connected to his living at a time when Nazis were describing not only homosexuals but also Jews as degenerate. Although heterosexual, Freud, as a Jew, was just as likely to be deemed a danger to society as homosexuals were, given his own supposedly racially 'degenerate' genes. As Foucault observes in the concluding sections of *The History of Sexuality*, eugenics and the theory of sexual perversion–heredity–degenerescence were entirely bound up with biological and biopolitical state racism, and it is to this concluding argument of *The History of Sexuality* that the next chapter turns.

SUGGESTIONS FOR FURTHER READING

Birman, Joël. 2007. *Foucault et la psychanalyse*. Lyon: Parangon.

Donzelot, Jacques. 1979. *The Policing of Families*. New York: Random House [first published in French in 1977].

Duschinsky, Robbie, and Leon Antonio Rocha (eds.). 2012. *Foucault, the Family and Politics*. Basingstoke, UK: Palgrave Macmillan.

Hook, Derek. 2007. *Foucault, Psychology and the Analytics of Power*. Basingstoke, UK: Palgrave Macmillan.

Knowles, Caroline. 1996. *Family Boundaries: The Invention of Normality and Dangerousness*. Peterborough, ON: Broadview Press.

4

SEX, RACISM AND DEATH

FROM SANGUINITY TO SEXUALITY

'Sex is boring,' Foucault said in a 1983 interview (Foucault, 1983, p. 229). Why, if sex is boring, was Foucault dedicating a whole series of books to the topic at the time that he made this statement? According to his own account, he did so because sex is a privileged site through which power works in biopolitical times, and cultivating different relations to sex might undo some of the effects of this power. As he writes in *The History of Sexuality*,

> [Sex] was at the pivot of the two axes along which developed the entire political technology of life. On the one hand, it was tied to the disciplines of the body: the harnessing, intensification, and distributing of forces, the adjustment and economy of energies. On the other hand, it was applied to the regulation of populations, through all the far-reaching effects of its activity. It fitted in both categories at once, giving rise to infinitesimal surveillances, permanent controls, extremely meticulous orderings of space, indeterminate medical or psychological examinations, to an entire micro-power concerned with the

body. But it gave rise as well to comprehensive measures, statistical assessments, and interventions aimed at the entire social body or at groups taken as a whole... This is why in the nineteenth century sexuality was sought out in the smallest details of individual existences; it was tracked down in behavior, pursued in dreams; it was suspected of underlying the least insanities, it was traced back into the earliest years of childhood; it became the stamp of individuality – at the same time what enabled one to analyze the latter and what made it possible to master it.

(Foucault, 1978, pp. 145–6)[1]

Sex in itself is not interesting to Foucault, and, indeed, he thinks that we must be very suspicious of the fact that we think it *is* interesting, since it is precisely this belief that sex is interesting that has incited us to speak so much about it, with all the power effects that this speech has had. It is *power* that is interesting, for Foucault, but 'sex' – as a social construct – needs to be studied because it is the primary avenue for the workings of power today.

In part V of *The History of Sexuality* Foucault describes the shift from sovereign power to biopower as a move from a 'symbolics of blood' to an 'analytics of sex'. Sovereign power was invested in blood relations, and its paradigmatic expression was bloodshed. As Foucault writes of sovereign power, 'Law cannot help but be armed, and its arm, par excellence, is death; to those who transgress it, it replies, with that absolute menace' (p. 144). Not just killing the enemy in war but ordering one's own citizens to risk their lives in battle is an exercise of sovereign power. Sovereign power, Foucault explains in part V of *The History of Sexuality*, is 'the right of death', and its ultimate manifestation is to kill:

[F]or a society in which famines, epidemics, and violence made death imminent, blood constituted one of the fundamental values. It owed its high value at the same time to its instrumental role (the ability to shed blood), to the way it functioned in the order of signs (to have a certain blood, to be of the same blood, to be prepared to risk one's blood), and also to its precariousness (easily spilled, subject to drying up, too readily mixed, capable of being corrupted). A society of blood – I was tempted to say, of 'sanguinity' – where power spoke *through* blood: the honor of war, the fear of famine, the triumph of death, the sovereign with his sword, executioners, and torturers: blood was *a reality with a symbolic function*.

(Foucault, 1978, p. 147, emphasis in original)

If societies characterized by sovereign power operated through a 'symbolics of blood', Foucault writes that

[w]e, on the other hand, are in a society of 'sex,' or rather a society with a 'sexuality': the mechanisms of power are addressed to the body, to life, to what causes it to proliferate, to what reinforces the species, its stamina, its ability to dominate, or its capacity for being used. Through the themes of health, progeny, race, the future of the species, the vitality of the social body, power spoke *of* sexuality and *to* sexuality; the latter was not a mark or a symbol, it was an object and target.

(Foucault, 1978, p. 147)

One effect of this shift is that modern Western subjects no longer identify who they are through their blood and blood relations but, rather, through their sexualities.

As seen in Chapter 2, biopower is 'power over life' rather than a 'right of death', and it is this kind of power, Foucault argues, that is 'on the advance' (2003b, p. 254). Consequently, for Foucault, 'it is no longer a matter of bringing death into play in the field of sovereignty, but of distributing the living in the domain of value and utility. Such a power has to qualify, measure, appraise, and hierarchize, rather than display itself in its murderous splendor' (1978, p. 144). A problem arises for the biopolitical state, however, when it wishes to wage war, kill or expose its own citizenry to death. How can a biopolitical state engage in these typically sovereign actions? How can a biopolitical state justify war, executions or letting certain segments of the population die when its function is to foster, manage and optimize life? This, Foucault argues, is where racism comes in.

Racism is 'primarily a way of introducing a break into the domain of life that is under power's control: the break between what must live and what must die' (Foucault, 2003b, p. 254). Racism allows the biopolitical state to divide the species into races, and into fit and unfit specimens of 'the race', the 'white race', the 'Aryan race', the 'Nordic race' or the 'human race'. This, in turn, allows the biopolitical state to designate certain populations or segments of its own population as biological dangers, and thus to warrant those populations' deaths, political or otherwise, in the name of the protection and management of life. Consequently, Foucault writes that '*whenever*...there was a confrontation, a killing or the risk of death, the nineteenth century was quite *literally obliged* to think about them in the form of evolutionism' (Foucault, 2003b, p. 257, emphasis in original). A kind of racism that was originally grounded in nineteenth-century biological theories of evolution, eugenics, heredity and the survival of the fittest is what allowed (and, in new guises, continues to allow) killing to be co-opted into the politics of life that characterizes societies such as ours. Moreover, even if much of this nineteenth-century science has now been repudiated, this kind of racism is likely to go on existing so long as we have biopolitical states, and these states feel the need to kill.

Although Foucault distinguishes between a sanguine power and a power that produces sexualities, he also writes that modern biopolitical racism has at times reactivated a symbolics of blood, fusing a symbolics of blood with an analytics of sex. Thus, for instance, although in general we have moved from identifying ourselves according to our blood to identifying ourselves by our sexual desires, some modern Western subjects have cared very much that their blood was European and, more specifically, that it was Northern European, Aryan or Nordic. Indeed, sexual and sanguine identities and practices have often been entangled in the course of recent centuries; for eugenicists, it was necessary for certain kinds of sex to take place and for other kinds of sex to be prevented, for some kinds of sexuality to be ensured and for others to be arrested, if Northern European, Aryan and Nordic bloodlines were to be kept pure and healthy. Concerns about blood could easily justify interventions in sex, and what kind of blood you had could determine whom you should have sex with, or whether you should have sex at all. The eugenics movement, especially in the form it took under National Socialism in Germany, combined the symbolics of blood with the analytics of sex with deadly consequences. As Foucault writes:

> Beginning in the second half of the nineteenth century, the thematics of blood was sometimes called on to lend its entire historical weight toward revitalizing the type of political power that was exercised through the devices of sexuality. Racism took shape at this point (racism in its modern, 'biologizing,' statist form): it was then that a whole politics of settlement [*peuplement*], family, marriage, education, social hierarchization, and property, accompanied by a long series of permanent interventions at the level of the body, conduct, health, and everyday life, received their color and their justification with the mythical concern of protecting the purity of blood and ensuring the triumph of the race. Nazism was doubtless the most cunning and the most naïve (and the former because of the latter) combination of the fantasies of blood and the paroxysms of a disciplinary power... A eugenic ordering of society, with all that implied in the way of extension and intensification of micro-powers, in the guise of an unrestricted state control [*étatisation*], was accompanied by the oneiric exaltation of a superior blood; the latter implied both the systematic genocide of others and the risk of exposing oneself to a total sacrifice. It is an irony of history that the Hitlerite politics of sex remained an insignificant practice while the blood myth was transformed into the greatest blood bath in recent memory.
>
> (Foucault, 1978, pp. 149–50)

Although there is a tendency to think of eugenics as a nineteenth- and early twentieth-century phenomenon that was repudiated after the Holocaust, Foucault was well aware that eugenics continued in more subtle forms and under new names ('genetic counselling', 'family planning', 'pro-family' politics) in the 1970s, and it continues in these forms today.

A 2014 article in *The San Francisco Globe*, titled 'How daughter with Down syndrome changed dad's life for the best', cites a father, Heath White, explaining why he was horrified to find out his wife was going to have a Down's syndrome child. White states: 'I've got genetically superior genes. I'm a winner with winner's blood'

(*San Francisco Globe*, 2014). It is not obvious what White means by 'superior genes' and 'winner's blood'. Presumably, however, he is referring to the fact that he is white, able-bodied, cognitively normal and middle class, and his wife mentions that they are both 'college graduates' and White considers himself 'perfect'. In other words, White is probably white supremacist, ableist and classist, but what is of interest is that he disguises at least some of these politically incorrect 'isms' in biological terms, speaking of his genes and blood instead of his race and class. White makes it clear that what most appalled him about the prospect of having a disabled child was that it would make people wonder what was wrong with him. As he states, 'My main concern was about what people would think about me... What weakness in me caused that?' For months, White thus urged his wife to have an abortion, though this went against her moral convictions. Although Jennifer White refused to have an abortion, and the newspaper article chronicles Heath White's eventual love for his Down's syndrome daughter, the majority of women in Jennifer White's situation *do* terminate their pregnancies, and the interview shows that the language of 'genes' and 'blood' and the logic of eugenics live on and inform these decisions.[2]

Today, unlike in Nazi Germany, the terminations of life that this eugenic logic mandates are not ordered by the state, but nor are these state mandates necessary. Biopolitics, or the disciplinary workings of medical power, have done their work, and the majority of prospective parents will terminate such pregnancies voluntarily, certain that they are making the socially responsible decision. In countries such as Canada the state *is* involved in facilitating and encouraging these abortions, insofar as it pays for and encourages (as standard medical practice) prenatal screenings for disabilities at a cost to taxpayers that outweighs the cost that the disabled children whose lives it prevents would have cost to the state had they been born (Withers, 2012). This indicates that the concern of the biopolitical state in preventing the births of disabled children is not primarily fiscal. Rather, what is at stake is the perpetuation of the eugenic dream of a genetically 'superior' race.

Although Foucault's comments on eugenics and race in the concluding pages of *The History of Sexuality* are frustratingly brief, he expanded upon the topic in several course lectures from the same period. In lecture 11 of *'Society Must Be Defended'* he reiterates the argument made in *The History of Sexuality*, while two earlier lectures in the *'Society Must Be Defended'* series (lectures 3 and 4) and lecture 11 in *Abnormal* provide what might be described as genealogies of racism in the 'modern, "biologizing," statist form' to which he refers in *The History of Sexuality*. As discussed in Chapter 1, genealogies, for Foucault, are counter-histories. They are written in opposition to a dominant view of history that makes some aspect of the present seem inevitable or acceptable, either by positing a continuity with the past and thus naturalizing the present, or by presenting the present as a pinnacle of progress. Although Foucault does not make his target explicit in his writings on racism, *The History of Sexuality*, *Abnormal* and *'Society Must Be Defended'* most probably resist a universalizing view of racism, or one that claims that racism, however loathsome, is inevitable, has always existed and always will. Today we can find countless articles written by scientists that argue that racism (like sexuality) is hard-wired, having served a useful purpose in our primitive past. Foucault's writings on racism rebut these claims. In the following section, I summarize Foucault's genealogies of racism in *Abnormal* and *'Society Must Be Defended'*, as these extend, contextualize and elucidate Foucault's discussion of racism in *The History of Sexuality*.

FOUCAULT'S GENEALOGY OF MODERN RACISM

As in *The History of Sexuality*, so in his 1975 lectures, *Abnormal*, Foucault discusses race only briefly and by way of conclusion. Race is thus not an abiding theme of either work, but nevertheless it seems significant insofar as it is the end point towards which each study tends. The primary goal of *Abnormal* is to trace the emergence of the concept of abnormality in psychiatric discourse and practice. In particular, these lectures examine the ways in which psychiatry transitioned from imitating medicine, or from treating mental pathologies, to managing abnormalities. Foucault considers the ways in which this transition from a psychiatry of mental illnesses to a psychiatry of abnormalities entailed a vast, and ultimately racist, expansion of psychiatry's power. Foucault is concerned in *Abnormal* to show that what is passed off as a medical activity is in fact a normalizing form of social control, with psychiatrists better perceived as self-appointed protectors of societal mores (and, in its racist version, of 'the race') than as scientists or medical practitioners.

According to Foucault, psychiatry first established its authority through a series of parallels with medicine, asserting its power to manage certain lives through the claims that *it too* had men in white coats who were treating 'pathologies' in institutions called 'hospitals'. While psychiatry's power over some lives was considerable, the strictly analogous model to medicine gave psychiatrists access only to the lives of subjects whose behaviour was extravagant enough for them to be deemed 'sick' and institutionalized, or 'the most embarrassing cases' (Foucault, 1988b, p. 180). Once its medical authority was established, however, Foucault shows that psychiatry would dispense with both illness and cure, coming instead to be the bearer of expertise on abnormal conditions, conditions that were often deemed hereditary or incurable. By the time heredity became caught up with psychiatric theory, psychiatry's inability to cure the hereditarily abnormal did not pose a threat to its power, since its role was quite overtly that of protecting society from perceived dangers, even if only by identifying those dangers in order to decide who should be incapacitated (institutionalized, sterilized, lobotomized). Thus, one no longer needs to be ill to become the object of psychiatric power; one can simply have a 'condition' or predisposition to an abnormal state against which, in the opinion of psychiatrists, society has the right to defend itself (Foucault, 2003a, p. 317). Psychiatrists are thus not best conceived as doctors but as experts on danger and protectors of society from its abnormal members. Taking 'abnormality' and 'conditions' rather than pathology and illness as its objects, Foucault observes, greatly expanded psychiatry's domain.

The psychiatric theory of 'conditions' was, Foucault argues, one way in which psychiatry penetrated the family, bringing this central institution under its control (2003a, p. 313). The family, or heredity, would take on 'an indefinite causal permissiveness' or would become the explanation for everything that is abnormal about individuals. The family could create abnormal individuals both through environmental influences and through the transmission of hereditary traits. Foucault writes: '[T]he theory of heredity allows the psychiatry of the abnormal to be... a technology of the healthy and the unhealthy, useful or dangerous, profitable or harmful marriage' (p. 315). This would give rise to the theory of degeneration and the eugenic management of populations, the regulation not only of who could marry and form families but, more fundamentally, who should reproduce at all. Psychiatrists became involved in eugenic means of preventing people from reproducing whose offspring would supposedly be predisposed to conditions deemed by psychiatry to be dangerous to society or a drain on its resources.

This account of the eugenic role of psychiatry brings Foucault to conclude his lecture course by positing a new form of racism in the modern age, which he calls 'racism against the abnormal'. As he writes:

> With this notion of degeneration and these analyses of heredity, you can see how psychiatry could plug into, or rather give rise to, a racism that was very different in this period from what could be called traditional, historical racism, from 'ethnic racism.' The racism that psychiatry gave birth to in this period is racism against the abnormal, against individuals who, as carriers of a condition, a stigmata, or any defect whatsoever, may more or less randomly transmit to their heirs the unpredictable consequences of the evil, or rather of the non-normal, that they carry within them. It is a racism, therefore, whose function is not so much the prejudice or defense of one group against another as the detection of all those within a group who may be the carriers of a danger to it. It is an internal racism that permits the screening of every individual within a given society.
>
> (Foucault, 2003a, pp. 316–17)

This internal racism, or racism against the abnormal, will, as in the Nazi case, interact with a more traditional, 'ethnic racism' but will not target only 'ethnic' groups. As Foucault writes: 'Certainly, there were very quickly a series of interactions between this racism and traditional, Western, essentially anti-Semitic racism, without, however, the two forms ever being coherently or effectively organized prior to Nazism' (p. 317). So, for instance, the Nazis manifested an 'ethnic racism' in their murder of Jews, but also applied an internal racism to Aryans who were deemed a genetic danger to the race (the mentally ill, the physically and cognitively disabled and the sexually abnormal).

Foucault's use of the term 'racism' in these pages may seem metaphorical rather than literal: prejudice against any abnormal group or carrier of 'stigmata' (homosexuals, the disabled) is, we might think, *analogous* to racism, but it is not racism per se since race is not what stigmatizes these people. Indeed, the claim that racism, in the modern age, is 'racism against the abnormal' seems oddly (and perhaps offensively) to dispense with race. This need not be racism against members of a stigmatized race, Foucault makes clear, but a racism that the white race turns against its own ('undesirable') members. In fact, however, what Foucault is calling an 'internal racism' *is* concerned with race insofar as it is a racism that seeks to protect 'the race' – the 'white race', the 'Aryan race', the 'human race' – even in cases when those it needs to protect itself against are its own deviant members. Although these members may be abnormal in terms of their sexuality or their cognitive or physical abilities rather than their race, they are still identified as a *racial* threat since the passing on of their genes purportedly undermines the future of the race. Thus, according to the logic of eugenics, while miscegenation may be *one* way that the race is threatened, another is the passing on of substandard Aryan or Nordic genes. Race remains central, therefore, even in the 'internal' form of racism that targets individuals who are bearers of abnormal conditions that are not themselves racial. As an example, we can return to the example of Heath White and his Down's syndrome daughter. The aptly named White states that he has 'superior genes' and 'winner's blood' and thus should not have a disabled daughter. White's high opinion of his 'genes' and 'blood' are most likely mere code words for race, however. The birth of a visibly 'abnormal' daughter is, he believes, humiliating, since it implies to all who see her that he has inferior genes, or is a substandard biological specimen and thus a biological threat to the race.

The following year, while concluding volume 1 of *The History of Sexuality*, Foucault would again provide a genealogical account of what, in *Abnormal*, he calls 'internal racism'. While in *Abnormal* Foucault seeks to connect the emergence of a biological and internal racism to the history of the expansion of psychiatric power, in lectures 3 and 4 of *'Society Must Be Defended'* he situates this particularly modern form of racism within a much longer history: the history of race war discourses beginning in the seventeenth century in Europe. Foucault starts his third lecture by once again noting nineteenth-century military strategist Carl von Clausewitz's famous statement 'War is a continuation of politics by other means'. While Clausewitz's phrase has often been inverted to say that it is politics that continues war by other means, Foucault suggests that Clausewitz's statement was itself an inversion. In other words, the idea that politics is war, and thus that war is perpetual, pre-dated Clausewitz and resonated throughout the seventeenth, eighteenth and nineteenth centuries. Indeed, Foucault argues, this claim was the rallying cry of a counterhistorical discourse that he calls 'race war discourse' and spends the next two lectures examining.

Medieval European society was, Foucault reminds us, a bellicose culture characterized by private warfare. This was an age in which day-to-day wars were waged between families. We might think of the House of Capulet and the House of Montague in Shakespeare's *Romeo and Juliet*, but also recall that the Prince of Verona had forbidden further warfare between these two houses on pain of death. By the late Renaissance, private warfare was being prohibited by sovereigns, and war became something that occurred between states or at a state's frontiers rather than within its borders. From this time onwards, only states could legitimately wage war, and today acts of war undertaken by non-state agents are called 'terrorism'. With the prohibition of non-state warfare, war was professionalized and a standing army was formed. Paradoxically, at this moment when society ceases to be saturated with internal or private warfare, a discourse develops that says that societies are in fact in a continual state of war. War, according to these discourses, is 'a permanent social relationship, the ineradicable basis of all relations and institutions of power'

(Foucault, 2003b, p. 49). Much as Foucault himself would argue in *The History of Sexuality*, these race war discourses insisted that politics is war.

Foucault's suggestion is that such 'perpetual war' discourses were a form of resistance to power, and to the monarch and his laws in particular. The aristocracy, the middle class and the working classes at different times would each use 'perpetual war' discourses to challenge the ruling party's power or the power of law. While the monarch wanted to present his power as one of peace, continuity, inevitability and divine right, the 'perpetual war' discourse undermined these claims and declared that this power was one of war, of oppression, in which a certain section of the population was enslaved, but planning to rise up; it insists that this law is not one of peace, is not inevitable, but is the result of temporary conquest and injustice. The 'perpetual war' discourse contends that the nation is not at peace even if it is not at war with other states: the monarch's power is not uncontested, but is violent and unstable.

Such was the language of English revolutionaries in the seventeenth century, and later of the French revolutionaries in the eighteenth century. While the monarch presents an image of his power as unified or as a tripartite pyramid – either as a Hobbesian Leviathan or the three estates of pre-revolutionary France – the 'perpetual war' discourse rejects these unified and tripartite ways of picturing power and declares that society is divided into two parts: them and us, oppressor and oppressed. Soon these binary parts are theorized as races. While this binary mode of dividing societies is a discourse of 'race war', Foucault stresses that 'races' in the seventeenth century did not refer to morphologically distinct groups but, rather, to cultures. A race was a people with its language, habits and religion. The Normans and the Saxons were, for instance, two races in early race war discourse, as were the Gauls and the Franks. These groups did not look different from one another, but they had different customs and spoke different tongues. These differences were understood to be bred rather than born, and a child born to Gauls but raised by Franks would be Frank. Another feature distinguishing the early notion of race from that of modern 'biologizing' racism was the fact that one race was not deemed superior to the other. The problem with people of the other race was not that they were biologically inferior but that they might steal one's land and conquer one's people.

By the eighteenth century the idea of 'race' began to change into an anatomical category. By this time there were debates about how many races there were, and philosophers such as Immanuel Kant weighed in on the number, counting people by anatomically distinct groups, such as yellow, red, white and black people. Now race had come to be about skin colour, bodies and morphologies, and not about customs or languages. A black person raised in a white society would still be black, and the problem with blacks, this racist discourse claimed, was not that they were conquerors or thieves but that they were anatomically and hence mentally and culturally inferior.

In the nineteenth century, Foucault notes, another development in discourses about race developed, and we find claims about divisions within races and not just between races. Not only are there hierarchical divisions between whites and blacks and whites and reds, but within the white population itself. There are the true representatives of the race and then there are the deviants, throwbacks and misfits: these are people who appear Aryan or Nordic but in fact represent an earlier evolutionary stage, or are closer to non-whites and non-human animals. At this point, biological theories of degeneracy and eugenic arguments developed, suggesting that some people were sub-specimens of a race. As he argues in *Abnormal*, Foucault contends in lecture 3 of *'Society Must Be Defended'* that an internal form of racism had emerged.

Having traced this history of race war discourse in lecture 3 of *'Society Must Be Defended'*, in lecture 4 Foucault worries that he may have seemed to be praising racist discourses. In fact, he clarifies, he is tracing the genealogy that led up to the biological racist discourses of the nineteenth and twentieth centuries, and, while the final forms of these discourses are pernicious, Foucault finds much that is admirable about their earlier forms. The earliest versions of race war discourse were the first historical discourses of political resistance to sovereign power. They undermined the continuity of power by unearthing the voices of those silenced by history and prophesizing a different future. Thus, Foucault *is* praising race war discourse in some of its forms; he also traces the way it was transformed, inverted, wrested from the margins and taken up by those in power, however. First, it was transformed from a race war discourse to a class war discourse in the early nineteenth century (Foucault, 2003b, p. 79). At this point, instead of Normans versus Saxons, we have workers versus property owners. First voiced by the revolutionary poor, this discourse was then inverted, taken up by the rich against the lower classes, and then against misfits of other kinds: the sexually deviant, the criminal and the mad. 'Race' is reintroduced as the name for this war, but now it is 'race' defined not as a cultural category but as a biological group. The misfits, many of whom are simply poor, are now deemed a sub-race. Race war discourse at this point has become an instrument wielded by the biopolitical state against its abnormal or marginalized members. Race war discourse has been turned into a normalizing discourse that justifies the exclusion and death of the abnormal as enemies of the state. In sum, race war discourse has been inverted by the late nineteenth century, and it is those at the centre who wield the discourse against those at the margins, reintroducing the language of race, superimposing it upon class and other forms of social deviance – except now the language of race means something else: race no longer refers to different but qualitatively neutral cultures but to hierarchically ranked biological groups.

When the discourse of race war is taken up from the centre, there is first a racist discourse about other races, and then a racist discourse directed at members within a given race. We see both moves in Nazi Germany, which posited a superior race that excludes Jews and gypsies while simultaneously defending itself against the Aryan ill, deviant and disabled. This is no longer a politico-historical discourse, the kind of discourse that Foucault finds laudable; rather, it is a biological discourse that he describes in his earlier course lecture as 'racism against the abnormal'. This discourse no longer makes claims about politics and history but is, rather, a discourse about human types, human physiology, biological ends, the survival of the fittest and the threat of racial degeneration. While the earlier version of race war discourse was spoken by those at the margins who needed to defend themselves against society, later versions of race war discourse would declare that it was *society* that needed to be defended *against* the abnormal. Thus, Foucault stresses, race war discourse is metamorphosing and circulating, appearing in different forms with different political functions over hundreds of years, first spoken by the enslaved, defeated and marginalized, and then used against them. Notably, for Foucault, it is only in its later forms that this discourse on race war is racist.

From this discussion, we can now see how Foucault's genealogy of modern biologizing racism rebuts the argument put forward by contemporary neuroscientists that humans are innately racist and can, at most, be socialized to resist our hard-wired racist instincts. For Foucault, the contrary is the case: race as we understand it is a recent concept, and racism in its morphologizing, biologist form is a mere 200-year-old phenomenon. Humans have not always been racist or distinguished between 'races' as we do; racism is a product of biopolitical societies and was unthinkable prior to the invention of sciences such as biology and psychiatry, with their theories of eugenics, heredity and degenerescence. For Foucault, it is the kinds of states we live in, the kinds of politics that we have and the kinds of 'expert discourses' that characterize our society that explain the prevalence of racism today. Foucault's arguments suggest that racism must be resisted not just at the level of individuals – with specific people identified as racist and then ostracized or reformed – but at the level of the state and broader social structures and workings of power.

FROM SPECTACLES OF DEATH TO GENOCIDAL DREAMS

In the final pages of *The History of Sexuality*, Foucault connects his discussion of the interpenetration of power, sex and racism to issues of major historical significance such as modern warfare, Nazism and genocide. He argues that, when power came to administer life, new relations to death resulted and new justifications to kill were required. For Foucault, understanding biopower and our changing relationship to death can help us to understand why the twentieth century was so bloody, and why it was characterized by genocides in particular. We are killing and dying differently today,

Foucault argues, and, specifically, 'never before did regimes visit such holocausts on their own populations' (1978, p. 137).

Throughout the Middle Ages and the Renaissance, the kinds of organized genocides that have marked the modern age were unknown, but death was an omnipresent, random and virtually uncontrollable feature of day-to-day life. Some 20 per cent of European women died in childbirth, 5 per cent of children died during birth and, in wealthy families, another 10 to 12 per cent died the following year, with infant mortality rates as high as 50 per cent among the poor and in foundling homes. Famines, epidemics and plagues ravaged the population. The Great Famine of the early fourteenth century reduced the European population by 10 per cent, while the Black Death killed another 30 to 60 per cent of the European population a few decades later. The constant threat of death and the helplessness of human beings in the face of death is reflected in the morbidity of medieval art – its *Triumphs of Death*, *Dances of Death* and *vanitas* – and in medieval literature: the *Decameron* opens with a description of the bubonic plague, which its characters have fled and await. Throughout the long Middle Ages and the Renaissance, almost no tactics existed for resisting death besides such flight, which often only spread the epidemic. Death could not be managed, and was viewed as God's will.

Just as death by plague, epidemics, famines and childbirth could be understood prior to the modern era only as the irresistible workings of a divine power, so too did secular power express itself through the threat and spectacle of death. Executions were public and drew crowds, and executed bodies were displayed for their exemplary value. While Hobbes understands the sovereign's right to kill disobedient subjects as an expression of the universal right to self-defence, in *The History of Sexuality* Foucault resists this reading: sovereigns could kill with impunity and other people could not (1978, p. 135). Anyone besides the sovereign who temporarily usurped the sovereign's power to kill, through suicide or homicide, risked being put in her place by the true sovereigns (king and God), punished with execution or damnation for her unlawful seizure of the right to shed blood. Sovereign power, the power to kill, was thus not a power that most people exercised (even over themselves), and was not a power that one ever escaped: death itself was understood as a transition from one kind of sovereign power (that of the king) to another (that of God alone). As a moment of transition from one power to the next, even the least dramatic of deaths was a semi-public affair and was ritualized with 'last words, last recommendations, last wills and testaments' (Foucault, 2003b, p. 248). A public and visible death was thus central to both power and life itself prior to the modern era.

All this would change in the eighteenth century. In *The History of Sexuality* Foucault writes:

> [T]hrough a circular process, the economic – and primarily agricultural – development of the eighteenth century, and an increase in productivity and resources even more rapid than the demographic growth it encouraged, allowed a measure of relief from these profound threats: despite some renewed outbreaks, the period of great ravages from starvation and plague had come to a close before the French Revolution; death was ceasing to torment life so directly. But at the same time, the development of the different fields of knowledge concerned with life in general, the improvement of agricultural techniques, and the observations and measures relative to man's life and survival contributed to this relaxation: a relative control over life averted some of the imminent risks of death.
>
> (Foucault, 1978, p. 142)

Foucault describes one impact of this shift as the 'disqualification of death' (p. 138). As he explains in a course lecture:

> [T]he great public rituals of death gradually began to disappear, or at least to fade away, in the late eighteenth century and... it is still doing so today. So much so that death – which has ceased to be one of those spectacular ceremonies in which individuals, the family, the group, and practically the whole of society took part – has become, in contrast, something to be hidden away. It has become the most private and shameful thing of all (and ultimately, it is now not so much sex as death that is the object of a taboo).
>
> (Foucault, 2003b, p. 247)

Foucault observes that, although death once had something of 'pageantry' about it, now it is seen as intensely 'private' (1978, p. 138). Even state executions are now performed discreetly within prison walls, with limited audiences, and the majority of us die in hospitals – sterile spaces far from the centre of life, surrounded only by those most intimate to us, our death agonies muted by medication.

As discussed in Chapter 1, Foucault argues at the outset of *The History of Sexuality* that silence and repression are not the most important way that power interacts with sex. In contrast, Foucault suggests that repression *is* the way that power now interacts with death, and death *is* something about which we are silent, that is censored or taboo. This 'disqualification of death', its transition from the centre to the margins of life, from our lens on the world to repression, censorship and taboo, is explained, for Foucault, by the prior move of death from the centre to the margins of power, its exchanging of positions with sex. New historical conditions had allowed for a new form of power: when death ceased to be omnipresent and random, life became a stable enough phenomenon that power could begin managing it. Now that we can assume life as a relatively stable phenomenon, we are concerned with controlling the form that such life takes. As Foucault writes:

> Western man was gradually learning what it meant to be a living species in a living world, to have a body, conditions of existence, probabilities of life, an individual and collective welfare, forces that could be modified, and a space in which they could be distributed in an optimal manner. For the first time in history, no doubt, biological existence was reflected in political existence; the fact of living was no longer an inaccessible substrate that only emerged from time to time, amid the randomness of death and its fatality; part of it passed into knowledge's field of control and power's sphere of intervention. Power would no longer be dealing simply with legal subjects over whom the ultimate dominion was death, but with living beings and the mastery it would be able to exercise over them would have to be applied at the level of life itself.
>
> (Foucault, 1978, pp. 142–3)

A receding relation to death thus allowed power to take hold of life rather than simply threatening to take it away. In the opening pages of *Discipline and Punish*, Foucault famously juxtaposes the execution of the regicide Damiens with the schedule of prisoners in a modern prison (Foucault, 1977, pp. 3–7). This example serves to contrast the exercises of sovereign and disciplinary power. Most notably, while the punishment of Damiens is a very public and spectacular death, death is not involved in the punishment of prisoners in the modern prison at all. Rather, every minute of the prisoner's life is regulated. As this example shows, in an age of biopower, death is no longer the paradigmatic expression of power; it is elided in favour of a total management of life.

EXECUTIONS

Although the biopolitical state manages mortality rates, Foucault argues that it no longer deals in death directly. On the contrary, since the function of biopower is to manage life, for the biopolitical state to kill is, Foucault writes, 'scandalous' (1978, p. 138). The consequence is not that biopolitical states do not kill, however, but that *when* they kill they justify their killings as 'vital' (p. 137). Although executions have become rare in the Western world, when they do occur they are no longer conceived as attempts to reassert the authority of the ruler through bloodshed, as was the case in the execution of Damiens. It is no longer political opponents and everyday lawbreakers who can be killed, therefore, but only those who can conceivably be seen as a threat to the life of the population. The death penalty once 'constituted the reply of the sovereign to those who attacked his will, his law, or his person. Those who died on the scaffold became fewer and fewer,' Foucault writes, for

> [h]ow could power exercise its highest prerogatives by putting people
> to death, when its main role was to ensure, sustain, and multiply life,
> to put this life in order? For such a power, execution was at the same
> time a limit, a scandal, and a contradiction. Hence capital punishment
> could not be maintained except by invoking less the enormity of the

crime itself than the monstrosity of the criminal, his incorrigibility, and the safeguard of society. One had the right to kill those who represented a kind of biological danger to others.

(Foucault, 1978, p. 138)

Foucault is noting that the use of the death penalty receded and changed under biopower. Whereas people were once executed for undermining the power of the sovereign, today executions have become rare in the West because the function of power is to manage life, not to seize it. On those occasions when Western states *do* execute people, it is said to be done in the name of life. While some of the cruellest executions were once for people who had opposed the political power of the sovereign, today no politician in the West could execute his political opponents. Those who are executed must be seen as vital threats not to the ruler but to the population, and are thus most often killers. One of the last women to be executed in France was 39-year-old housewife Marie-Louise Giraud, who was guillotined in 1943 for performing 27 abortions. In a generation of world wars and massive losses to the French population, whose birthrate was already low compared to its German enemy, escalating numbers of abortions could plausibly be viewed as a threat to the population. As many foetuses were being aborted as babies were being born in France during World War II; in this context, an impoverished *faiseuse d'anges* could be construed as a biopolitical threat.

Biopolitical decisions to kill are fused with racism in the case of state executions: while Marie-Louise Giraud was viewed as a biopolitical threat because she was aborting the foetuses of able-bodied, white French women, those executed today are disproportionately racialized subjects. In the United States (the only Western country that still uses the death penalty on its own citizens), there are more black and Latino prisoners on death row than white prisoners, though white people make up 77.7 per cent of the US population. African Americans account for about a half of murder victims, but 80 per cent of state executions involve cases with white victims. Since the death penalty was restored in 1976 there have been 31 white defendants executed for killing black people, but 294 black defendants executed for killing white subjects, suggesting that the latter kind of crime is considered far more troubling to the US state. In cases in which white subjects are executed, it is often necessary to construct them as degenerate, even monstrous individuals (Taylor, D., 2010).

SUICIDE

According to Foucault, biopower has not only changed how we kill others and how seriously these killings are taken but also how we kill ourselves. Unlike executions, suicide has long been a scandal in Western societies, a scandal of power; it was once a scandal of power of a different sort, however. Saint Augustine's *The City of God* includes a chapter descriptively titled 'That Christians have no authority for committing suicide in any circumstances whatever' (Augustine, 1950, p. 65). As Augustine's title makes clear, what was once at stake with suicide, as with other killings, was who had the right of death. Under sovereign power, it is the sovereign alone – whether king or God – who has this authority. Subjects of the sovereign do not have the right to shed blood, not even their own. Throughout the Christian era, the bodies of suicides were posthumously punished – dragged through the streets face down and then hung by their feet, their property confiscated – and were not granted Christian burials (Minois, 1999; Tierney, 2010). This was because they had unlawfully seized the power to kill. Suicide was called self-murder and was worse than murders of other sorts. Under biopower, the problem would be different. If power is no longer the right to kill but, rather, aims to manage every instant and aspect of life, then, Foucault argues, death is the moment one escapes power rather than the moment of transition to another power. Suicide is thus a withdrawal of one's life from the tactics of biopower. It is perhaps the *only* way to escape biopolitical regulation through our own agency. Suicide is hence a problem for power today, but it is a problem of evasion rather than seizure. Suicide is now a problem for sociologists and psychiatrists, not for the law.[3] As Foucault writes in *The History of Sexuality*:

> It is not surprising that suicide – once a crime, since it was a way to usurp the power of death which the sovereign alone, whether the one

here below or the Lord above, had the right to exercise – became, in the course of the nineteenth century, one of the first conducts to enter into the sphere of sociological analysis; it testified to the individual and private right to die, at the borders and in the interstices of power that was exercised over life. This determination to die, strange and yet so persistent and constant in its manifestations, and consequently so difficult to explain as being due to particular circumstances or individual accidents, was one of the first astonishments of a society in which political power had assigned itself the task of administering life.

(Foucault, 1978, p. 139)

One effect of the biopoliticization of suicide is not only that the state invests money for suicide research and suicide prevention programmes, in an effort to impede the suicides of some segments of the population, but that it allows, facilitates or refrains from preventing suicides in other segments of society. For instance, in 2015 the Supreme Court of Canada lifted a ban on what was once called 'physician-assisted suicide', which was simultaneously renamed 'physician-assisted death'. This renaming is significant: replacing the term 'suicide' with the more neutral word 'death' represents an effort to destigmatize the decision to die on the part of terminally ill patients, which facilitates these decisions. The Canadian state has decided to allow voluntary death in cases of terminally ill patients, but, significantly, the deaths involved are those of disabled, ill and often elderly people. Voluntary death continues to be called 'suicide' among other, more valued segments of the population, and in these cases continues to be prohibited and prevented when possible by the state.

WAR

Foucault argues that biopower has changed not only the reasons states execute and the ways they respond to suicide but also, most importantly, how they wage war. Leaders of nations no longer ostensibly take their people to war for personal glory, to expand their borders or to loot and pillage, but because the life of the population is threatened. Like the criminal who goes to his death, the enemy is not just someone who has land or resources one wants but is construed as an incorrigible threat to the nation, to the West, to the values we hold dear: 'Wars are no longer waged in the name of a sovereign who must be defended,' Foucault writes. Rather, 'they are waged on behalf of the existence of everyone; entire populations are mobilized for the purpose of wholesale slaughter in the name of life necessity' (1978, p. 137).

Foucault came of age in Nazi-occupied France, and when he writes of war in *The History of Sexuality* it is World War II and the Holocaust that are primarily on his mind: the Holocaust had been justified in the name of German life and health, the well-being of the Aryan race and the nation. To show the continued relevance of Foucault's claims about war, however, we may consider the ways that the 2003 US-led invasion of Iraq was justified by the claim that Iraq had weapons of mass destruction and was affiliated with Al-Qaeda. War in this latter case was endorsed in the name of protecting American life through 'a pre-emptive strike', because Iraqi president Saddam Hussein, it was insisted, was preparing to 'strike' the United States. As Foucault writes,

It is as managers of life and survival, that so many regimes have been able to wage so many wars, causing so many men to be killed. And through a turn that closes the circle, as the technology of wars has caused them to tend increasingly toward all-out destruction, the decision that initiates them and the one that terminates them are in fact increasingly informed by the naked question of survival.

(Foucault, 1978, p. 137)

When no weapons of mass destruction were found in Iraq and no link with Al-Qaeda could be established, the Bush and Blair administrations shifted tactics, emphasizing the massacres that Hussein had visited on his own people. Now the invasion of Iraq was recast as a civilizing and charity mission: its purpose had not been to protect American lives so much as to save Iraqi lives. While it seems clear that this claim, like the claims about weapons of mass destruction, was a pretence, the important point is that governments now *need* pretences to wage war and need, in particular, to show that their wars are *vital*. For most of history, armies could invade foreign countries without such hypocrisy. The ancient Romans felt no need to pretend they were liberating people through their military conquests; they could be upfront about their objectives as they sacked and pillaged. It would never have occurred to them to disguise war as self-defence or humanitarian effort, as we do now, even when our first acts are to slaughter thousands of people, turn millions more into refugees and immediately secure the oil fields. Today, however, nations must justify their slaughters in the name of life.

Foucault argues that there will, paradoxically, be more wars and genocides under biopower than under sovereign power. He writes:

> If genocide is indeed the dream of modern powers, this is not because of a recent return of the ancient right to kill, it is because power is situated and exercised at the level of life, the species, the race, and the large-scale phenomena of population.
>
> (Foucault, 1978, p. 137)

When a racist state aims to manage the population, to purify that population of racial elements that are construed as contaminating, genocidal forms of racial violence can be justified. As Foucault writes in a *'Society Must Be Defended'* course lecture, the logic of biopolitical racism is this:

> If you want to live – the other must die. The more inferior species die out, the more abnormal individuals are eliminated, the fewer degenerates there will be in the species as a whole... the more I – as species rather than individual – can live, the stronger I will be, the more vigorous I will be.
>
> (Foucault, 2003b, p. 255)

Put otherwise, when the purity, health, well-being and thriving of the race or species is seen to be at stake, states are licensed to engage in 'wholesale slaughter' of subpopulations as they never were previously. As Foucault makes clear, however, 'wholesale slaughters' are not the only way that biopolitical states kill. At least as often, states kill by 'disallowing' life to the point of death, depriving certain people of the conditions necessary for their social or biological survival. Foucault describes this phenomenon as 'letting die'.

LETTING DIE

As Foucault explains in both *The History of Sexuality* and *'Society Must Be Defended'*, death need not entail 'murder as such, but also every form of indirect murder: the fact of exposing someone to death, increasing the risk of death for some people, or, quite simply, political death, expulsion, rejection' (2003b, p. 256). As political theorist Janine Brodie elaborates,

> It is at this point, Foucault argued, that state racism was engraved onto the practices of government. States sorted subpopulations into biological continuums of good and bad, ascribing hierarchies of superior and inferior, and sorted groups and behaviors that needed protection and promotion, things that 'must live,' in contrast to things to 'let die,' things identified as threats to a vibrant population, as degenerate and abnormal, including those deemed as inferior races.
>
> (Brodie, 2012, p. 97)

As an example of such 'letting die', in this section I consider the Canadian state's biopolitical practices with respect to indigenous peoples over the course of its history; this history, as Brodie argues, serves to 'remind us that, in contrast to dominant narratives about the recognition and accommodation of diversity, Canadian citizenship politics continues to be shaped by the biopolitical imperatives of categorization, racialization, and selective exclusion' (p. 108).

One way that the biopolitical Canadian state has and continues to 'let die' its indigenous population is through cultural assimilation. The Gradual Civilization Act was passed in 1857 with the explicit aim of assimilating indigenous people into the settler colonial culture. Residential schools for indigenous children were established in the 1840s and continued until 1996, with the goal of assimilating indigenous people into the dominant culture. In the residential schools, indigenous children were converted to Christianity and forced to speak English, prohibited from

speaking their native languages or practising their own faiths, separated from their families for ten months at a time or for years
on end and prevented from interacting with their siblings of the
opposite sex. Some 30 per cent of indigenous children in Canada
were placed in the residential school system between the 1840s
and 1996, which, in Brodie's words, 'integrat[ed] indigenous children into the dominant norms and expectations of settler citizenship' (2012, p. 106).

Although indigenous children were being assimilated through
this school system into settler culture, this is not to say that their
lives were valued and fostered in the same way as the lives of settler
children. Residential schools for indigenous children had astonishingly high mortality rates, ranging from 30 to 60 per cent of
students dying within five years in western Canadian residential
schools, and with 69 per cent of students dying within five years
at one residential school. Over 3,000 children are believed to have
died in the residential school system, with 6 to 12 per cent of the
children dying each year (Truth and Reconciliation Commission
of Canada, 2015a; 2015b). The residential schools were over-
crowded, unsanitary and poorly heated, and lacked medical care,
and many children died from diseases such as tuberculosis and
influenza. Dying children were forced to sit through classes rather
than receiving medical care. Although most of these children were
not directly murdered, their lives were disallowed to the point of
death: they were not provided with the care necessary to survive
and their lives were undervalued, with lethal effects. Even in cases
in which children survived the schools, many had lost contact
with their families, forgotten their languages and lost knowledge
of their faiths and traditions. Many survivors of the residential
schools had been psychologically, physically and sexually abused
by their caretakers and teachers and would pass the legacy of this
trauma on to their children (Truth and Reconciliation Commission
of Canada, 2015c). With the overt objective of cultural assimilation and mortality rates as high as 69 per cent, the residential
schools can be said to have practised not only cultural genocide
but also eugenics. Indeed, the residential schools practised eugenics overtly, sterilizing many of the children in their 'care'. In the

province of Alberta, the sterilization of children in the residential schools was compulsory.

Another manner in which indigenous people were 'let die' by the Canadian state is through dispossession. The 1878 Throne Speech announced a 'Treaty with the Blackfeet, Blood and Piegan Indians, by which "*the Indian is extinguished* over a territory of 51,000 square miles"' (emphasis in original). Although settler Canadians congratulated themselves for eliminating 'Indians' from the land with less direct violence and bloodshed than their neighbours to the south, they nevertheless pursued the same ends as the US settler state by 'depriving [indigenous people] of their traditional livelihood, culture and autonomy' (Brodie, 2012, p. 104). Indigenous people were progressively dispossessed of their land and cut off from traditional forms of subsistence. The result was starvation for many indigenous people, for which the state then provided a limited amount of 'relief', even while stating that, to avoid the necessity of such 'relief' in the future, indigenous people would need to begin practising agriculture. Through imposed starvation, indigenous people were thus forced to adapt to European forms of subsistence. The Throne Speech of 1880 states that 'no effort will be spared to induce the whole of the indigenous population to betake themselves to agricultural pursuits' (Brodie, 2012, p. 106). The 1882 Throne Speech similarly states:

> Every exertion has been made to settle the Indian Bands on Reserves, and to induce them to betake themselves to the raising of cattle and cultivating the soil... [W]e can only expect by a long continuance of patient firmness to induce these children of the Prairie and the Forest to abandon their nomadic habits, become self-supporting, and ultimately add to the industrial wealth of the country.
>
> (in Brodie, 2012, p. 106)

The government's objective was to culturally annihilate traditional hunter-gatherer societies. The options offered to indigenous people were, essentially, to either starve or contribute to the wealth and expansion of the settler state that was dispossessing them.

Indigenous people in Canada were also 'let die' by being legally disqualified as persons. Section 12 of the [Canadian] Indian Acts of 1886 and 1927 both explicitly restrict the meaning of 'person' to non-'Indians', thus enacting a kind of political death (Brodie, 2012, p. 105). By simultaneously impounding indigenous people on reservations, the state performed a typically biopolitical sub-division of the population, marking off those intended for iso-lation, rejection, exclusion and death from those who could be part of the nation-building project (Brodie, 2012, pp. 106–7). As Brodie argues, 'The extinguishment of Aboriginal title and of per-sonhood are two biopolitical mechanisms of letting some groups die (indigenous peoples) in order to make others live (settlers and selected immigrants)' (p. 105).

Although the residential school system has now been abol-ished, many indigenous children continue to be removed from their families by child welfare authorities, often to be raised in group homes run by non-Native adults, perpetuating the cultur-ally genocidal role of the residential schools. Many of the children coming out of these homes quickly end up in other state-run insti-tutions: prisons. Moreover, schools on Indian Reserves in Canada receive significantly less funding than schools elsewhere in Canada (Sniderman, 2012). Given what scholars have called the 'school to prison pipeline', this systematic under-education of indigenous children in Canada not only perpetuates the poverty of indigenous people but channels them into futures of incarceration (Erevelles, 2014, p. 91). Prisons in Canada, as Robert Nichols has argued, serve a colonial purpose and have taken over the role of residen-tial schools in containing, isolating and preventing the biological and social reproduction of indigenous peoples (Nichols, 2014). These sex-segregated institutions function today to bring about the social and cultural death of the racialized segments of the population that they disproportionately house, preventing their biological and social reproduction. With the closing of residential schools, indigenous people are now sentenced to prisons at seven to eight times the rate of other Canadians. Indigenous people make up only 4 per cent of the Canadian population, but in 2010 they 'comprised 27% of the total adult population in provincial or territorial custody and 20% in federal custody', with Native women making up 33.6 per cent of federally sentenced women in Canada (Nichols, 2014, p. 436).

The Canadian state also continues to systematically 'let die' indigenous segments of the population through what are now well-documented practices of perpetuating suicide-inducing conditions of poverty and despair and non-intervention in their murders. The suicide rate for indigenous people in Canada is twice that of the general population, and the suicide rate for Inuit people is more than ten times the national average. Critical suicidologists have directly linked these high suicide rates to the biopolitical effects of colonization (Kral *et al.*, 2009; Kral and Idlout, 2009). Indigenous women in Canada between the ages of 25 and 44 are five times more likely to be victims of sexual violence and homicide than other Canadian women, and their assaults and murders are systematically under-investigated by the Canadian police and relatively ignored by the Canadian media (Gilchrist, 2010; Jiwani and Young, 2006).

In sum, the Canadian settler colonial state has been and remains an example of biopolitical racism insofar as it disallows indigenous lives to the point of death, whether this death is a literal, biological death or social, cultural or civil. It does this by systematically refraining from intervening in the murders of indigenous people; by creating and perpetuating living conditions that encourage the suicides of indigenous people; by condemning indigenous people to social and cultural death in the form of dispossession and isolation on reserves, poverty and incarceration; and through practices of cultural annihilation, expectations of cultural 'adaptation' and rendering impossible traditional ways of life.

Foucault has argued in the first four parts of *The History of Sexuality* that it was by describing sex as dangerous – dangerous to one's immortal soul, dangerous to one's health, dangerous to the gene pool, dangerous to society – that priests, doctors, teachers and the state could justify not only the extraction of sexual confessions but also interventions in the sexual bodies and practices of the population. Insisting that sex is dangerous has been a ruse of power, Foucault insists. Although Foucault is thus suspicious of the claim that sex is dangerous, in part V of *The History of*

Sexuality he shows just how dangerous the *deployment* of sexuality has been. As the above discussion of settler colonial biopolitics in Canada has described, in the last two centuries this deployment has been lethal. In particular, the deployment of sexuality has justified *racial* killings ranging from genocidal wars to the 'letting die' of biopolitically unvalued segments of the population.

DE-SEXING SEXUALITY

How did a book that was supposed to be about sex end up being about racial genocide? In concluding volume 1 of *The History of Sexuality* Foucault anticipates the kind of resistance that his relentless politicization (and hence denaturalization) of sex will inspire. He imagines an interlocutor complaining:

> Before Freud, one sought to localize sexuality as closely as possible: in sex, in its reproductive functions, in its immediate anatomical localizations; one fell back upon a biological minimum: organ, instinct, and finality. You, on the other hand, are in a symmetrical and inverse position: for you there remain only groundless effects, ramifications without roots, a sexuality without a sex. What is this if not castration once again?
>
> (Foucault, 1978, p. 151)

In other words, this interlocutor might grant that pre-Freudian accounts of sexuality that reduced everything to biology, anatomy and the physical body were naïve, yet complain that Foucault has gone too far in the opposite direction, refusing to grant any significance to the body at all. For Foucault, sexuality appears to be determined by social forces, power and history, and he ultimately writes more in volume 1 about genocide than genitals. Foucault explains sexuality without giving any space to biological sex, hormones or erogenous zones. Indeed, Foucault explicitly argues that we must not imagine a biological 'sex' that is the ground for a socially constructed 'sexuality'. As he writes, 'We must not place sex on the side of reality, and sexuality on that of confused ideas and illusions; sexuality is a very real historical formation; it is what gave rise to the notion of sex, as a speculative element necessary to its operation' (1978, p. 157).

Both sex and sexuality are thus real today, for Foucault, but they are both *historically constructed realities*. Moreover, rather than sexuality being a later invention that gets projected onto a pre-existing sex, Foucault insists that '"sex" is historically subordinate to sexuality' (p. 157). Put otherwise, for Foucault, biological 'sex' is just something that needed to be invented for the deployment of sexuality to function. In describing sex this way, Foucault anticipates the charge that matter – the material body – doesn't *matter* to his account. According to Foucault's imagined critic, he ought to have admitted that the body, sex or biology is at least a foundation, 'ground' or 'root' to sexuality, even if these substrata are overlaid by social constructs, political investments and power effects. Denying the significance of sex, sex organs and matter, and insisting instead on a purely social causality for sexuality, Foucault figuratively 'castrates' the body, cutting physical sex organs out of his account.

Foucault was correct that this would be a common critical response to *The History of Sexuality*, and the apparent denial that matter *matters* is a fault for which Foucauldian feminists and queer theorists have also stood accused. Against this accusation, Foucault insists that he has provided a history *of the body*, and has attended far more to the body than is typically done in philosophy. Far from ignoring the body, Foucault has scrutinized the body's politicization, medicalization and sexualization, demonstrating that the body is a key site of both power and resistance. This is akin to the defence against similar accusations put forward by Foucauldian philosopher Judith Butler in her aptly titled book *Bodies that Matter* (Butler, 1993a). Bodies *do* matter, both Foucault and Butler insist. Nevertheless, what both Foucault and Butler mean by this is that bodies have been *made* to matter, through the social and political forces that have been invested in them, and not because of anything inherent to their physicality. Although bodies matter for Foucault and Butler, they do not matter intrinsically. What each of these authors has done is to historicize the ways in which bodies have been made to matter, and to problematize these historical formations. Drawing on authors such as Butler, the next two chapters discuss feminist and queer appropriations of volume 1 of Foucault's *The History of Sexuality* as these have pursued and extended Foucault's denaturalization of sex.

NOTES

1 I am translating *folies* as 'insanities' rather than 'follies' as I think this better conveys Foucault's point.
2 For feminist critical disability studies and discussions of reproductive autonomy, see Hubbard (2013); Saxton (2013); and Piepmeier (2013).
3 The Suicide Act of 1961 decriminalized suicide in England and Wales, though assisting in a suicide remains illegal. Attempting suicide was removed from the Canadian Criminal Code in 1972, though counselling (or aiding and abetting) suicide remains a criminal act. In the United States, suicide was once considered a felony in some states, but these laws were rarely enforced. In 1963 only six states considered suicide a crime; by the 1990s only two states considered suicide a crime, and these laws have now been repealed.

SUGGESTIONS FOR FURTHER READING

Marsh, Ian. 2010. *Suicide: Foucault, History and Truth*. Cambridge: Cambridge University Press.

Mitchell, David T., with Sharon L. Snyder. 2015. *The Biopolitics of Disability: Neoliberalism, Ablenationalism, and Peripheral Embodiment*. Ann Arbor, MI: University of Michigan Press.

Nichols, Robert. 2010. 'Postcolonial studies and the discourse of Foucault', in *Foucault Studies*, no. 9: 111–44.

——. 2013. 'Of first and last men: contract and colonial historicality in Foucault', in Amy Swiffen and Joshua Nichols (eds.), *The Ends of History: Questioning the Stakes of Historical Reason*. New York: Routledge: 64–83.

——. 2014. 'The colonialism of incarceration', in *Radical Philosophy Review*, vol. 17, no. 2: 435–55.

Schotten, C. Heike. 2015. 'Against totalitarianism: Agamben, Foucault, and the politics of critique', in *Foucault Studies*, no. 20: 155–79.

Tremain, Shelley (ed.). 2015. *Foucault and the Government of Disability*, 2nd edn. Ann Arbor, MI: University of Michigan Press.

Yeng, Sokthan. 2013. *The Biopolitics of Race: State Racism and US Immigration*. Langham, MD: Lexington Books.

5

THE HISTORY OF SEXUALITY AND FEMINIST THEORY

The first volume of Foucault's *The History of Sexuality* is one of the most influential philosophical works of the twentieth century. As Janet Halley writes, 'Volume One of Michel Foucault's *History of Sexuality* was read and read again by feminists, gay activists, and emerging queer theory makers. No one could be indifferent to this book' (Halley, 2006, p. 119). Most notably, *The History of Sexuality* is, without a doubt, *the* foundational text of queer theory. As Jana Sawicki and Shannon Winnubst write in their editors' introduction to a special topics issue on queer theory in the journal *Foucault Studies*, 'Historian of sexuality David Halperin half-jokingly dubbed Foucault the patron saint of this nascent critical project. If Foucault was its saint, *History of Sexuality*, Volume I became its bible. To put it inaptly, Foucault was a seminal figure in queer theory' (Winnubst and Sawicki, 2012, p. 4). Similarly, in *Mad for Foucault*, Lynne Huffer argues that queer theory has been little more than a (problematic) fusion of Foucault's *History of Sexuality* and psychoanalysis (Huffer, 2009). Queer theorist Gayle

Rubin stated in a 1997 interview with Judith Butler, 'I was really, just totally hot for that book' (Rubin and Butler, 1994, p. 72).

More ambivalently, feminist theorists have felt the need to engage extensively with volume 1 of *The History of Sexuality*, even if, ultimately, they are as likely to critique Foucault's book as to endorse it. More recently, Foucault's analysis of normalization in *The History of Sexuality* has been appropriated by critical disability scholars such as Shelley Tremain, and his analysis of biological racism and eugenics in part V of volume 1 has been taken up by postcolonial and critical race scholars such as Ann Laura Stoler, Ladelle McWhorter and Jasbir Puar (Stoler, 1995; McWhorter, 2009; Puar, 2007). Foucault's *The History of Sexuality* is read and continues to influence scholarship in a range of disciplines beyond philosophy, including sociology, anthropology, literary and film studies, and political science, providing political theorists, social theorists and students of history and culture generally with crucial insights into modern power and its relation to knowledge. Although the legacy of Foucault's *The History of Sexuality* is too vast to be catalogued in two chapters, by focusing on a few key Foucauldian texts, this chapter and the next consider the reception and influence of this work in feminist and queer theory.

FEMINIST TENSIONS

The History of Sexuality has been a fraught work for feminist theorists. By the 1970s feminist scholars had identified sexuality as a primary site of women's oppression, and had closely associated sexuality with gender. Feminists such as Catharine MacKinnon argued that '[s]exuality is to feminism what work is to Marxism: that which is most one's own, yet most taken away' (MacKinnon, 1982, p. 515). As MacKinnon elaborates, '[F]eminism fundamentally identifies sexuality as the primary sphere of male power' (p. 529). Since they saw sexuality as the crux of women's oppression, feminists claimed authority on sexual oppression. The fact that Foucault wrote three volumes on sexuality in the midst of the second wave of the feminist liberation movement with virtually no discussion of women or gender was thus a move bound to offend feminist sensibilities. As will be seen in Chapter 7, volumes 2 and 3 of *The History of Sexuality* focus exclusively on the practices of elite male philosophers, and thus do not concern women at all. Volume 1, on the other hand, promises but does not deliver on an analysis of the hysterization of women and the regulation of sexual reproduction. As it stands, volume 1 pays no particular attention to women's sexuality or the history of male control over women's reproductive capacities, and never mentions men's sexual domination of women. Volume 1 describes a growing medical regulation of both men's and women's sexuality, but does not discuss the many ways in which the historically male-dominated medical profession has controlled women's sexuality. Although feminist scholars, like Foucault, were critical of the increasing medical control of bodies in the nineteenth and twentieth centuries, it is significant to feminists that this was largely a control exercised by male doctors over female bodies (Ehrenreich and English, 2005), and Foucault fails to attend to this fact.

Despite feminist objections to this move, Foucault's *The History of Sexuality* provided an influential demonstration that one could engage politically and critically with sexuality in a sustained manner without theorizing gender. In the wake of volume 1, gay and lesbian scholars argued that feminists might be the experts on gender oppression, but sexuality, while related to gender, was a separate domain, and it was gay and lesbian scholars who examined sexuality. As Rubin writes in her 1984 article, 'Thinking sex',

> I want to challenge the assumption that feminism is or should be the privileged site of a theory of sexuality. Feminism is the theory of gender oppression... Gender affects the operation of the sexual system, and the sexual system has had gender-specific manifestations. But although sex and gender are related, they are not the same thing.
>
> (Rubin, 2006, p. 169)

Almost without exception, gay and lesbian theorists in the late 1980s and 1990s took up volume 1 of *The History of Sexuality* in order to extend the break announced by Rubin between feminism and sexuality studies. While MacKinnon would write that 'sex inequality takes the form of gender; moving as a relation between people, it takes the form of sexuality. Gender emerges as the congealed form of the sexualization of inequality between men and women', queer theorists following Rubin would contest such an understanding of the relationship between sexuality and gender. Butler, for instance, highlights not only the presumed heterosexuality behind MacKinnon's formulation but also its tautological nature, in which gender hierarchy both produces and presupposes gender. While, for Butler, we cannot divorce sexuality from gender, nor can we reduce the latter to the former.

Beyond introducing a painful but productive rift between feminism and sexuality studies, *The History of Sexuality* also contains Foucault's controversial discussion of Charles Jouy, the 'simple-minded' peasant who sexually assaulted a young girl, and Foucault's description of this assault as 'inconsequential', 'bucolic' and 'pastoral pleasures'. As discussed in Chapter 1, this passage has given rise to forty years of sustained feminist outrage, beginning with Monique Plaza's 1978 article 'Nos dommages et leurs intérêts' ('Our damages and their compensations') (Plaza, 1978). It is indeed ironic that, although Foucault's point in *The History of Sexuality* was to problematize the extraordinary amount of 'expert discourse' that Jouy's sexual assault on Sophie Adam generated in the middle of the nineteenth century, his own remarks on this previously forgotten case have led to far more ink on Jouy and Adam than was spilled in 1867. As feminist philosopher Shelley Tremain writes, 'No aspect of Foucault's corpus has been more consistently subjected to the charges of masculinism and male bias than his example of the nineteenth-century farmhand Charles Jouy' (Tremain, 2013, p. 801). It is due to his discussion of Jouy, and his neglect of gender throughout the three volumes, that feminist scholars, unlike queer theorists, have by and large not loved Foucault's *The History of Sexuality*.

Although *The History of Sexuality* is thus a complicated work for feminists, one of my aims in earlier chapters has been to provide feminist applications of points Foucault makes in volume 1; these examples indicate the volume's relevance to feminist scholarship, despite Foucault's undeniable failure (or decision not) to attend to gender. Interestingly, Foucault himself praised the women's liberation movement, in contrast to the sexual and gay liberation movements, for insights that are linked to his own arguments in *The History of Sexuality*. As he stated in an interview,

> The real strength of the women's movement is not that of having laid claim to the specificity of their sexuality and the rights pertaining to it, but that they have actually departed from the discourses conducted within the apparatuses of sexuality... [This constitutes] a veritable de-sexualization, a displacement effected in relation to the sexual centering of the problem, formulating the demand for forms of culture, discourse, language... which are no longer part of that rigid assignation and pinning down to their sex.
>
> (Foucault, 1980a, pp. 219–20)

In other words, although the feminist movement identified women as sexually oppressed, it did not do so by claiming that women had an innate sexuality that was being repressed by men. Although, as discussed below, the women's movement has often auto-critiqued itself for *gender* essentialism, it did not tend towards essentialism about sexuality. As Foucault observes, the feminist movement did not ground its struggles in claims about a particularly female sexuality. Feminist demands did not focus on claims about a biological or natural female sexuality and women's right to express it, the way that the gay liberation movement focused on homosexuality as an innate orientation and gay people's right to live that orientation openly. Feminist political campaigns at the time Foucault was writing focused on rights such as reproductive autonomy and the need for equity in employment to liberate women from marriage and compulsory heterosexuality. Such campaigns aimed to free women sexually, and as a sex, from male control, but they say nothing about female sexuality or what it would look like in the absence of this control. Moreover, many feminist demands – such as their insistence on transformations in culture and language – have nothing to do with sex. Although women, like gays and lesbians, were saturated with sex by medicine, in striving for women's liberation the feminist movement, unlike the gay and lesbian movement, did not reproduce this sexualization. For Foucault, feminist strategies thus represented a model for sexual liberation that did not reinforce the constitutive power of the sexual sciences. Building on Foucault's own insight into the connections between his work and the women's liberation movement, the following sections explore some of the ways in which the relationship between *The History of Sexuality* and feminist theory has been productive.

THE REPRESSIVE HYPOTHESIS, IDENTITY POLITICS AND THE FEMINIST SEX WARS

In 'Identity politics and sexual freedom', feminist philosopher Jana Sawicki draws on Foucault's discussion of power as productive in *The History of Sexuality* to critique both camps in what she calls the 'feminist sex debates' (Sawicki, 1991). These debates, often referred to as the 'feminist sex wars,' were waged throughout the 1980s and early 1990s and polarized feminists between so-called 'sex positive' and 'sex negative' camps. The primary issues at stake in these 'wars' were pornography, prostitution, sadomasochism and lesbian sexuality, but they also involved disagreements around such issues as transsexuality, gay male 'cruising', intergenerational sexual relations and public sex (Ferguson, 1984; Duggan and Hunter, 2006).

On one side of this 'war', radical feminists such as Andrea Dworkin, Catharine MacKinnon, Carole Pateman, Janice Raymond and Adrienne Rich took negative views of transgressive sexual practices and gender identities such as sex work, pornography, sadomasochism, adult–child sexual relations, casual and public sex, and transgender issues (MacKinnon, 1991; Dworkin, 1981; 2006; Raymond, 1979; Rich, 1980; Pateman, 1988). Each of these practices and identities, radical feminists argued, reflected and entrenched male 'sex right' and the objectification of women and children. The radical camp in the feminist sex wars attended to sexual violence and the harms that emerge from sex and sexual pleasure in a society defined by male sexuality, and the ways that these harms are disproportionately inflicted on women and children. Because of their negative or critical views of many transgressive sexual practices and identities, these authors were labelled 'sex negative' by the opposing feminist camp, which often ignored sexual harm in order to celebrate sexual pleasure and freedom.

Feminists in the radical, 'sex negative' camp argued in favour of censoring pornography and criminalizing prostitution, because they saw these as ways in which women were victimized and exploited by male pornographers, clients and pimps, and also as practices through which the idea of male sexuality as a natural 'right' and women as mere objects for male consumption were reinforced. Pornography was seen as a major player in the construction of female sexuality as passive and masochistic, and in the construction of women as objects for male pleasure with no sexual agency of their own. As Robin Morgan puts it, 'Pornography is the theory, and rape the practice' (Morgan, 1974, p. 169). For 'sex negative' feminists, prostitution epitomized the exploitation of women by men; even if sex work could be regulated to ensure the safety of workers, it was harmful to women in general since it perpetuated the ideas of male sex right and of women as objects for male consumption.

Male sexuality was described by these radical feminist authors as essentially aggressive, exploitative, violent, lustful, promiscuous, genital-focused and orgasm-driven. Female sexuality, in contrast, was primarily described as exploited and repressed by these authors, but, in those rare situations (such as egalitarian lesbian relations) in which female sexuality could exist apart from male exploitation and patriarchal gender roles, women's sexuality was described as gentle, nurturing, monogamous and neither genital-focused nor orgasm-driven. Lesbians were described by authors such as Adrienne Rich as being more interested in forging emotional bonds than with genital pleasure, and were contrasted with gay men in this respect (Rich, 1980). For Rich, lesbian politics should not be annexed to gay male politics, because gay men – as men – had different values from lesbians. Lesbianism, for Rich, was comparable to maternity: it was an experience of women, and was thus better allied with feminism than with the male-dominated gay liberation movement (Rich, 1980). Lesbian relationships that broke with the nurturing ideal described by Rich, or that appeared to reproduce masculine/feminine gender roles and masculine sexual aggression, were criticized by radical feminists for reproducing the patriarchy. Lesbians who engaged in sadomasochism and butch/femme roles, for instance, were seen as having internalized heterosexual gender roles and to be perpetuating patriarchal oppression within lesbian relationships.

The radical or 'sex negative' feminist literature of this time was also characterized by transphobia. Transwomen were viewed as having internalized misogyny to such an extent that they wanted to be men, while transmen were seen as hostile interlopers who made a mockery of femininity, threatened to invade safe, female-only spaces and could never in fact know what it meant to be a woman because they had been raised with male privilege and were thus not 'survivors of girlhood' (Raymond, 1979).[1] Radical feminism was in this way caught up in the 'identity politics' of what it meant to be a 'woman' and, in some cases, a 'lesbian', the correct way to live these identities and the policing of who could claim these identities.

On the other side of the battle, 'sex positive' feminists criticized 'sex negative' feminists for displaying typically 'feminine' puritanism and maternalistic moral authoritarianism (Rubin, 2006; Califia, 1981). Self-described 'pro-sex' or 'sex positive' feminists – whom Sawicki, following Ann Ferguson, calls 'libertarian feminists' – critiqued radical or 'sex negative' feminists for bolstering the conservative sexual morality of a repressive society, and for participating in the villainization and marginalization of sexually oppressed minorities such as gay men, many lesbians (such as those in butch/femme and BDSM relationships) and trans people. According to 'sex positive' feminists such as Gayle Rubin, resisting sexual repression and puritanical sexual morality is a feminist issue because women's sexual pleasure, as well as men's, has been repressed by this moralizing tradition (Rubin, 2006).

Libertarian feminists such as Rubin can be seen as part of the sexual liberation movement that Foucault is engaging with in volume 1 of *The History of Sexuality*: although in her canonical essay 'Thinking sex: notes for a radical theory of the politics of sexuality' Rubin acknowledges Foucault's critique of the 'repressive hypothesis', she nevertheless insists that our political focus should be on the ways that sexuality remains repressed in a neo-Victorian society, and, like the Marxist-Freudians, she focuses on how this repression is harmful to, rather than constitutive of, sexually 'deviant' subjects. As Sawicki observes, Rubin, like many feminist scholars of this time, was aware of critiques of biological essentialism and Foucault's account of the social construction of sexualities, but this did not allow her to evade essentialism altogether. Rubin's objective, like that of Reich and Marcuse, was to liberate sexuality in all its forms, including the most transgressive – sadomasochistic sex, commercial sex, 'cruising' and man–boy love – rather than to show the contingency and historically constituted nature of these desires and the identities that went with them.

Although 'sex positive' or libertarian feminists acknowledged that much pornography is misogynist, and that sex workers are frequently exploited and harmed, they thought that the dangers of censoring and criminalizing politically incorrect expressions of sexuality outweighed the benefits. For these feminists, creating pornography and erotica for women was more important than censoring misogynist pornography, and they defended prostitution by stressing the agency of sex workers – some of whom might actually *enjoy* their work – as well as the positive tasks that sex workers accomplish within a sexually repressive society. For instance, it is often only with sex workers that individuals can explore their otherwise repressed sexual desires. Libertarian feminists thus defended a positive notion of sex work, in contrast to the 'sex negative' view of sex workers as exploited victims whose occupation harms other women. Some 'sex positive' feminists granted that prostitution should be regulated to improve the working conditions and ensure the safety of sex workers, but they rejected the radical feminist argument that prostitution should be criminalized or abolished.

Drawing on volume 1 of Foucault's *The History of Sexuality*, Sawicki points out that both the radical and libertarian feminist positions within the 'sex wars' rely on a version of the repressive hypothesis. In other words, although the debates appear polarized, both positions are in fact alike in how they imagine power working in relation to sex. In particular, and despite Foucault's praise for the anti-essentialism of feminist theory, both camps see at least some kinds of sexuality as natural or innate, and understand power as a force that represses sexuality. This is the case even if, in many cases, radical and libertarian feminists recognized socially constructed forms of sexuality that are imposed on top of the innate sexualities they aimed to liberate. For instance, in 'Compulsory heterosexuality and lesbian existence', Rich describes the ways that patriarchy constructs female sexuality as heterosexual, passive, masochistic and objectified; nevertheless, beneath this socially constructed version of female sexuality Rich assumes an innate, woman-oriented, nurturing female sexuality. Moreover, Rich does not consider how male sexuality is socially constructed, and seems to imply that what she describes as the aggression and promiscuity of male sexuality comes naturally to men. As Sawicki writes, '[T]he process through which *male desire* has been constructed remains unanalyzed' in the 'sex negative' feminist literature (Sawicki, 1991, p. 38, emphasis in original).

Libertarian feminists, on the other hand, argue that a sexually repressive, conservative and neo-Victorian society, with the recent collaboration of radical feminists, constructs women's sexuality to be monogamous and vanilla, but suggests that other, less politically correct forms of sexuality are being repressed. In other words, the vanilla, monogamous, nurturing sexual relations that radical feminists assumed to come naturally to women are precisely what the libertarian feminists viewed as the social construct of a dominant, puritanical society. Conversely, while radical feminists saw women's natural sexuality being repressed by the sadomasochistic forms of sexuality that patriarchy imposes, sadomasochistic sexuality is one of the forms of sexuality that libertarian feminists considered repressed. For the libertarians, the sexual ideal of radical feminism correlated almost exactly with that of a puritanical society, with the exception of egalitarian/ non-role-playing lesbian relations, which stood at the top of the sexual hierarchy for these feminists. All forms of sexuality that did not conform to the conservative ideal of the dominant society, and of radical feminism, were repressed, according to libertarian feminists. Although their view of what is constructed versus what is repressed is thus almost completely reversed, both camps in the feminist 'wars' imply that *some* kind of sexuality is innate, and that power currently represses our natural sexual desires in ways that are deleterious.

For Sawicki, turning to Foucault offers us a way out of the impasse posed by this polarized feminist debate. In particular,

Foucault's refutation of the repressive hypothesis and his argument that power is constitutive of sexualities allows us to reject the sexual essentialism of both the radical and libertarian views of sexuality. Indeed, when asked in an interview about radical feminist arguments about the purported differences between lesbian and gay men's sexual practices and relationships, Foucault's first reaction was to laugh, after which he rejected the empirical claims behind these arguments and noted that what differences do exist can be attributed to contingent social causes.[2] Moreover, Foucault's historicization of sexuality offers us an alternative way to approach the sexual issues that were at stake in the 'sex wars'. Sawicki argues that Foucault's historical approach to sexuality allows us to retain what is useful about both the radical and libertarian positions. In particular,

> like radical feminist theory, it politicizes the personal domain and thereby avoids the liberal trap of conceiving of our personal desires and relationships as outside power. But unlike radical feminist theory, it does not locate power in a monolithic structure or central institution such as pornography or compulsory heterosexuality.
>
> (Sawicki, 1991, p. 44)

While the libertarian feminist blanket endorsement of sexual freedom is problematic insofar as it often refuses to critique any sexual practices in which 'consenting adults' (and, indeed, 'consenting' minors) choose to engage – thus failing to question the political conditions that produce the appearance of consent or to analyse power relations – radical feminists identify a single locus of oppression in patriarchy, neglecting the claims of other sexually marginalized groups. Foucault's politicization of the personal, combined with his view of power as diffuse and complex, helps us to address both these sets of shortcomings, even while maintaining the strengths of each feminist position.

Sawicki also argues that radical feminists risk becoming trapped in 'identity politics'. By focusing on their identities as women or lesbians, they fail to recognize the historically constituted nature of these identities, or to build alliances with other sexually oppressed groups. As Sawicki writes, 'Individuals involved in such conflicts sometimes become preoccupied more with bolstering their own identities than with their political goals. Such identity politics can be self-defeating insofar as they often lead to internal struggles over who really belongs to the community', as was seen in radical feminist hostility towards trans people (1991, p. 45). Foucault's historical approach to sexuality provides a way out of this divisive identity politics, for it helps us to 'recognize that identities are historically constituted', and thus to accept their contingency (p. 46). As Sawicki writes,

> We might even be prepared for the dissolution of feminism or lesbianism as we understand them in the future and thus not attach ourselves to our identities so rigidly. I am not suggesting that we can will them away, but rather that we might be more effective if we become less concerned with preserving them or imposing them on others and more concerned with eliminating injustices wherever they arise.
>
> (Sawicki, 1991, p. 46)

Foucault offers feminists a 'politics of difference', Sawicki argues, which allows women to build alliances with other sexually oppressed groups, such as gay men and trans people, without obliging them to accept that 'anything goes', as occurred with libertarian feminism. As Sawicki demonstrates, we therefore do not need to choose between the polarized options of libertarian and radical feminism as these played out in the 'sex wars'. Foucault offers feminists a third, and more satisfactory, approach to sexual politics.

CONSCIOUSNESS RAISING, CONFESSION AND EXPERIENCE

In his introduction to *The Use of Pleasure*, Foucault describes the three volumes of *The History of Sexuality* as a genealogy of the modern experience of sexuality. This raises a question, which has been crucial for feminist readers of Foucault, of how Foucault understands experience. Are our experiences entirely the result of historical discourses and political constructions, or can our experiences be dissonant with the discourses that describe us? Does

Foucault's invocation of 'bodies and pleasures' as 'the rallying point for the counterattack against the deployment of sexuality' suggest that our experiences of bodies, sexual pleasures and, importantly, sexual *dis*pleasures might be more than how the discourses of sex-desire construct them to be? Is it the potential dissonance between how we experience ourselves and how we are described by experts that produces resistance? For example, do historical constructions of what it means to be a woman completely determine how female humans experience themselves? Insofar as some women fail to identify or associate with expert discourses on womanhood or femininity, what explains this discord, and is it this rupture between discourse and experience that gives rise to feminist resistance? With respect to the experience of sexuality, do expert discourses on sex completely exhaust the meanings that sexual experiences have for us? If not, what explains the disparity between how sex is described by experts and how we experience sex ourselves? What epistemological status should we give to our experiences? Do our experiences give us unmediated access to the truth of ourselves, or are they of little epistemological value insofar as they may be no more than contingent historical constructs?

These philosophical questions are particularly significant when we consider experiences such as sexual assault, sexual harassment and child molestation. These are all experiences that for most of history were hardly theorized and, in some cases, had no names. Sex with 13-year-olds is now called 'child molestation' and 'paedophilia', for instance, but 13 was once a standard age of sexual initiation and marriage in Western societies, and continues to be in many parts of the world. Moreover, the historical descriptions that we do find of some sexual experiences have been misogynist and victim-blaming ones. If we take the apparently Foucauldian perspective that sexual experiences are the result of social constructs and discourses, must we conclude that women and girls did not experience (what we now call) sexual assault, sexual harassment and child molestation as sexual harms before they were named and formulated as such? Alternatively, should we take the position that, although women and girls in earlier historical periods would have been impacted by historical discourses (or the lack thereof) on experiences such as these, they would *also* have had visceral and emotional experiences of sexual assault, sexual harassment and sexual molestation as personally harmful, much as women and girls do today? Might these experiences have existed even if women and girls in previous eras lacked vocabularies for these experiences, and venues in which to express them?

These questions about the limits of social constructionism and the epistemic value of experience track a long debate between feminist theorists on the evidentiary status of women's experiences. Participation in consciousness-raising groups was a common feminist activity in the late 1960s and 1970s, and provided a forum in which women could discuss their individual experiences of sexism with other women. The practices of speaking and listening in these groups allowed women to realize that they were not alone in their experiences of, for instance, sexual assault, domestic violence, harassment in the workplace and in school, unhappy marriages, conflicts with men, a lack of fulfilment in motherhood, frustration as housewives, negative perceptions of their own bodies and sexual dissatisfaction. Recognizing that other women shared their experiences made the personal political, according to a feminist slogan of the time. Through consciousness-raising practices, women realized that these gendered experiences were the result not of personal failings or individual bad luck but of structural oppression.

In her 1982 article 'Feminism, Marxism, method, and the state', MacKinnon argues that consciousness raising was central to feminist theory and method. As she writes,

> Consciousness raising is the major technique of analysis, structure of organization, method of practice, and theory of social change of the women's movement. In consciousness raising, often in groups, the impact of male domination is concretely uncovered and analyzed through the collective speaking of women's experience, from the perspective of that experience.
>
> (MacKinnon, 1982, pp. 519–20)

For MacKinnon, 'feminism... is the theory of women's point of view... Consciousness raising is its quintessential expression' (p. 535). MacKinnon is arguing against the appropriation of a non-feminist method, such as Marxism, to analyse women's oppression. She contends that feminism has its own method, and this is consciousness raising: 'Consciousness raising not only comes to know different things as politics; it necessarily comes to know them in a different way. Women's experience of politics, of life as sex objects, gives rise to its own method of appropriating that reality: feminist method' (p. 535). For MacKinnon, the practice of consciousness raising allows women to analyse their experience as 'the starting point for individual and social change' (p. 515). MacKinnon thus argues that consciousness raising is not merely an activity in which feminists engage but *the* method of feminist theory and practice, comparable to dialectical materialism for Marxism.

MacKinnon's argument that we should take women's experiences as a starting point for theory 'challenges traditional notions of authority and objectivity' (p. 515). Usually academics claim to be objective and neutral in their enquiries, using the plural 'we' or avoiding first-person pronouns altogether. In contrast, feminist theory has tended to ground arguments in personal experience and to write in an unapologetically subjective voice, often drawing on the author's own experiences as evidence. Feminist philosophers have argued that their use of the subjective voice and first-person pronouns does not render their work less 'objective' or 'neutral' than that of male scholars. On the contrary, the work of male scholars is just as subjectively biased as feminist work, even if male authors do not acknowledge this fact and actively try to obscure it. Feminists have acknowledged and demonstrated the political and epistemic value of experience, and MacKinnon is adamantly defending these feminist tendencies and perspectives.

At the end of 'Feminism, Marxism, method, and the state', MacKinnon connects the sexual objectification of women to the supposedly 'objective' method of knowledge production that has characterized scientific and academic writing, arguing that there is a connection between the sexual objectification *of* women and objective knowledge *about* women.

> Having been objectified as sexual beings while stigmatized as ruled by subjective passions, women reject the distinction between knowing

> subject and known object – the division between subjective and objective postures – as the means to comprehend social life. Disaffected from objectivity, having been its prey, but excluded from its world through relegation to subjective inwardness, women's interest lies in overthrowing the distinction itself.
>
> (MacKinnon, 1982, p. 536)

Patriarchy objectifies women, makes women into sexual objects and then studies them as objects. Through this process, patriarchy 'objectively' proves that women are precisely the sexual objects that patriarchy has made them to be. As MacKinnon writes, '[M]en *create* the world from their own point of view, which then *becomes* the truth to be described' (p. 536, emphasis in original). In contrast, a feminist method does not claim objective knowledge about women, since this would merely objectify them again. Instead, it starts with women's point of view and women's own accounts of their experiences. It thus begins with, and functions as, consciousness raising.

MacKinnon stresses that consciousness raising is not the mere or naïve expression of women's experiences, taken to be transparent revelations of the truth. Rather, consciousness raising involves both the expression and the political analysis of women's experiences, or their 'deconstruction' (p. 536). As MacKinnon describes it, consciousness raising is the 'collective critical reconstitution of the meaning of women's social experience, as women live through it' (p. 543). In other words, women do not just speak the 'truth' of their experiences in consciousness raising but recognize, through the collective, feminist analysis of these experiences, the socially constituted nature of how they had initially interpreted them. Consciousness raising does not just allow women to give voice to their experiences but enables them to understand their experiences differently from how they did previously, and thus to change them. For instance, while women in a consciousness-raising circle might initially describe experiences of sexual assault by expressing feelings of self-blame, guilt and shame, having their consciousness raised about rape myths and the systematic nature of men's violence against women transforms the way these women experience and understand sexual assault. Although

MacKinnon's account of women's experience and the function of consciousness raising is, therefore, a social constructivist account, she believes that feminism can help women to deconstruct these social constructs and reconstruct their experiences in more empowering ways.

Although MacKinnon's view of experience is thus not an essentialist account, Foucauldian feminist historian Joan Scott challenges the privileging of experience that we find in feminist practices and writings such as hers. In her 1991 article 'The evidence of experience', Scott critiques the ways in which historians of 'difference' turn to first-person accounts of experience for evidence (Scott, 1991). The assumption on the part of these historians is that, if they can unearth women's, gay men's, lesbians' or working-class people's own accounts of their lives, they can say something about the truth of these people then and now. Scott raises two problems with this kind of assumption: first, it essentializes the subjects it is describing; second, experience is taken as a bedrock of knowledge, or as a foundation for truth. In fact, however, all that these first-hand accounts of experience tell us is how a particular identity was socially constructed in a particular time, or how it was experienced under certain historical conditions. For instance, because same-sex love was forbidden, it was forced into hiding in certain historical periods. If we find first-hand accounts of closeted love between women in historical archives, this does not tell us the truth of 'lesbian experience', therefore, but only about the effects of closeting and repression on the experience of same-sex love between women in a certain time and place. While first-hand accounts of 'gay' and 'lesbian' experience are taken by historians to reveal foundational truths about these sexual identities, Scott thus cautions that all they really tell us is about how the need to remain hidden constitutes particular experiences. There is no natural identity – such as lesbian or homosexual – that was hidden historically but that we can now reveal through the personal narratives of the lives of those hidden people. Rather, the hiding itself constituted the experience of being what we now call a lesbian or a homosexual. As Scott says, 'It is not individuals who have experience, but subjects who are constituted through experience' (p. 779).

Scott would thus argue against MacKinnon that taking women's points of view as authoritative is problematic since these viewpoints may be mere constructs of patriarchy. Indeed, drawing on Foucault's discussion of confession, we might criticize consciousness raising as confessional, or as social construction in action. If gender is socially constructed and women experience the world through their gender, their own experiences – and their experience of confessing these experiences – may simply reaffirm and extend the 'objective' claims of patriarchy about women. For example, patriarchy constructs women's sexuality to be passive and subordinate to the task of pleasing men. Male scientists' studies of women's sexuality then, predictably, show that female sexuality is (often) passive and aimed at pleasing men. As MacKinnon points out, objectification followed by 'objective' analysis is mutually reinforcing. If we start with the subjective female point of view instead, however, we may not do much better. If we ask women what they desire and how they experience their own sexuality, we may well find that what many women desire is to be passive, to find a dominant man, to please that man and to feel themselves desired by such a man. These women's very acts of 'confessing' such sexual 'truths' may be erotic acts that reinforce those 'truths'. Engaging in consciousness raising, women may very well insist that they still experience their sexuality as heterosexual, passive, other-oriented or masochistic, and seek affirmation for these socially constituted identities from their consciousness-raising circles. From a Foucauldian perspective, such scenarios come as no surprise, since this is how women's sexuality has been constructed in a patriarchy, and a few rounds of consciousness raising will not be enough to undo lifetimes of socialization. Thus, turning to women's subjective descriptions of their own experiences of sexuality, even following consciousness raising, may simply reinforce the 'objective' claims of patriarchy.

For Scott, turning to women's accounts of their experiences may not therefore function as an effective feminist method, unless we argue that there is something about experience that escapes social construction, or that there is some aspect of female sexuality that resists masculinist constructions. This is not entirely implausible from a Foucauldian perspective, since, as Foucault says, '[w]here there is power, there is resistance'. Thus, it may be that power constructs women's sexuality to be passive and subordinate to male desires, and yet it may also be that there is always a part of women's 'bodies and pleasures' that resists this subordination. From a Foucauldian perspective, however, this resistance may not be due to the recalcitrance of bodies that are expressing an innate sexuality; on the contrary, such resistance may be a simple reaction to the workings of power.

The question of experience has been particularly significant to feminist engagements with Foucault's discussion of the case of Charles Jouy. Feminist philosopher Linda Alcoff reads Foucault's discussion of this case in volume 1 of *The History of Sexuality* to suggest that Foucault saw the legal and medical responses to Jouy's crime as an overreaction to a harmless situation, given that Sophie Adam was uninjured and unperturbed by the events. According to Alcoff, post-structuralists such as Foucault believe that 'experience and subjectivity are produced through the interplay of discourses' (Alcoff, 2000, p. 39) and thus cannot 'dissociate dominant discourses and bodily sensations. This results in his simply ignoring the relevance of any subjective description of experience' (Oksala, 2011b, p. 209). Therefore, according to Alcoff, Foucault assumes that, because no discourses on the psychosexual harms of sexual assault or child–adult sex existed in the middle of the nineteenth century, Sophie Adam would not have felt harmed by the rape, and this explains her apparently nonchalant post-rape behaviours. For Foucault, on Alcoff's interpretation, it is only later medicalizing discourses that insist that sexual assault and adult–child sex are psychologically traumatic and sexually damaging that have led us to experience such events in these ways. Put bluntly, for Foucault, as Alcoff understands him, child molesters do not cause the harms of child molestation; medical discourses on child molestation do. For Alcoff, however, the harms of rape and child–adult sex exist independently of whether and how anyone is talking about them, and arise from the phenomenology of sex itself. According to Alcoff, Adam would have been harmed by being raped by Jouy, in the same way that girls are harmed by such crimes today, even if there were no legal or medical discourses at the time that formulated these harms, simply because rape and adult–child sex are – and always have been – harmful. Because the rape was surely harmful to Adam, according to Alcoff, she argues that the legal and medical responses to the situation were not absurd, as Foucault assumes, even if they were not yet attentive to the needs of the victim either.

Alcoff insists that to understand the experiences of rape and child–adult sex we need to listen to the accounts of victims of these experiences, and she provides a number of first-hand narratives of the harms of child molestation, including her own. This is not to say, for Alcoff, that these first-hand accounts of sexual experience are entirely unmediated by discourses and history; women and children can, for instance, experience themselves as responsible for their own rapes because of victim-blaming constructs of sexual crime. Nevertheless, first-hand accounts of sexual experience provide us with insights that legal and medical discourses about these situations miss. Notably, Alcoff thinks that contemporary accounts of sexual assault by survivors of child molestation can shed light on what Sophie Adam would have experienced in 1867 (Alcoff, 2000, p. 54).

In 'Sexual experience', feminist philosopher Johanna Oksala grants Alcoff's point that Foucault's interpretation of the Charles Jouy case is 'sexist' (Oksala, 2011b). Oksala readily concedes that Foucault has no interest in the experience of Sophie Adam, and feels no sympathy for the female child, due to his adult and male arrogance. For Oksala, as for Alcoff, Foucault problematically assumes that Adam more or less 'asked' to be raped and was in any case unharmed by the events. His interest is entirely in the experience of the male adult with whom he is sympathetic. Oksala, understandably, has no interest in defending Foucault on this matter, but she does want to defend the view that a Foucauldian approach to experience remains useful for feminist theory. In particular, she disagrees with Alcoff that Foucault reduces experience and subjectivity to discursive or historical constructs. As she argues, although Foucault took no interest in the subjective experience of Adam, this does not mean that he took no interest in subjective experience at all, or that he thought that such experience was epistemically irrelevant. Indeed, Oksala argues that, in order for us to understand Foucault's project in *The History of Sexuality* (and throughout his oeuvre) as social critique rather than mere historical description, we must recognize the manner in which he sees experience as more than, and dissonant with, discursive constructs.

Contra Alcoff, Oksala insists that 'Foucault does not hold experience and language to be ontologically coextensive, nor does he ignore the epistemic importance of subjective experience' (2011b, p. 209). As Oksala notes, Foucault defines experience in volume 2 of *The History of Sexuality* as 'the correlation, in a culture, between fields of knowledge, types of normativity, and forms of subjectivity' (Foucault, 1985, pp. 4–5, cited in Oksala, 2011b, p. 210). As Oksala writes, this means that '[a]ny analysis of experience must proceed along disparate axes that are mutually dependent on, but irreducible to, one another. Experience is inherently heterogeneous because it emerges from the interplay of distinct elements: domains of knowledge (objectification), practices of power (coercions), and reflexive relations to oneself (subjectivation)' (p. 210). While Foucault's earlier work focused on the first two axes of experience – domains of knowledge (discourse) in works such as *The Order of Things*, and practices of power in works such as *Discipline and Punish* – in his *The History of Sexuality* series, Foucault attempts to take the third axis of experience, or self-reflexivity, into account. Oksala suggests that we understand the three axes of experience as a 'series of foldings: the subject must fold back on itself to create a private interiority while being in constant contact with its constitutive outside. The external determinants or historical background structures of experience and the internal, private sensations fold into and continuously keep modifying each other' (p. 211).

As evidence of Foucault's nuanced view of experience, Oksala cites a 1984 encyclopedia entry that Foucault wrote on himself, in which he describes his own philosophy of experience as follows:

> The discourses of mental illness, delinquency, or sexuality say what the subject is only within a very particular truth game; but these games do not impose themselves on the subject from the outside in accord with necessary causal or structural determinations. Instead they open up a field of experience in which subject and object alike are constituted

> only under certain simultaneous conditions, but in which they go on
> changing in relation to one another, and thus go on modifying this
> field of experience itself.
>
> (Foucault, 1996, pp. 317–18, cited in Oksala, 2011b, p. 212)

Experience, for Foucault, including the experience of sexuality, should thus not be imagined as something directly and unilaterally constituted through expert discourses, such as those of the sexual sciences, but, rather, as a multidimensional field in which such discourses, manifold power relations and the subject's own relation to herself continually interact. As Oksala argues, experience is not reducible to discourse or coextensive with language, as Alcoff assumes, because it is produced through both discursive and non-discursive practices, and, moreover, 'always incorporates modes of self-awareness and critical self-reflexivity. Individual experiences are constituted by games of truth and power, but they in turn affect and modify these practices' (Oksala, 2011b, p. 213).

As Oksala notes, Foucault published two memoirs – those of a nineteenth-century parricide, Pierre Rivière, and those of a nineteenth-century intersexed individual, Herculine Barbin – alongside the expert discourses on these subjects' lives, precisely to show the discrepancies between 'objective' and 'subjective' (or third-person and first-person) accounts of the same lives, and the ways that the third-person, medical or legal accounts do material violence to the human beings they dissonantly describe (Foucault, 1975; 1980b). In Barbin's case, the dissonance between how the subject experienced hir own body and how that body was described by doctors contributed to the tragedy of hir life and, ultimately, hir suicide. At the same time, Foucault does not suggest that Rivière's and Barbin's accounts of their own lives were purely self-derived, or ahistorical. On the contrary, he emphasizes the ways that Rivière's narration of his life and crimes was influenced by his reading of history, the Bible and contemporary flysheet reports of sensational murders. Barbin's memoir, in turn, while divergent from the reports of doctors, was informed by hir reading of Ovid's *Metamorphosis* and sentimental literature, as well as the gendered influences of the convent and women's boarding schools in which ze had lived. As Oksala writes, 'Bodies always assume meaning through a complex process in which competing discourses, conceptualizations, and cultural practices intertwine with private sensations, pleasures, and pains' (Oksala, 2011b, p. 218). While Rivière's and Barbin's accounts of their own lives are thus contrasted by Foucault with the reports of medical and legal authorities, he does not suggest that they came out of nowhere or spoke the innate truths of the subjects. On the contrary, Rivière and Barbin exercised some critical self-reflexivity in selecting other contemporary discourses on which to draw in describing their own lives – discourses that apparently resonated better, or in more empowering ways, with their experiences than did the discourses of doctors and lawyers – but these alternative discourses on which they drew were limited to those on offer in their circumscribed cultural milieus. While Rivière and Barbin drew on these resources, and interpreted them in their own ways, in order to resist the authoritative discourses of medicine and the law, medical and legal experts would scrutinize Rivière's and Barbin's memoirs. In time, the personal accounts of criminals and sexual 'deviants' would shape what criminologists and sexual scientists said about such subjects as much as delinquents and 'deviants' would appropriate, internalize and transform what criminologists and sexual scientists were saying about them. These complex and interactive feedback loops between experts and the 'human kinds' about which they write are consistent with Foucault's theory of power in *The History of Sexuality*.

With this more complex understanding of the interplay between first-person and third-person accounts in the production of experience, we can understand how medical discourses on homosexuality would constitute 'homosexuals', even while those individuals so constituted could reflect on, respond to and transform the meaning of the experience of homosexuality for themselves, for the medical profession and for society at large. The consequently transformed medical and social discourses on homosexuality would then continue to impact the experiences of 'homosexuals', who would also continue to reflect on, respond to and transform these discourses again through what Foucault calls 'reverse discourses'. Similarly, for Foucault (and contra Alcoff's interpretation of Foucault), the experiences of rape and child–adult sex

are an ever-changing sum of what is being said about these situations by experts, how these situations are impacted by power
relations and practices and how survivors take up and respond
to these discourses and practices. This sum would have been
different for Sophie Adam from how it was for Linda Alcoff,
given the differences in their historical contexts, but this is not
to say that what was being said about adult–child sex in 1867
correlates with Adam's experience of her interactions with
Charles Jouy either.

According to Oksala, this non-correlation between discourse
and experience is crucial to understanding Foucault's discussion
of the case itself. Adam, we are told, joked with another girl
about masturbating Jouy, telling a village woman that they had
played a game of 'curdled milk'. This woman told the girls they
were 'little horrors', but did not, apparently, take the situation
very seriously. Although Adam did not joke about or otherwise
report the incident in which Jouy later raped her, Foucault again
implies that her experience of this event was dissonant with the
responses of her parents and authorities. Adam ran to a fair
and bought almonds directly after the assault, and did not tell
her parents what had happened because she thought she would
be slapped if she did. This, for Foucault, indicates that Adam
did not take the incident very seriously. In contrast, her parents, the mayor and doctors viewed the incident as a grave event
requiring far more drastic interventions than Adam anticipated.
Foucault's references to Adam's joking, the village woman's
cavalier scolding and Adam's (debatably) nonchalant post-rape
behaviour could be interpreted as an attempt to highlight the
ways in which Adam's experiences diverged from those of the
sexual authorities and experts of the time. As Oksala observes,
Foucault was even keener to show that Jouy's experience of
the events in question was dissonant with how authorities
described them. While feminists have read Foucault's descriptions of 'bucolic', 'pastoral', 'innocent' and 'ordinary pleasures'
as Foucault's own view of the incidents in nineteenth-century
Lapcourt, France, Oksala suggests that these are Foucault's ren-
derings of how Jouy saw the events. It is for Jouy, Oksala argues,

that the 'curdled milk' and rape incidents were 'ordinary' events in 'village sexuality', and this was in striking contrast with the manner in which the mayor, law and medicine interpreted his acts as deviant and dangerous.

Thus, even in his discussion of the case of Charles Jouy, Foucault emphasizes discrepancies between subjective experiences and discourses and power relations. Our experiences, including our experiences of sexuality, may be 'socially constructed', for Foucault, but they are not ontologically coextensive with discourses or entirely determined by them. More complicatedly, discourses and power relations inform and transform our experiences, even while, in what Ian Hacking describes as a 'looping effect' (Hacking, 1995b), our self-narrations of our experiences inform and transform what 'experts' and 'authorities' say and do. Oksala thus writes that, 'while the personal, lived, or subjective experience is not ontologically or epistemically foundational or self-sufficient in Foucault's analyses, it is nevertheless indispensable. If Foucault held that subjective experiences were simply coextensive with dominant expert discourses, as Alcoff claims, there would be no need, or possibility, for him to undertake a critique of them' (Oksala, 2011b, p. 214). As Oksala says, 'In exactly the same way that Foucault's critique of psychiatry relies on the recognition that dominant discourses and the subjective experiences they constitute are not seamlessly aligned, the Foucauldian feminist critique of patriarchal discourses and attitudes to rape must recognize the correlation, but also the discrepancy, between discourse and experience' (p. 215). Such a nuanced, Foucauldian approach to experience, Oksala argues, allows us both to draw on girls' and women's experiences of sexual violence to critique gendered ideologies about rape (such as victim blaming and rape myths) and to recognize the ways that these ideologies may be internalized by victims and perpetrators alike. Foucault's own analysis of an incident of rape in *The History of Sexuality* is thus notoriously egregious, but Oksala nevertheless argues that this same volume provides feminists with indispensable tools for critiquing gendered experiences of sexual violence and transforming a rape culture.

FEMINIST BODIES AND PLEASURES

In a brilliantly playful article, 'Coming to understand: orgasm and the epistemology of ignorance', feminist philosopher of science Nancy Tuana takes up some of the epistemological aspects of *The History of Sexuality* for feminist purposes (Tuana, 2004). As seen, in volume 1 of *The History of Sexuality* Foucault shows that what we have a will to know about, and what we thus end up knowing about, is an effect of power. This means that the truths we have, including the kinds of scientific knowledge we have, are caught up in relations of power. We see this point in detail in Foucault's discussion of the sexual sciences and their sexual taxonomies. We now have considerable knowledge about sexual identities or sexualities, but Foucault shows that it is in part the practices of scientists that produced the facts that we now understand to be truths. In some cases, the knowledge and truth claims of sexual scientists are shown by Foucault to be political fictions. In other cases, while scientists may have uncovered objective facts – for instance, about the ways that reproduction works – there were political motives behind their quests for these particular truths, which were pursued at the expense of other truths or other potential areas of knowledge.

This brings up an epistemological argument that is not thematized by Foucault but is nevertheless implicit throughout his work. This is: it is not only the knowledge we have but also the knowledge we do *not* have that is an effect of power. Foucault makes a closely related point with respect to silence in *The History of Sexuality* when he writes: 'Silence itself – the things one declines to say... – is less the absolute limit of discourse, the other side from which it is separated by a strict boundary, than an element that functions alongside the things said, with them and in relation to them within over-all strategies' (Foucault, 1978, p. 134). While scientists have a will to know certain truths, such as truths about sexual taxonomies, they *lack* a will to know other truths, and are thus silent on these topics. Indeed, scientists may have actively willed *not to know* about certain potential domains of knowledge. Ignorance, like silence, is not just an absence of knowledge or discourse, in other words, but is actively constructed and preserved for political purposes. As Tuana writes, 'Ignorance, far from being a simple lack of knowledge that good science aims to banish, is better understood as a practice with supporting social causes as complex as those involved in knowledge practices' (2004, p. 195).

One example of such politically willed epistemologies of ignorance – one that has been examined by critical race theorists such as Charles Mills, Linda Alcoff and Shannon Sullivan – is the ignorance on the part of Americans about the United States' history of racism (Mills, 2007; Alcoff, 2007; Sullivan, 2007). In 'White ignorance and colonial oppression: or, why I know so little about Puerto Rico', Sullivan, for instance, undertakes an incisive study of why she, as a highly educated American, nevertheless knew virtually nothing about Puerto Rico, including its official status and relationship to the United States (Sullivan, 2007). Through an examination of US educational curricula, Sullivan demonstrates that her ignorance about Puerto Rico was not accidental, but had been actively cultivated for political purposes.

In *Epistemology of the Closet*, Eve Kosofsky Sedgwick notes: 'Such ignorance effects can be harnessed, licensed, and regulated on a mass scale for striking enforcements – perhaps especially around sexuality.' For example,

> The epistemological asymmetry of the laws that govern rape... privileges at the same time men and ignorance, inasmuch as it matters not at all what the raped woman perceives or wants just so long as the man raping her can claim not to have noticed (ignorance in which male sexuality receives careful education)... Or again, in an ingenious and patiently instructive orchestration of ignorance, the US Justice Department ruled in June, 1986, that an employer may freely fire persons with AIDS exactly so long as the employer can claim to be ignorant of the medical fact, *quoted in the ruling*, that there is no known health danger in the workplace from the disease. Again, it is clear in political context that the effect aimed at... is the ostentatious declaration, for the private sector, of an organized open season on gay men.
> (Kosofsky Sedgwick, 1990, p. 5, emphasis in original)

Although we are more familiar with the idea that 'knowledge is power', Kosofsky Sedgwick notes that, in many cases, 'obtuseness itself arms the powerful against their enemies' (p. 7).

In 'Coming to understand', Tuana, like Sedgwick, examines the epistemology of ignorance about sexuality. In particular, she considers the scientific and lay ignorance about female genitals, orgasms and sexual pleasure. While Foucault's focus with respect to the sexual sciences in *The History of Sexuality* is the knowledge that these sciences produced about sexual identities, Tuana thus chooses a different focus. She asks: what facts about sexual pleasure have the sexual sciences had a will to know, and what facts about sexual pleasure have they had a will to remain ignorant about? What have been the power effects of these wills to know and to remain ignorant about different aspects of sexual pleasure? In what kinds of truth, and in what kinds of ignorance, have these wills to know, and to not know, resulted? What kinds of sexual ignorance have been socially constructed in the preceding centuries? As Tuana shows, even while the sexual sciences have had a will to know about sexual taxonomies or identities, they have had a will *not to know* about female pleasure or orgasm, and this has had the effect of producing ignorance on these topics on the part of the general public.

Tuana describes her experience teaching a large course on sexuality at her university, and finding that, while her students come to class already knowing a considerable amount about the male genitals, they know relatively little about the female genitals. Moreover, what they do know about the female genitals is related to their reproductive role (menstruation, pregnancy) rather than their pleasure capacities. Both female and male students have a better sense of what the vagina, fallopian tubes, uterus and ovaries look like and do than about the clitoris, and 'both men and women alike typically know far more about the structures of the penis than they do about those of the clitoris' (Tuana, 2004, p. 198). Tuana relates this ignorance about the clitoris on her students' part to the apparent lack of desire on the part of scientists to know about the pleasure sites of the female genitals. Tuana argues that, although it was long believed that orgasm was related to conception for both men and women, once female orgasm was dissociated from reproduction, male scientists took little interest in women's sexual pleasure.

Tuana's careful consideration of medical drawings of the male and female genitals show that scientists have developed considerable anatomical knowledge about the male genitals and about the female reproductive system, but often either fail to represent the clitoris at all or depict it as 'a simple nub' with relatively little attention to detail (2004, p. 200). In particular, this 'nub' tends to be represented as largely external, with scant interest in its extension beneath the skin. Historically, as Tuana discusses, the clitoris was assumed to be a 'diminutive homologue' of the penis, and was represented as such, with no apparent desire to examine the clitoris and note the ways in which it is, in fact, different from the penis (p. 200). At times, we see medical writers and illustrators refusing to discuss or depict this 'obscene part' at all (p. 200). Even contemporary anatomical drawings give the clitoris 'short shrift' compared to the female reproductive organs and the male genitals. In line with their lack of interest in the human female's clitoris, Tuana observes that male scientists have also demonstrated an active will not to know about clitoral stimulation, orgasm and female sexual pleasure on the part of our 'simian sisters' (p. 219). Indeed, against considerable evidence to the contrary, male primatologists have denied that female primates other than humans have orgasmic capabilities (p. 221).

Tuana's explanation for the lack of interest in the clitoris in historical anatomical drawings, and the lack of scientific interest in female pleasure and orgasm more generally, is that scientists understood the purpose of sex – at least for females – to be reproduction, and, since they had divorced female orgasm from reproduction, the clitoris and female orgasm were irrelevant. For Freud, the clitoral orgasm was immature in comparison with the (possibly non-existent) vaginal orgasm. Beyond this, female sexual desire was long considered to be a danger to men, and so the clitoris, being linked to that desire, was best ignored. What scientific interest *was* paid to the clitoris was not motivated by a will to know about the female orgasm or pleasure but by a will to know about sexual deviance. As Tuana discusses, female 'inverts' were believed to have abnormal genitals, including erectile and enlarged clitorises, distensible vaginas, protruding labia, small uteruses and insensitive hymens. An examination of a woman's clitoris was one means among others to test for signs of degeneration. Scientists did, therefore, occasionally attend to the clitoris, but they did not do so with a will to know about female pleasures.

Tuana contrasts this state of affairs with the interest taken in the clitoris by the feminist health movement that emerged in the 1970s. In particular, she compares historical and contemporary scientific drawings of the female genitals with the anatomical drawings produced by feminists. As Tuana notes, the 'nub that tended to disappear in standard anatomical texts took on complexity and structure in the hands of these feminists', and, in particular, it came to be depicted as a largely internal organ (Tuana, 2004, p. 200). In feminist works such as *Our Bodies, Ourselves*, the clitoris was 'loving[ly]' rendered and 'expanded in size and configuration to include three structures: the shaft, the glans, and the crura' (p. 203). Now that feminists were studying the female genitals, we learned that the crura of the clitoris alone has twice the number of nerve fibres as the entire penis, and is an impressive organ of pleasure indeed. In addition, the feminist health movement highlighted other pleasurable parts of the female anatomy that had gone entirely overlooked in both historical and contemporary medical drawings, such as the 'G-spot' and urethral sponge.

Despite these interventions in knowledge on the part of the women's health movement, the ignorance of Tuana's students regarding the clitoris indicates that the scientific will not to know about female pleasure continues to construct ignorance about women's bodies and pleasures. As Tuana notes, ignorance about women's bodies and pleasures results, concretely, in less pleasure for those bodies. Although women were long believed to enjoy sex more than men, in the last century women have consistently reported a lack of pleasure in their bodies compared to men. In particular, Tuana cites studies of twentieth-century American women who report high levels of disinterest in sex and an absence of pleasure in the sex they do have. Many of these women report that they do not ever have orgasms (Tuana, 2004, p. 213). Given women's multi-orgasmic capabilities, Tuana does not believe that women's current lack of sexual pleasure has anything to do with the limitations of their bodies compared to men's bodies, or with the 'truth' of female sexuality. Rather, she sees women's lack of pleasure in their bodies today to be a consequence of the scientific will not to know about the pleasure capacities of these bodies.

Tuana presents her article as following 'Foucault's admonition' in volume 1 of *The History of Sexuality* 'to attend to bodies and pleasures rather than sexual desire' (p. 197). Specifically, her aim is 'to trace bodies and pleasures as a source of subversion'. As she writes, 'The bodies of my attention are those of women, the pleasures those of orgasm [and] it is women's bodies and pleasures that I embrace' (p. 196). Tuana is cautious, however, not to suggest that the bodies and pleasures she is describing are the 'truth' of female sexuality. On the contrary; as she writes, 'Bodies and pleasures, as Foucault well knew, have histories... Bodies and pleasures are not natural givens, not even deep down' (p. 197). For example, Tuana does not suggest that feminist depictions of the female genitals, or the insistence of women primatologists that non-human female primates *do* have orgasms, or her own insistence on women's multi-orgasmic capabilities, represent the 'truth' of female sexuality that male scientists have long suppressed. Rather, these feminist drawings, primatological arguments and Tuana's own descriptions are just as politically motivated – and as motivated by desires to know and not know – as those of male scientists.

Although Tuana's attention to women's bodies and pleasures does not, therefore, reveal the truth of their 'sex-desire', it does aim to subvert their sexual normalization. In particular, it aims to subvert contemporary reductions of women's sexuality to reproductive acts, organs and capacities, and contemporary beliefs in the inferior pleasurable capacities of women compared to men. By attending to anatomical knowledge of the female genitals usually left out in scientific textbooks, feminist depictions of the female genitals, women's multi-orgasmic abilities, the sex lives of female bonobos and other primates (such as the female chimpanzee who laughs softly as she masturbates) and ancient celebrations of women's vulvas, Tuana works to transform our ignorance of women's bodies and pleasures into politically inflected knowledge. In the process, she provides us with kinds of knowledge that are both pleasurable and empowering. As she writes, '[W]omen's bodies and pleasures can, at this historical moment, be a wellspring for resisting sexual normalization' (Tuana, 2004, p. 197).

NOTES

1 For an excellent feminist critique of transphobia in radical feminist theory, see Heyes (2003).

2 In 'Sexual choice, sexual act', an interviewer says to Foucault: 'There is a growing tendency in American intellectual circles, particularly among radical feminists, to distinguish between male and female homosexuality. The basis of this distinction is two-fold. If the term homosexuality is taken to denote not merely a tendency toward affectional relations with members of the same sex but an inclination to find members of the same sex erotically attractive and gratifying, then it is worth insisting on the very different physical things that happen in the one encounter and the other. The second basis for the distinction is that lesbians seem in the main to want from other women what one finds in stable heterosexual relationships: support, affection, long-term commitment, and so on. If this is not the case with male homosexuals, then the difference may be said to be striking, if not fundamental. Do you think the distinction here a useful and viable one? Are there discernible reasons for the difference noted so insistently by many prominent radical feminists?' Foucault's response to this question is: '(Laughs.) All I can do is explode with laughter.' When prompted to say more, he states: 'Well… I find it very amusing… What I will say is that the distinction offered doesn't seem to me convincing, in terms of what I observe in the behavior of lesbian women. Beyond this, one would have to speak about the different pressures experienced by men and women who are coming out or are trying to make a life for themselves as homosexuals. I don't think that radical feminists in other countries are likely to see these questions quite in the way you ascribe to such women in American intellectual circles.' See Foucault (1989b: p. 325).

SUGGESTIONS FOR FURTHER READING

Diamond, Irene, and Lee Quinby (eds.). 1988. *Feminism and Foucault: Reflections on Resistance*. Boston: Northeastern University Press.

Hekman, Susan J. (ed.). 1996. *Feminist Interpretations of Michel Foucault*. University Park, PA: Pennsylvania University Press.

McLaren, Margaret A. 2002. *Feminism, Foucault, and Embodied Subjectivity*. Albany, NY: State University of New York Press.

McNay, Lois. 1992. *Foucault and Feminism*. Cambridge: Polity Press.

Oksala, Johanna. 2016. *Feminist Experiences: Foucauldian and Phenomenological Investigations*. Evanston, IL: Northwestern University Press.

Rubin, Gayle, and Judith Butler. 1994. 'Sexual traffic', in *differences: A Journal of Feminist Cultural Studies*, vol. 6, nos. 2/3: 62–99.

6

THE HISTORY OF SEXUALITY
AND QUEER THEORY

FROM FEMINISM TO QUEER THEORY

As seen in Chapter 5, feminist theorists were critical of *The History of Sexuality* for failing to attend to gender. In 1990, in what could be seen as an unexpected response to this criticism, Judith Butler published *Gender Trouble*, which took up *The History of Sexuality* to do for gender what Foucault had done for sexuality. Butler thus provided the Foucauldian analysis of gender that Foucault's own volume lacked and that feminists had demanded, but she dismantled a widely accepted feminist understanding of gender in the process. While Butler aimed to intervene in feminist theory in writing *Gender Trouble*, and intended to challenge the heteronormativity of feminist theory in particular, she did not anticipate that she would simultaneously be authoring a foundational work in what was to become queer theory. This is what happened, however, and today, as Tamsin Spargo writes, *Gender Trouble* 'is arguably the most influential text in queer theory' (Spargo, 1999, p. 52).

The term 'queer', as used in queer theory, activism and communities, is the subversive appropriation of a label once used to denigrate people considered abnormal, strange or eccentric in their sexual practices or gender expression. Although many older gays and lesbians who have been deeply injured by this term continue to find it too painful to appropriate, a younger generation has embraced the label (Clare, 1999). Against the assumption that to be deemed abnormal – or queer – is an insult, self-described queers took up the term with pride, thus undermining the normalizing assumption tacit in its original usage. As Spargo writes, within queer theory '[q]ueer can function as a noun, an adjective, or a verb, but in each case is defined against the "normal" or "normalising"' (Spargo, 1999, pp. 8–9). The first sentence of the first chapter of queer theorist Ladelle McWhorter's first book, *Bodies and Pleasures*, asserts that she 'was not a well-adjusted child' (McWhorter, 1999, p. 1), while the final sentence of McWhorter's second book, *Racism and Sexual Oppression*, exhorts readers to 'never, ever adjust' (McWhorter, 2009, p. 331). In this typically queer anti-normativity stance – the refusal to become 'well adjusted' to the norms of a homophobic, gender-oppressive, racist, ableist, neoliberal, capitalist, militaristic and carceral society – queer theory distinguishes itself from what Lisa Duggan has described as the 'homonormativity' of gay and lesbian politics (Duggan, 2003). In Duggan's words, 'homonormativity' is 'a politics that does not contest dominant heteronormative assumptions and institutions – such as marriage, and its call for monogamy and reproduction – but upholds and sustains them while promising the possibility of a demobilized gay constituency and a privatized, depoliticized gay culture anchored in domesticity and consumption' (Duggan, 2002, p. 179).

Although the gay liberation movement started out, like the feminist movement, by demanding radical or revolutionary social change, over time, according to Spargo,

> the model of liberation through transforming the system gave way ... to a different conception of gay and lesbian politics that had more in common with what is known as the 'ethnic' model. This presented gays and lesbians as a distinctive minority group, equal but

different, and worked to achieve rights and legal protection within
the existing order.

(Spargo, 1999, p. 29)

In the course of the late 1960s and the 1970s the objective of mainstream gay and lesbian politics, dominated by middle-class white
gays and lesbians, came to be 'equality' rather than the assertion of
difference (or the affirmation of abnormality), and this was often
achieved by assuring straight people that at least some (white,
middle-class) gays and lesbians are normal, law-abiding citizens,
who want the same things in life as straight people, including
monogamous marriage, children and a white picket fence (Lenon,
2012; 2011). As Dean Spade persuasively argues, mainstream gay
and lesbian politics came to be dominated by demands for rights
that were primarily advantageous to white, middle-class gays and
lesbians, such as marriage (with the property rights and tax breaks
for high-income-earning couples that this institution entails) and
shared health care benefits for same-sex couples (which assumes
the kind of employment that comes with such benefits), thus dis-
tancing itself from the more urgent political needs of the majority of non-heterosexual people, who are marginalized along other
axes of identity such as race, class and ability (Spade, 2011). Jasbir
Puar contends that the focus of mainstream gay and lesbian politics on the right to marry is 'fueled by conscious and unconscious
yearnings to reinstate the privileges of whiteness, in fact, white
Americanness' (Puar, 2007, p. 128). As many queer theorists have
thus argued, in the course of the 1970s mainstream gay and lesbian politics ceased to challenge the dominant society and simply
asked to be accepted by it. Increasingly, white, middle-class gays
and lesbians gave up resisting dominant sexual and social mores
and tried instead to reassure straight people that they already con-
formed to those mores, but simply did so with a person of the
same sex. In 1968 the Gay Liberation Front, imitating the Black
Liberation slogan 'Black is beautiful', assured people that 'Gay is
good' (Halperin, 1995, p. 61).

In contrast, queer politics does not ascribe any definitional content to homosexuality, good or otherwise, but affirms its marginality (Halperin, 1995, p. 61). Queer politics is first and foremost an

anti-normative politics, a politics from the margins. To be queer is not to be a 'natural kind' or an object of knowledge but in an oppositional position in relation to the norm (Halperin, 1995, p. 61). Foucault's *The History of Sexuality* became the 'Bible' of this movement in part because it is here that Foucault theorizes biopolitics as a normalizing form of power, and calls for resistance to biopolitical normalization. Following Foucault's critiques of sexualization and identity politics, queer politics has focused less on sexuality and more on resisting homophobia, heteronormativity and other 'regimes of normalcy' (Winnubst and Sawicki, 2012, p. 4). In Danielle Peers' scintillating phrase, '[Q]ueer is not whom you fuck, it's what you fuck up.'[1]

In this chapter I first examine the ways that *Gender Trouble* challenged and advanced feminist theory, while simultaneously contributing to the foundation of queer theory and the canonical status of Foucault's *The History of Sexuality* within this new field. Following this discussion of Butler, I turn to several other appropriations of *The History of Sexuality* within queer theory.

TROUBLING GENDER

By the time Butler wrote *Gender Trouble*, feminists in the Anglo-American tradition had long defined gender as the social and cultural interpretations of sex, while accepting sex as the natural or biological distinction between male and female. Feminists in this tradition focused their attention on critiquing the more misogynist aspects of gender interpretations, leaving the givenness of sex unchallenged. Although feminists were invested in showing that gender was a patriarchal construct, or that sex could be interpreted otherwise, Butler points out that they themselves often wanted to believe that, beneath these impositions of patriarchy, one could unearth a pre-discursive experience of women. Feminists themselves assumed or sought some shared feature that united women as a group, whether this was a maternal drive, or simply a shared experience of oppression that resulted from the biological facticity of their sex. Butler writes, for instance, of feminist approaches to psychoanalysis that essentialized the maternal experience, as well as feminist anthropological studies that attempted to recover a matriarchal past. Feminists thus sought femininity in its pure form, untampered by patriarchy, deep in the female psyche or in the distant past. As Butler writes,

> [T]his recourse to an original or genuine femininity is a nostalgic and parochial ideal that refuses the contemporary demand to formulate an account of gender as a complex cultural construction. This ideal tends not only to serve culturally conservative aims, but to constitute an exclusionary practice within feminism, precipitating precisely the kind of fragmentation that the ideal purports to overcome.
>
> (Butler, 1999, pp. 46–7)

More insidiously, as Butler points out, by accepting the views that sex is a biological fact and that there is a relationship between sex and gender, feminists continued to naturalize the gender categories they aimed to politicize. For instance, by defining gender as the way a culture interprets biological sex, while accepting that sex naturally comes in only two forms (male and female), feminists assumed that gender was also binary (masculine/feminine), with masculinity correlating with maleness and femininity correlating with femaleness. As Butler writes, this 'binary, heterosexist framework... carves up genders into masculine and feminine and forecloses the kinds of subversive and parodic convergences that characterize gay and lesbian cultures' (1999, pp. 84–5). Writing from the perspective of these cultures, Butler challenges the view that sex is a pre-discursive or apolitical fact on which genders are superimposed. Instead, she follows Foucault in arguing that sex is a by-product of the deployment of sexuality.

Butler opens chapter 1 of *Gender Trouble* with an epigraph from *The History of Sexuality*, citing Foucault's claim that '[t]he deployment of sexuality... established this notion of sex' (p. 3). This means that ' "female" no longer appears to be a stable notion, its meaning is as troubled and unfixed as "woman"' (p. xxix). In chapter 3 of her book, Butler elaborates on Foucault's argument, writing:

> In opposition to this false construction of 'sex' as both univocal and causal, Foucault engages a reverse-discourse which treats 'sex' as an

effect rather than an origin. In the place of 'sex' as the original and continuous cause and signification of bodily pleasures, he proposes 'sexuality' as an open and complex historical system of discourse and power that produces the misnomer of 'sex' as part of a strategy to conceal and, hence, to perpetuate power-relations. One way in which power is both perpetuated and concealed is through the establishment of an external or arbitrary relation between power, conceived as repression or domination, and sex, conceived as a brave but thwarted energy waiting for release or authentic self-expression. The use of this juridical model presumes that the relation between power and sexuality is not only ontologically distinct, but that power always and only works to subdue or liberate a sex which is fundamentally intact, self-sufficient, and other than power itself. When 'sex' is essentialized in this way, it becomes ontologically immunized from power relations and from its own historicity. As a result, the analysis of sexuality is collapsed into the analysis of 'sex,' and any inquiry into the historical production of the category of 'sex' itself is precluded by this inverted and falsifying causality. According to Foucault, 'sex' must not only be recontextualized within the terms of *sexuality*, but juridical power must be reconceived as a construction produced by a generative power which, in turn, conceals the mechanism of its own productivity.

(Butler, 1999, p. 121, emphasis in original)

Sex itself is a social construct, for Butler and Foucault, or has always been what feminists call 'gender'. Everything that we say and think about 'sex' – including the idea that there are two (and only two) sexes – is already a gendered interpretation. There is no biological substratum to gender, therefore, but only gender interpretations all the way down. Butler argues that, just as disciplinary power functions, for Foucault, by obliging subjects to repeat practices until these practices are internalized as habits and dispositions, so gender identities, far from being grounded in facts about biology or the body, are simply the result of repeated, compulsory performances of gender mandated by the constructs and socio-political norms of sex and sexuality. In this way, and drawing on Foucault, Butler puts forward what has been called the 'performativity theory' of gender.

Butler's view of gender as nothing more than the congealed product of stylized repetitions of acts that are themselves mandated by historically contingent norms of sex and sexuality challenged forms of feminism that were grounded in identity politics, or that required 'woman' to be a stable category, grounded in femaleness, that feminism could represent. As Spargo observes,

> Like Foucault's analysis of the interimplication of knowledge and power in the production of subject positions, gender performativity literally destroys the grounds of political movements whose goal is the liberation of repressed or oppressed natures, whether gendered or sexual, but opens up possibilities of resistance and subversion closed down by identity politics.
>
> (Spargo, 1999, p. 57)

Butler thus threatens the theoretical ground of feminist movements that claim to speak for and defend women as a natural group. This does not make her work anti-feminist, however, but just draws upon a different feminist tradition. As Butler demonstrates in chapter 1 of *Gender Trouble*, Foucault's argument about the political nature of sex resonates with French-language feminist philosophers such as Simone de Beauvoir, Luce Irigaray, Julia Kristeva and (especially) Monique Wittig, who each argued that 'woman' – or the category of sex more generally – is not a biological given but a political fiction and construct of patriarchy. As Butler describes her intentions in writing *Gender Trouble*, 'As I wrote it, I understood myself to be in an embattled and oppositional relation to certain forms of feminism, even as I understood the text to be part of feminism itself' (1999, p. vii).

With the publication of *Gender Trouble*, Butler thus deprived Anglo-American feminists of their cherished understandings of sex and gender, and of their ability to claim to represent 'women'. Beyond this, however, Butler expanded on Foucault's argument in *The History of Sexuality* to contend that feminists, in producing authoritative discourses on 'women', contribute to the social construction of the very subjects for whom they purport to speak. As Butler observes, 'Foucault points out that... systems of power produce the subjects they subsequently come to represent... And the feminist subject turns out to be discursively constituted by the very political system that is supposed to facilitate its emancipation' (p. 4). In arguing that feminism contributes to the constitution of the subjects it purports to represent (i.e. women), Butler is self-consciously echoing Foucault's argument that the sexual sciences produced the subjects that they categorize and describe (e.g. homosexuals), and that the constitutive role of the sexual sciences was extended by the sexual liberation movement. Indeed, Butler writes that 'the problem is even more serious', as the *way* that feminism constructs the category of women is 'an unwitting regulation and reification of gender relations' (pp. 8–9). For instance, Butler analyses feminist accounts of 'women' that assume experiences of heterosexuality and maternity, in this way contributing to the construction of heterosexuality and motherhood as gender norms, and other ways of being a woman as aberrant or abnormal. This power move on the part of feminism – its disciplining of gender, or contribution to the constitution of the category of 'women' – gives rise, as Foucault notes power always does, to resistance, generating 'multiple refusals to accept the category' on the part of subjects who feel excluded from the category of 'women' as feminism describes it. These exclusions and acts of resistance, Butler argues, reveal the feminist construction of gender to be 'coercive and regulatory... even when the construction has been elaborated for emancipatory purposes' (p. 7).

While some feminists have taken the view that it is necessary for feminism to assume an essential gender – or to assume the category of women – in order to struggle for the emancipation of women, in *Gender Trouble* Butler resists even a strategic gender essentialism. As she observes, any constitution of a subject position, including a feminist constitution of women, will be exclusionary. Extended sections of *Gender Trouble* examine the ways that non-heterosexual women are excluded from feminist discourses, for instance in the heterosexist feminist psychoanalysis of Julia Kristeva. In representing women in a certain way, other ways of being, such as queer ways of being, will not be represented, or will be excluded from what it means to be a 'woman'. As Butler observes, the history of Western feminist discourses and practices has demonstrated this point time and again, with white, heterosexual, First World feminists consistently if tacitly excluding non-Western women, women of colour, trans women and lesbians, among others, from their understandings of what it means to be a 'woman' and a 'feminist'. As Butler argues, such exclusions are inevitable when politics is understood as representational, or identity politics. Such a politics functions within a 'heterosexual matrix' and directly against feminist goals (pp. 8–9). For Butler, therefore, feminism should be less invested in speaking for and about women, and should instead be critiquing and undermining the categories of sex. As she writes, 'It is not enough to inquire into how women might become more fully represented in language and politics. [Beyond this, f]eminist critique ought also to understand how the category of "women," the subject of feminism, is produced and restrained by the very structures of power through which emancipation is sought' (p. 5).

In the original, 1990 preface to *Gender Trouble*, Butler asks: 'What happens to the subject and to the stability of gender categories when the epistemic regime of presumptive heterosexuality is unmasked as that which produces and reifies these ostensible categories of ontology?' (p. xxviii). For Butler, such an unmasking is what *The History of Sexuality* begins to do, and what *Gender Trouble* perseveres in doing. Foucault shows that sexualities are socially constituted, with heterosexuality produced as a norm through the production of homosexuality as its abnormal opposite. As Butler shows, how sexualities such as heterosexuality and homosexuality are understood entails and produces assumptions about what it is to be a man or a woman, or what it means to be masculine or feminine. Far from sex being a biological given that causes or explains both gender and sexuality, it is the biopolitical implantation of sexualities that requires and produces our current understandings of gender and sex.

As Butler argues, the way to continue the unmasking of 'the epistemic regime of presumptive heterosexuality' that *The History of Sexuality* begins is not to speak on behalf of (and thus reinforce) a given category of sex or gender but, rather, to trouble our categories of sex and gender. This troubling can be done, Butler argues, through the Foucauldian method of genealogy. As she writes: 'To expose the foundational categories of sex, gender, and desire as effects of a specific formation of power requires a form of critical inquiry that Foucault, reformulating Nietzsche, designates as "genealogy"' (p. xxix). In arguing that sex is gender and gender is performative, Butler shows gender to be a political and contingent construct, and one that is, moreover, interwoven with the regulatory constructs of sex and sexuality that Foucault describes. As she writes,

> The notion that there might be a 'truth' of sex, as Foucault ironically terms it, is produced precisely through the regulatory practices that generate coherent identities through the matrix of coherent gender norms. The heterosexualization of desire requires and institutes the production of discrete and asymmetrical oppositions between 'feminine' and 'masculine,' where these are understood as expressive attributes of 'male' and 'female.'
>
> (Butler, 1999, p. 23)

We live in a society that, as Butler puts it, 'heterosexualizes' desire. We see this in the assumption that males naturally desire (feminine) females, and females naturally desire (masculine) males, that to be male is to be masculine and to be female is to be feminine, and thus a woman who desires a woman has somehow, unnaturally, been 'masculinized' and a man who desires a man has somehow, unnaturally, been 'feminized'. For instance, children are presumed to be heterosexual and cisgendered until proved otherwise. Like Foucault's own discussion of genders in ancient Greece, to be discussed in Chapter 7, Butler's *Gender Trouble* contributes to a genealogy of gender as we know it, showing the contingency of each of these assumptions.

Straight feminist readers of *The History of Sexuality* had noticed – and been critical of – the absence of gender analysis in this book. What they imagined Foucault should have done, however, was to integrate into his historical descriptions observations of how the medicalization and disciplining of sex was primarily a male control of female bodies. Butler, a queer feminist, does not raise this criticism, but sees a different potential for gender analysis in Foucault's work. Butler's Foucauldian queer feminist reading of *The History of Sexuality* does not simply add gender to the volume and stir; instead, it uses Foucault to challenge feminist understandings of both gender and sex. Why did Butler see a different and more radical potential for gender analysis in *The History of Sexuality* than straight feminists saw? Why did she recognize the potential to take up and deploy *The History of Sexuality* for the purpose of gender politics, rather than simply critiquing the absence of such politics in Foucault's volume? In a plausible response to these questions, several queer theorists have argued that *The History of Sexuality* is a queer book, and that queer readers recognize political implications and strategies in its pages that straight readers miss. In the following sections, I examine two arguments to this effect, as they are articulated by queer theorists Ladelle McWhorter and David Halperin.

'A QUEER VOICE'

In *Bodies and Pleasures: Foucault and the Politics of Sexual Normalization*, Ladelle McWhorter describes growing up queer in the 1970s in Decatur, Alabama. At 12 years old, already romantically and erotically involved with another girl, she discovered the word 'homosexual', and asked her mother what it meant. She was told that a homosexual is 'a kind of person that falls in love with a person of their own sex'. This was the first time McWhorter realized that, in our times, the sex of the people with whom one falls in love makes one a 'kind of person'. Because her mother's apparently innocuous definition of 'homosexual' was spoken with such disgust, McWhorter simultaneously realized that she had to hide from her mother that she *was* this 'kind of person'. From that time onwards, McWhorter carefully attended to what was said about 'homosexuals'. As she describes, she learned that

homosexuals are sick people whose brain chemistry drives them to their unnatural and repulsive acts but who may be controlled with hormone injections. I learned that homosexuals are child-molesters who should be executed – extralegally if need be. I learned that homosexuals are ridiculous people – weak, manipulable, pathetic, worthless – who deserve whatever bad things happen to them. Finally,

> I learned that homosexuals are only homosexuals, never neighbors or
> Presbyterians or dentists or secretaries or citizens or mothers or peo-
> ple whose hobbies include anything beyond the consumption of por-
> nographic material. Queers are nobody, just queer, one-dimensional.
> When somebody finds out you're queer, they forget everything they
> ever knew about you; or, if they remember anything about you at all,
> the things they remember just get reinterpreted as nothing more than
> symptoms of your disease.
>
> (McWhorter, 1999, p. 2)

McWhorter soon learned that, if it was discovered that she was
this 'kind', all of her interests and achievements would be reduced
to symptoms and signs of her 'diseased' sexuality. Although as a
presumably straight child she was able to have many attributes,
such as being a good student, an athlete and a creative writer, once
it was known that she was a 'homosexual', each of these aspects
of her identity would be reduced to symptoms of her perverted
sexuality: her achievements in science class and her athleticism
would be reinterpreted as signs of masculinity or inversion, and
her creative writing talent would be attributed to the supposed
homosexual inclination to dissimulate (McWhorter, 1999, p. 2).
Although she quickly realized that 'homosexuals' are reduced to a
pathologizing understanding of their sexuality, McWhorter never
stopped being perplexed that this is the way things are. After all,
she was many other things besides the love she felt for and the sex
she had with another girl. Why were none of these other aspects
of her life considered as significant as her sexuality?

Because to be a homosexual was to be reduced to sexual sickness, to be loathed and objectified, McWhorter understandably
did not want to identify as a homosexual. She simply wanted to
be who she was. This included being a girl who desired and made
love with other girls, but McWhorter did not see why she had to be
reduced to and labelled by that desire, let alone subjected to violence on this basis. Although she therefore did not want to identify
as a homosexual, and spent years trying to avoid this identification, McWhorter found that her sexuality saturated her existence
precisely because she had to make such persistent efforts to hide
it from those who would harm her if they found out. She herself

could not maintain the view that her sexual desires were only a small part of herself, when she was obliged to spend so much of her energy hiding this part. As she explains, it was precisely the obligation to hide her sexuality that turned her into a homosexual: 'I did not want to be a homosexual. But gradually they – peers, teachers, ministers, therapists – made me' (p. 3).

Although homosexual is what McWhorter was made to be, she also describes homosexuality as a nearly impossible position *to* be. Since to be a homosexual was to be objectified, or reduced to a thing that was considered an aberration, to be a subject who identified as this object – this object that should never exist at all – was a contradiction in terms. To identify as homosexual was to identify as being nothing more than something that, according to society, ought to be eradicated from the world if possible. A homosexual was not a subject, a being with a point of view, but an object of derision, hatred and study for the sexual sciences. As McWhorter writes,

> Queers were surfaces merely, across which gender transgressions were written. It was as though to 'be queer' was to be some sort of puppet whose strings were pulled by sexuality alone. Queers did nothing but perform – gaily of course. Real feelings, thoughts, assessments, decisions, dreams, hopes, and ideas were only for straight people; only straight people actually had a point of view.
>
> (McWhorter, 1999, p. 4)

McWhorter argues that it is the apparent impossibility of being both a homosexual and a subject, along with the sheer violence perpetrated against queer people, that drives so many queer youth to take their lives. Indeed, Foucault himself 'flirted with suicide in his youth', and his biographers have speculated that it was his struggle to accept a homosexual identity that was the cause (Halperin, 1995, p. 130). As McWhorter describes, she herself eventually felt unable to avoid the 'logical conclusion' of what society was telling her: that she could not exist, that she should die.

McWhorter's conclusion that it was impossible to be a homosexual and a subject led to an episode of suicidality in her adolescence, which resulted in her being hospitalized for months. While in the psychiatric hospital, McWhorter was advised: 'Don't ever study philosophy.' Nonetheless, upon her release, study philosophy is exactly what McWhorter did: she went to university, she took philosophy courses, and eventually she came across the writings of Michel Foucault. She describes this memorable occasion:

> Then, on January 7, 1983, I read Foucault's *The History of Sexuality* in its entirety, and for the first time in my life I heard something I believed it was impossible to hear: the articulation of a homosexual point of view. I had believed that it was impossible to speak as a homosexual, from a homosexual perspective, because I had believed there was no way to be a homosexual except to be totally objectified. But Foucault's book proved me wrong. I was excited. I was overjoyed. Never have I been so happy with a book between my hands.
>
> (McWhorter, 1999, p. 9)

The History of Sexuality demonstrated to McWhorter that one could be both a homosexual and have a point of view, since this book reflected, on her reading, a homosexual point of view. In *Saint Foucault*, David Halperin argues that the demonstration of such a point of view is one of the main objectives of gay and lesbian politics; for Halperin, this politics insists that homosexuality can be 'a position from which one *can* know' rather than simply a position of being known, a '*condition* of knowledge' rather than a mere object of knowledge (Halperin, 1995, p. 60). For McWhorter, Foucault's book showed that it was not a contradiction in terms to be homosexual and a knower, to be a homosexual and to live, think and be. As McWhorter writes, 'Foucault's book defies the political odds and emerges as a queer voice – an event that is in itself politically powerful and that had a tremendously empowering impact on me' (McWhorter, 1999, p. 9).

McWhorter suggests that *The History of Sexuality* had a similar impact on other queer readers as well. Although heterosexual political philosophers of the time, working at high levels of abstraction, warned readers that Foucault's work was politically useless if not dangerous, queer readers – oblivious to or uninterested in these critiques – were finding an important political resource in Foucault's book. As McWhorter describes:

[W]hile Rorty, Walzer, Moi, Dews, Taylor, Fraser, and countless others offered warnings to activists not to waste their time getting sidetracked by theories that in the end would be useless to them, not to get seduced, not to get mired in Foucault's nihilistic muck, scores of gay bookstores quietly stocked and sold Foucault's books. While relatively mainstream philosophers, historians, and political theorists insisted that Foucault's work could never form the basis for or even aid any successful political movement, queer readers were making Foucault a part of their intellectual lives. And, given the extremely politically ramified conditions under which non-heterosexual people live, making Foucault a part of their intellectual lives usually meant making him a part of their political lives... Most of those readers never thought to seek out a professional political theorist to help them decide whether Foucault had something valuable to say. They just read Foucault.

(McWhorter, 1999, p. xv)

Halperin similarly observes that mainstream, heterosexual political theorists and philosophers of the 1980s and 1990s, such as Charles Taylor and Richard Rorty, dismissed Foucault's work as nihilistic and politically useless, even while members of the politically militant and impactful LGBTQ AIDS activist group, AIDS Coalition to Unleash Power (ACT UP), consistently named volume 1 of *The History of Sexuality* as the book that influenced their political activism the most (Halperin, 1995, pp. 15–16). What was it about *The History of Sexuality* that spoke to queer readers, including McWhorter and Halperin, and that straight political theorists were missing? How and why did this work concretely empower LGBTQ activists, even while heterosexual philosophers assured readers that, for theoretical reasons, it could never do so?

In fact, it may not be immediately obvious why McWhorter would have recognized *The History of Sexuality* as a 'queer voice', or as a work that expresses a 'homosexual point of view'. After all, volume 1 of *The History of Sexuality* does not involve any extended discussions of homosexuality. Although it promises a future volume on the 'sexual pervert', it does not deliver on this promise, and there are many forms of so-called 'perversion' besides homosexuality. Although volume 1 includes Foucault's brief description of the 'homosexual' as a 'species', it does not include any detailed discussions of same-sex desire. Foucault writes in passing of 'the sensuality of those who did not like the opposite sex', but this is in a list of phenomena that were simultaneously being medicalized, including 'the sexuality of children, mad men and women, and criminals... reveries, obsessions, petty manias, or great transports of rage' (Foucault, 1978, pp. 38–9). The short case study of a sexually pathologized subject in *The History of Sexuality* is Charles Jouy, who had sexual relations not with another man but with a girl. So why was Foucault's book so useful to ACT UP activists, and why was McWhorter immediately convinced that this volume demonstrated the possibility of a 'homosexual point of view'? Might we even worry that, in making this claim, McWhorter is herself reducing Foucault to his sexuality? Might calling *The History of Sexuality* a 'homosexual' book be indicative once more of the tendency, which McWhorter fiercely critiques, to reduce everything homosexual people do to symptoms of their sexual desires?

McWhorter reads *The History of Sexuality* as expressing a homosexual point of view in part because it provides answers to questions that one would probably never ask if one were heterosexual. For example, *The History of Sexuality* is driven by the same questions that perplexed McWhorter as a child growing up in Alabama: 'Why do I have to be judged as a sexual being at all? Why does that have to be the most important thing about me? Why can't I be defined by something else, some other aspect of my personality or my daily life?' (McWhorter, 1999, pp. 9–10). As McWhorter writes, this question simply 'isn't likely to enter the mind of a well-adjusted heterosexual person, not because well-adjusted heterosexual people are not judged by their sexuality (they most certainly are) but because the judgement is positive' (p. 10). For example, if a landlord discriminates against homosexuals, refusing to rent to them, the people who are discriminated against are made aware of how their sexuality is impacting their lives. They at least suspect that they are being judged by and detrimentally reduced to their sexuality, and are thus likely to wonder why things need to be this way. Such subjects must constantly decide whether to try to pass as heterosexual, or refuse to do so and suffer the consequences of discrimination. In contrast, the heterosexual tenants whose rental application is accepted tend not to be aware of the ways that they are being privileged by their sexuality, and how their sexuality is impacting their lives, since it does so only in positive ways. Although all of us are judged by our sexualities, this fact, and why it is problematic, is most conspicuous to those for whom these judgements are detrimental. As McWhorter writes,

> We queers tend to see very clearly that sexuality is central to the disposition of everybody's life, not just to homosexuals. So we are apt to ask, 'Why does it have to be this way? Why do we all have to be judged by our sexuality rather than something else?' This question is queer in the sense that being situated in the world as a queer person is what is most likely to motivate someone to ask it and look for an answer. And it is this question that motivates Foucault's whole book, provides its energy and direction throughout.
>
> (McWhorter, 1999, p. 10)

Importantly, however, the question that drives Foucault's book is not 'homosexual' or 'queer' in any essential sense. It is not the case that someone who loves or desires people of the same sex in any time and place would ask the question that Foucault poses. It is only a person who loves or desires people of the same sex in a culture that reduces one to that love and desire, and stigmatizes one for it, who would ask this question; and, as Foucault's book makes clear, it is only recently and contingently the case that we live in a society such as this. McWhorter is thus identifying Foucault's question as one that only a sexual 'deviant' would ask, but she does so without essentializing the subject position from which she recognizes that Foucault, like she herself, writes.

For McWhorter, *The History of Sexuality* is also written from a homosexual point of view because it is critical of practices, such as sexual confession, that are accepted as therapeutic by most straight people but that non-heterosexual people know to be dangerous and harmful to their well-being. While Foucault's narrative might not resonate with a straight reader, McWhorter recognizes the significance of the story of sexual repression and the allegedly curative practice of sexual confession that is a central theme of Foucault's book. As she writes,

> This tale of a natural (hetero)sexuality that needed to be rescued from Victorian bondage was a story I knew well. By the time I reached puberty in the 1970s, even Alabamians were aware that we were supposed to liberate ourselves by exploring our sexual feelings rather than repressing them, supposed to affirm our sexuality, supposed to manage its more dangerous potentials through the transformative power of confessional speech.
>
> (McWhorter, 1999, p. 12)

Although a heterosexual Alabamian adolescent was likely to accept this story at face value, McWhorter already knew as a teenager that sexual confession would not, in fact, be liberatory for *her*. On the contrary, she was already 'intimately acquainted with the grim realities consequent upon sexual confession':

> Unless you're straight-**straight**-*straight*, if you're honest about your sexuality, liberation is not what follows: lock up is. The truth does not make deviants free. For any sexual deviant, confession, whatever its benefits, comes at an extremely high price. To name oneself queer in our society is to put one's job, one's family, one's freedom, and even one's life on the line.
>
> (McWhorter, 1999, p. 13, emphasis in original)

A heterosexual person might not question the story we are told about sexual confession, because confession might actually seem to function for the straight person as it is promised to do. Straight people might not even be aware of how often they are expected to confess their sexuality, since their sexual revelations are relatively inconsequential, and are seamlessly received. For non-heterosexuals, however, sexual confessions can and often do have life-altering impacts, costing them jobs, friendships, families, homes, safety and freedom. Although McWhorter thus knew from a young age to keep her sexual desires and practices secret, she describes in her book the process of eventually being worn out by hiding and evading the compulsion to confess:

> I didn't surrender to her. I didn't confess. But after a few years of unremitting surveillance and subtle and not-so-subtle threats, you get tired. The thing you fight, the thing you fear, gradually stops seeming so frightful after all. You can't go on alone. You really do need help. What's the difference, either way? So eventually you find yourself in somebody's badly furnished office, huddled on a chair, saying the words they want you to say. And they listen. And they are interested. And that's a relief; it feels good. They ask questions. At times you hesitate. Some questions seem irrelevant; some embarrass you. They insist, gently. You refuse. They suggest that you are resisting therapy, don't really want help, want to persist in your illness. If you still won't answer they take your clothes, lock you up in a cubicle with nothing but a mattress, watch you through a two-way mirror, and write down all the nasty words you say. They ask more questions, make you draw pictures, administer drugs. They acquire your medical records, look in your mouth, take samples of blood, give you intelligence tests and plug you into electroencephalographs. They watch you interact with peers, listen to your phone calls, withhold your mail because unmonitored interactions will impede therapy. They bring in your family, videotape you together while they question them, and study your facial expressions while you listen to their answers. Then they tell you whether you're really gay or not.
>
> (McWhorter, 1999, pp. 27–8)

As is clear, the sexual confessions of a straight adolescent would neither be extracted the way McWhorter's were nor would they be scrutinized in such detail and with such invasive consequences, since the straight adolescent's confessions, unlike McWhorter's, would not be deemed symptomatic of a social danger. Although sexual confessions are required of us all, they are particularly demanded from and have the most devastating impacts upon those who are considered 'deviant'.

Halperin similarly describes the disappointing consequences of the sexually confessional practice of 'coming out':

> The point of coming out, I had thought, was precisely to deprive other people of their privileged knowingness about me and my sexuality; coming out had seemed to me to furnish a means of seizing the initiative from them, a means of claiming back from them a certain interpretative authority over the meaning of my words and actions. As I discovered to my cost, however, it turns out that if you are known to be lesbian or gay your very openness, far from preempting malicious gossip about your sexuality, simply exposes you to the possibility that, no matter what you actually do, people can say absolutely whatever they like about you in the well-grounded confidence that it will be credited.
>
> (Halperin, 1995, p. 13)

As Halperin explains, far from being a straightforward liberation from the dangers and constraints of the closeted life,

> to come out is precisely to expose oneself to a different set of dangers and constraints, to make oneself into a convenient screen onto which straight people can project all the fantasies they routinely entertain about gay people, and to suffer one's every gesture, statement, expression, and opinion to be totally and irrevocably marked by the overwhelming social significance of one's openly acknowledged homosexual identity.
>
> (Halperin, 1995, p. 30)

This does not mean, for Halperin, that one should *not* come out but, rather, that one should be prepared to find that coming out is an act of resistance rather than liberation. Coming out resists a normalizing form of power by affirming what is constructed as abnormal, but it does not liberate a person from oppression or set him apart from power. To some extent, Foucault shows that coming out is a submission to a normalizing power that requires us to identify with a sexuality and confess to it, but it is also what Foucault calls a 'reverse discourse', an act of defiance insofar as it declares one's refusal to strive for the sexual norm.

As the complex politics of coming out illustrates, and as McWhorter observes, the fact that Foucault makes confession a central theme of his study of sexuality, and is concerned to debunk the myth that confessions are liberatory, is, once again, indicative of his experience as a homosexual. Indeed, McWhorter argues that gays and lesbians are aware that the experience of being made homosexual in a heterosexist society is less about what kinds of pleasures you are having with what kinds of people than it is about who knows what about you, and trying to control this information. The experience of being 'homosexual' is, as Eve Kosofsky Sedgwick's *Epistemology of the Closet* brilliantly describes, first and foremost an epistemological experience. For instance, writing of the consequences – for both himself and Foucault – of being both a public intellectual and an openly gay man, Halperin writes:

> The problem of authorization... dramatizes the more general social and discursive predicament of lesbians and gay men in a world where a claimed homosexual identity operates as an instant disqualification, exposes you to accusations of pathology and partisanship ... and grants everyone else an absolute epistemological privilege over you.
>
> (Halperin, 1995, p. 8)

Because the experience of homosexuality is so intertwined with the politics of knowledge, Halperin writes that LGBTQ politics has 'consisted largely in the story of how lesbians and gay men fought to wrest from non-gay-identified people control over such matters as who gets to speak for us, who gets to represent our experience, who is authorized to pronounce knowledgeability about our lives' (pp. 56–7). The experience and politics of homosexuality are thus more about knowledge than pleasure, and this, McWhorter argues, is why Foucault's *The History of Sexuality* is an epistemological work that attends to practices of knowledge production such as confession.

McWhorter also recognizes a homosexual point of view in Foucault's interest in the surveillance of childhood, which, as he describes, originated in the medical crusade against masturbation but did not stop there. Readers who grew up, as McWhorter puts it, 'straight-**straight**-*straight*' may have sailed through childhood relatively unaware of the intense scrutiny placed on children's sexual practices, since this scrutiny did not result in drastic interventions in their cases. These readers might find Foucault's account of the sexualization of childhood and the biopolitical regulation of the family to be surprising and unfamiliar, or even paranoid and exaggerated. In contrast, McWhorter writes: 'It was in great part this vast surveillance system, rooted in the war on masturbation, that made my life so very miserable through adolescence. I recognized Foucault's descriptions immediately. That was my world, all right' (McWhorter, 1999, p. 22). Finally, McWhorter recognizes her own experience of being saturated by sexuality and forced to take on the identity of 'homosexual' in Foucault's account of the 'perverse implantation'. As she writes, 'Here, in those five pages of Foucault's little book, I saw described, for the first time, the world in which I struggled to survive' (p. 24). Although born decades apart, in different socio-economic milieus and on different continents, McWhorter is arguing that she and Foucault, and other queer readers, shared a world – albeit a contingent, unhappy and historically constituted world – and this is why she recognized in his writing what a straight reader might miss, and what she had thought it was impossible to hear: 'a queer voice'.

CANONIZING FOUCAULT

Butler's and McWhorter's discussions of Foucault both give us a sense of the canonical status of the philosopher in queer theory. Not all gay and lesbian scholars were impressed by Foucault, however. In *Gay Ideas*, philosopher Richard Mohr objects to the idea that sexuality is socially constructed and to the influence of Foucault in popularizing this view among gay and lesbian writers. Mohr singles out for particular criticism queer classicist David Halperin, whose 1990 book *One Hundred Years of Homosexuality* contributed, in Mohr's view, to the banefully 'hagiographical' status of Foucault among gay and lesbian scholars. In Mohr's scathing words, Halperin was guilty of engaging in 'generic worship of Saint Foucault' (Mohr, 1992, p. 282, n. 2). In a considered response to Mohr, Halperin would take up the gauntlet, publishing a book titled *Saint Foucault: Towards a Gay Hagiography*, wherein he writes: 'So let me make it official. I may not have worshipped Foucault at the time I wrote *One Hundred Years of Homosexuality*, but I do worship him now. As far as I'm concerned, the guy was a fucking saint' (Halperin, 1995, p. 6). Like McWhorter, Halperin expresses a deep sense of self-recognition in Foucault's life and work, for which reason he, like McWhorter, experiences mainstream criticisms of Foucault as odious and, indeed, as personal attacks. Writing of his feeling of identification with Foucault, Halperin goes so far as to declare: '*Michel Foucault, c'est moi*' (1995, p. 8).

Halperin, like McWhorter, offers a number of explanations as to why queer readers have been enamoured of *The History of Sexuality*, and why they have found in this small book so much political potential when many straight readers saw only political nihilism or despair. One of these explanations is that the AIDS crisis that emerged shortly after the publication of *The History of Sexuality* made Foucault's arguments strikingly clear to the gay and lesbian community. As Halperin writes, '[I]t would be difficult to imagine a more powerful or urgent demonstration than the AIDS crisis of the need to conceptualize sexuality, after the manner of Foucault, as "an especially concentrated point of traversal... for relations of power"' (p. 27). In particular, Foucault's arguments about the interrelations between medical knowledge and power and his theory of biopower helped to make sense of many aspects of how the AIDS catastrophe unfolded. As the gay community suffered devastating losses that were exacerbated by social stigma and a failure to mobilize medical resources and knowledge, many of Foucault's arguments in *The History of Sexuality* were painfully illustrated. In the course of the catastrophe, power did not simply or primarily work through laws and elected officials, or in a juridico-legal manner. Rather, the struggles of the gay community were first and foremost for access to knowledge and medical treatment and against forms of prejudice and stigma that came from innumerable different directions, many of them administrative, bureaucratic and medical (Castiglia and Reed, 2011; Cohen, 1999; Epstein, 1998; Gould, 2009; Shotwell, 2014; Triechler, 1999; Stoller, 1998; Patton, 1985; Gossett, 2014).

As the death toll rose, gay men struggled to access medical knowledge about the disease, and it was a political act to fight for and distribute safer-sex knowledge among their communities. It was also very clear to those who were dying and to their communities that medicine and scientific knowledge would have been mobilized in very different ways had the demographic primarily struck by AIDS been heterosexual. Far from the resources and uses of medicine, science and knowledge being neutral or objective, these were deployed differentially as a result of the socially undesired nature of the populations (homosexuals, drug users, sex workers) who were primarily being extinguished by AIDS. The view that AIDS was God's or nature's punishment for the sinful or unnatural acts of homosexuality was widespread, leading to an apathetic (or murderous) unwillingness to intervene in 'God's will'. Foucault writes of 'genocidal dreams' as characteristic of biopower in *The History of Sexuality*, and Halperin describes the biopolitical response to the AIDS crisis as both genocidal and ubiquitous. Put simply, the reaction to AIDS was a 'letting die', and it came not 'from above' but 'from everywhere'. In this biopolitical context, the struggle of gay men was not for sexual 'liberation' or to be able to express their sexuality freely and authentically; the struggle was, rather, to resist by remaining alive – to survive.

More hearteningly, Foucault's *The History of Sexuality* illuminates not only how power operated during the AIDS catastrophe but also how such power could be resisted. AIDS activists recognized that they had to struggle not against the workings of a juridico-legal power but against what Foucault had called biopower. As trans theorist Dean Spade also emphasizes, this insight gave queer activists a crucial piece of strategic advice: not to waste time on struggles for legal rights that, history has shown, do little to actually improve the life chances of populations that are biopolitically devalued (Spade, 2011). The Black liberation movement, for instance, has been successful in obtaining legal rights for people of colour, but this has not meant that they are no longer subjected to systematic murder, poverty and incarceration. Rather than wasting activist energy and resources on legal battles for rights (such as the right to marry, the right to serve in the military or the right to be recognized in hate crime legislation) that merely reinforce the (racist, homophobic, transphobic, militaristic and carceral) status quo, Spade, like Halperin, follows Foucault in arguing that we need to be resisting biopower as it regulates our lives and distributes life chances. As Spade notes, this means that queer politics must be more invested in resisting normalizing institutions such as marriage than in fighting for the right to marry, and more invested in abolishing the military and penal systems than in contributing to their expansion.

For ACT UP, as Halperin describes, the recognition that power functions primarily through regulatory rather than juridico-legal avenues meant finding 'ways of breaking down monopolies of professional expertise, ways of democratizing knowledge, and ways of credentializing the disempowered so that they can intervene in the medical and governmental administration of the epidemic' (Halperin, 1995, p. 28). Beyond this, it meant contesting the workings of power at multiple sites, including

> immigration policy, public health policy (including such matters as anonymous HIV-antibody testing and needle exchange), the practice of epidemiology and clinical medicine (right down to the determination of optimum dosage levels for new drugs), the conduct of scientific research (the elimination of placebo trials in experiments on human subjects), the operation of the insurance and pharmaceutical industries, the role of the media in representing the epidemic, the decisions of rent control boards, the legal definition of 'family,' and ultimately the public and private administration of the body and its pleasures.
>
> (Halperin, 1995, p. 28)

As Halperin writes,

> Foucault's *History of Sexuality, Volume I*, had already treated the body as a site of political struggle. ACT UP – which had led a kind of uprising of the sick against their doctors, insurers, health care providers, blood banks, public welfare administrators, prison wardens, medical researchers, drug vendors, and media experts, not to mention their employers and landlords – would seem to furnish a perfect example of

> a strategic power reversal, a form of resistance made possible by the
> very apparatus of power/knowledge it was invented to resist.
>
> (Halperin, 1995, pp. 28–9)

The strategies of ACT UP were not strategies of liberation, Halperin argues, but strategies of resistance to the 'genocidal dreams' of a homophobic society.

Beyond informing, or simply resonating with, the political strategies of ACT UP, Halperin argues that Foucault offers queer theorists and activists a strategic lesson in how to approach authoritative discourses. That is, Foucault teaches us to engage less with the content of 'expert' discourses and more with what they are doing and the power effects that they are having. Throughout Foucault's own oeuvre, whether he is considering the discourses of social scientists on 'human kinds', the discourses of psychiatry on mental illness or the discourses of doctors on sexuality, Halperin observes that 'Foucault's example teaches us to analyze discourse strategically, not in terms of what it *says* but in terms of what it *does* and how it *works*' (p. 30, emphasis in original). Foucault refers dismissively to the content of these discourses as *bavardage*, or chatter, and teaches us that we waste our time if we try to engage with this chatter on its own terms. Rather, we need to see how such chatter is politics – which is to say: war – and to engage with it at the level of strategy, or battle. Foucault thus instructs us not to become entangled in the details of the 'expert' *bavardage* about homosexuality but, instead, to ask: what are these arguments *doing* and how might we resist their effects?[2]

One way to resist the effects of these discourses is, Foucault's work shows us, to demystify them. As Foucault writes in *The History of Sexuality*, power's 'success is proportional to its ability to hide its own mechanisms' (cited in Halperin, 1995, p. 51). Halperin argues that all of Foucault's work was politically strategic insofar as it aimed to expose the mechanisms of power and thus to reduce the proportion of that power's success. In unmasking the political nature of what psychiatry does to and says about the mentally ill, criminals and sexual 'deviants', for instance, Foucault made it more difficult for psychiatrists to go on doing what they were doing and to go on saying what they were saying. Similarly, Halperin argues that queer theory learned from Foucault not to take on the task of refuting each of the (pseudo-) scientific claims that were being made about homosexuality but, rather, to reveal the political nature of these claims and thus to dismantle the authority of those making such claims.

Finally, in *Saint Foucault* Halperin distinguishes between 'gay' and 'queer' by arguing that 'gay' politics follows the sciences of sex in accepting homosexuality as both an identity and an essence, whereas 'queer' politics follows Foucault's arguments in *The History of Sexuality* in accepting homosexuality as an identity but *not* as an essence. Queer politics radically resists the sciences of sex, therefore, while gay politics is at most a reverse discourse that functions on the terms of these sciences (Halperin, 1995, pp. 61–2). According to Halperin,

> Unlike gay identity, which though deliberately proclaimed in an act of affirmation, is nonetheless rooted in the positive fact of homosexual object-choice, queer identity need not be grounded in any positive truth or in any stable reality... Queer is by definition whatever is at odds with the normal, the legitimate, the dominant. *There is nothing in particular to which it necessarily refers.* It is an identity without an essence.
>
> (Halperin, 1995, p. 62, emphasis in original)

As Halperin insists, identifying as queer is thus not restricted to gays and lesbians, or even to those marginalized due to their sexual practices. The term allows us to define queer not as a 'thing' but as a 'resistance to the norm', including norms that are not obviously sexual (p. 66). In this sense, he argues that ACT UP was a more queer political movement than Queer Nation, since Queer Nation was organized around sexual orientation, whereas ACT UP brought together 'all the constituencies affected by the AIDS catastrophe', including those who were exposed to AIDS due to race, poverty, sex work, prison or intravenous drug use (p. 63). In responding to the AIDS catastrophe, ACT UP also took on many political battles, not only those directly related to sexual practices and identities. For instance, ACT UP was deeply invested in struggles concerning immigration, poverty, drug use, incarceration, sex work and health care. Similarly, Spade argues that queer (and particularly trans) politics must not be limited to resisting norms of sexuality and gender, but must also resist norms of race, class and ability. For Spade, a *critical* queer and trans politics is thus necessarily embedded in struggles against racism, capitalism, immigration policies, privatized health care, the prison and military industrial complexes and criminalization (Spade, 2011). While, from the perspective of some gay and lesbian politics, such 'desexualizing' understandings of queer politics as we find in Halperin and Spade may seem problematic, we have seen that, for Foucault, what we need to do is not so much affirm our sexualities as recognize sexualization as a product of biopower, and to resist biopower by refusing normalization.

For Halperin, so crucial is Foucault to queer theory and activism that, 'if Michel Foucault had never existed, queer politics would have had to invent him' (1995, p. 120). In particular, and still thumbing his nose at Mohr, Halperin writes that Foucault is 'the patron saint of queer activism'. Contra the straight, liberal, humanist philosophers who saw in Foucault only a theory of political despair, Halperin claims that, for queer theorists, 'Foucault is not only our Marx but also our Freud'. Put otherwise, Foucault provides queer theory not only with its canonical account of power, but also with its canonical account of sexuality (pp. 120–1).

'THE IMPERIAL PRUDE'

Foucault's thesis that biopower, the invention of sexuality and the historical emergence of biological racism are interrelated phenomena has given rise to a body of critical race theory that draws on Foucault's introductory volume to *The History of Sexuality*, and that has recently intersected with queer theory in powerful ways. Some of this literature examines, expands on, nuances and applies what Foucault has to say about race in *The History of Sexuality* (Feder, 2007; McWhorter, 2009; 2011; Medina, 2011; Stone, 2011; Sheth, 2011; Mader, 2011), but some critical race scholars have been just as concerned with what Foucault does not say about race as what he does say. In particular, although the first paragraph of *The History of Sexuality* includes the ironic statement that 'the image of the imperial prude is emblazoned on our restrained, mute, and hypocritical sexuality' (Foucault, 1978, p. 3), this is the first and last time that imperialism is mentioned in Foucault's book. For Foucault, the racism in question in volume 1 of *The History of Sexuality* was always Nazism, an internal European racism, and not the racism of Europe's imperial ventures. Ann Laura Stoler thus criticizes Foucault's discussions of race in *The History of Sexuality* and his related course lectures for failing to consider empire. As she writes,

> Europe's eighteenth- and nineteenth-century discourses on sexuality, like other cultural, political, or economic assertions, cannot be charted in Europe alone. In short-circuiting empire, Foucault's history of European sexuality misses key sites in the production of that discourse, discounts the practices that racialized bodies, and thus elides a field of knowledge that provided the contrasts for what a 'healthy, vigorous, bourgeois body' was all about.
>
> (Stoler, 1995, p. 7)

Stoler observes that a consideration of empire requires that we add at least one more figure to Foucault's discussion of 'four objects of knowledge' of nineteenth- and twentieth-century Western sexual sciences; in addition to the masturbating child, the hysterical woman, the 'pervert' and the reproductive couple, there was also the sexualized 'savage' (Stoler, 1995, pp. 6–7). The non-Western 'savage' was used 'to bolster Europe's bourgeois society and to underscore what might befall it in moral decline' (p. 7). The 'primitive' 'other' embodied the sexual threat of degeneration for white, Western, bourgeois subjects – both as an alluring contaminant and as what Europeans could become should they fall prey to this allure.

Although Foucault failed to recognize the imbrications of East and West in the form of empire (and several postcolonial scholars have even charged Foucault with orientalism for his facile contrasting of Western *scientia sexualis* and Eastern *ars erotica*: Puar, 2007, pp. 75, 94), *The History of Sexuality* has nevertheless provided useful theoretical tools for examining the racial dynamics of both European and American imperialism. This is demonstrated by Stoler's watershed study *Race and the Education of Desire: Foucault's* History of Sexuality *and the Colonial Order of Things* and, more recently, by queer theorist Jasbir Puar's influential monograph *Terrorist Assemblages: Homonationalism in Queer Times* (Stoler, 1995; Puar, 2007). Focusing on the Dutch East Indies in her study of the 'colonial order of things', Stoler provides a Foucauldian examination of the ways that Europeans struggled to regulate relations between colonial subjects and native concubines, wives, servants[3] and mixed-race subjects, constituting themselves and their 'others' in the process. Like Stoler, Puar expands on Foucault's examination of the biopolitical co-constitution of sexualities and races in *The History of Sexuality*, but she does so in the more recent context of post-9/11 US politics. While queer theorists such as Butler, McWhorter and Halperin have all discussed the ways that biopolitics has systematically exposed non-heterosexual people to death,[4] Puar examines the more recent phenomenon of homosexuals being folded back into life. Those homosexuals who have been recuperated – and indeed mobilized – by biopolitics are the ones who, in Duggan's terms, have been 'homonormalized'. More specifically, Puar shows that the *ways* these homonormalized gays and lesbians have been recuperated within biopolitical regimes has been instrumental to contemporary US imperialism and the war on terror. Indeed, Puar coins the term 'homonationalism' to refer to the ways in which 'an exceptional form of national heteronormativity is now joined by an exceptional form of national homonormativity'. For Puar, homonationalism is a 'brand of homosexuality' that 'operates as a regulatory script not only of normative gayness, queerness, or homosexuality, but also of the racial and national norms that reinforce these sexual subjects' (Puar, 2007, p. 2).

Following the attacks of 11 September 2001, Americans were urged to shop. Rather than staying at home and grieving, Americans were instructed that the ultimate patriotic act was to contribute to the US economy through consumption. In this context, certain gay and lesbian subjects, far from being biopolitically undesirable, came to be 'embraced by biopolitical incitement to life', with 'life' figured as domesticity and consumption

(Puar, 2007, p. xiii). Gay and lesbian Americans have, on average, higher levels of education – and thus income – than their straight counterparts, as well as fewer children – and thus more disposable income. Indeed, it seems that gays and lesbians are particularly active contributors to some segments of the US economy, such as tourism. A certain type of gay and lesbian subject – white, middle-class, homonormative (partnered, monogamous, propertied) – therefore became a model of citizenship in post-9/11 biopolitical times. As Puar observes, this marks a moment in which '[t]he terms of degeneracy have shifted such that homosexuality is no longer *a priori* excluded from national formations' (p. 2). The 'outlaw' status of homosexuals was 'mediated' in the 1980s and 1990s not only through gains in legal rights but also through 'the rise during the 1980s and 1990s of the gay consumer, pursued by marketers who claimed that childless homosexuals had enormous disposable incomes' (p. 4). In contrast, the sexuality of terrorists – and, by extension, of Muslims, Arabs and all those mistaken for Muslims or Arabs, such as Sikhs – was constructed as decidedly abnormal (repressed, polygamous) or racially queer (p. xii). Puar's book thus charts the differential ways in which some non-heterosexual subjects – homonormative US nationals, or 'homonationals' – were folded into the biopolitical regulation of life, while other sexual deviants – the racialized and 'perverse terrorist' and other objects of Islamophobia – were folded 'out of life, out toward death' (p. xii).

Despite ongoing oppression of non-heterosexual people in the United States, ranging from violent hate crimes to the very recently criminal status of sodomy (pp. 114–64), Puar's book thus charts numerous ways in which US, European and Israeli racism, xenophobia, war and imperialism have been justified by the supposedly exceptional sexual tolerance of the West in comparison to the exoticized homophobia of the Middle East. Puar opens her book, for example, with a discussion of protests that occurred across the Western world in 2006 in response to the executions of two gay youth in Iran, while similar executions of gay youth in Nigeria went all but unnoticed, and the homophobia of the US military exposed in 2004 at Abu Ghraib failed to result in similar protests. As Puar observes, this begs the questions '[w]hy now?' and '[w]hy

Iran?' Puar's answer is that Iran had recently been named by then US president George W. Bush as part of the 'axis of evil', and condemnations of Iran's homophobia fuelled Islamophobia, 'the war on terror' and the political push for a US invasion of Iran. The supposedly exceptional sexual tolerance of Western countries was thus contrasted with the repressive, homophobic nature of non-Western countries – and of Muslim countries on the United States' enemy list in particular – as evidence of the sexually exceptional status of the West and the 'backwardness' of its enemies. As Puar describes, the 'repressive hypothesis' is now projected not onto ourselves but onto non-Western others, and onto Muslims (and those mistaken as Muslims) in particular. Terrorism is causally linked by security 'experts' not to US imperialism but to sexual repression arising from religious taboos. Thus, in response to scandals such as Abu Ghraib, we heard not about the homophobia of the US military that the photos documented but, rather, about how such torture was particularly egregious given the sexual repression and homophobia *of Muslims*, for whom, we were told, being naked in the presence of women and being forced to simulate homosexual acts was the ultimate shame. As Puar argues, these commentaries on Abu Ghraib reinforce orientalist, othering views about the sexual backwardness of 'Arabs' compared to the supposed sexual tolerance of the West, and do so in manners that reinforce xenophobia and the war on terror (p. 139). With similar logic, we see Israel promoted as a desperately needed enclave of sexual tolerance in the Middle East, and Islamophobic demands for immigration restrictions that would protect the values of the sexually exceptional West from homophobic and perverse Muslim immigrants.

Puar's insights build on those of feminist scholars who have noted the ways that feminist agendas have been co-opted by non-feminists for the purposes of Western empire and war (pp. 5–7).[5] In both the nineteenth and twentieth centuries, the oppression of women in non-Western countries was selectively mobilized to justify military and colonial incursions by imperial powers. For example, nineteenth-century British men who were on record for vehemently opposing women's suffrage in the United Kingdom simultaneously exploited the 'primitive' oppression of women in countries such as India to justify colonial rule (Oliver, 2007). Western countries with long and ongoing histories of resisting feminist social transformation nevertheless mobilize Western feminist inroads to justify their control of more 'backward' countries, with primitivism correlated with the relative status of women. Empire has in this way been recast as a feminist mission, with, in Gayatri Spivak's famous words, 'white men... saving brown women from brown men' (Spivak, 1988). The exploitation of feminism for imperialism and war was seen recently when the situation of women in Afghanistan under the Taliban was taken advantage of by the US administration of George W. Bush to justify military incursions in that country, even while the same administration opposed feminist political movements back in the United States and remained indifferent to comparable gender oppression in countries it had no investment in invading (Oliver, 2007). Postcolonial feminist scholarship, like postcolonial queer scholarship such as Puar's, thus builds on Foucault's work by demonstrating the ever-shifting and adaptive nature of biopower and its continual deployment of race. In particular, this scholarship teaches us to attend to the ways that even those groups that have been socially and politically marginalized may be selectively folded back into a biopolitical regime for the purposes of racism and empire. Puar's work, like much contemporary queer scholarship, is less explicitly invested in canonizing *The History of Sexuality* than the 1990s writings of Butler, McWhorter or Halperin, and yet it demonstrates the pervasive and ongoing fecundity of Foucault's influence on queer theory today.

NOTES

1 Danielle Peers used this phrase in a presentation titled 'Desiring disability: supercrips and revolting gimps', presented at the (Dis)ability? Queer and Feminist Perspectives symposium, which took place in Edmonton, Alberta, in October 2012.

2 As Halperin notes, Sedgwick's *Epistemology of the Closet* (Sedgwick, 1990), which takes *The History of Sexuality* as 'axiomatic', is a brilliant example of this strategy.

3 As Stoler describes, in the biopolitical regulation of colonial sexuality, native nursemaids of European children were considered a particularly

vexing problem, and were regularly blamed for initiating their charges in sexual debauchery (Stoler, 1995, pp. 140, 155).

4 McWhorter discusses the ways in which queer people are biopolitically driven to suicide, while both Butler and Halperin argue that queer people were 'let die' through non-interventionist responses to the AIDS catastrophe: see Butler (1993b).

5 Puar's arguments also resonate with those of postcolonial critical animal theorists, who have critically scrutinized the ways that Western countries mobilize the abuse of animals in non-Western cultures to justify their ongoing xenophobia, even while slaughtering and experimenting upon unparalleled numbers of animals raised in draconian of conditions with virtually no legal constraints: see Kymlicka and Donaldson (2014); Deckha (2012); and Kim (2015).

SUGGESTIONS FOR FURTHER READING

Davidson, Arnold I. 2004. *The Emergence of Sexuality: Historical Epistemology and the Formation of Concepts*. Cambridge, MA: Harvard University Press.

Eribon, Didier. 2013. *Réflexions sur la question gay*. Paris: Flammarion.

Foucault, Michel. 1989. 'Friendship as a way of life', in Sylvère Lotringer (ed.), *Foucault Live: Collected Interviews, 1961–1984*. New York: Semiotext(e): 308–12.

——. 1989. 'Sexual choice, sexual act', in Sylvère Lotringer (ed.), *Foucault Live: Collected Interviews, 1961–1984*. New York: Semiotext(e): 322–34.

——. 1989. 'Sex, power and the politics of identity', in Sylvère Lotringer (ed.), *Foucault Live: Collected Interviews, 1961–1984*. New York: Semiotext(e): 382–90.

Huffer, Lynne. 2009. *Mad for Foucault: Rethinking the Foundations of Queer Theory*. New York: Columbia University Press.

Nichols, Robert. 2012. 'Empire and the disposif of queerness', in *Foucault Studies*, no. 14: 41–60.

Roach, Tom. 2012. *Friendship as a Way of Life: Foucault, AIDS, and the Politics of Shared Estrangement*. Albany, NY: State University of New York Press.

Schotten, C. Heike. 2014. 'Homonationalist futurism: "terrorism" and (other) queer resistance to empire', in *New Political Science*, vol. 37, no. 1: 71–90.

——. 2016. 'Homonationalism: from critique to diagnosis, or, we are all homonational now', in *International Feminist Journal of Politics*: 1–20, http://dx.doi.org/10.1080/14616742.2015.1103061.

Stein, Edward. 2001. *The Mismeasure of Desire: The Science, Theory, and Ethics of Sexual Orientation*. Oxford: Oxford University Press.

Warner, Michael. 2000. *The Trouble with Normal: Sex, Politics, and the Ethics of Queer Life*. Cambridge, MA: Harvard University Press.

7

A GENEALOGY OF THE DESIRING SUBJECT

REVISING THE PROJECT

As noted in Chapter 4, in 1976 Foucault's intention was to write five more volumes of *The History of Sexuality*, and the topics of these volumes were to be the hystericization of women's bodies, the pedagogization of children's sex, the control of fertility and the race, the psychiatrization of perversions and an exploration of the Christian concept of 'the flesh'. In the first course lecture in *'Society Must Be Defended'*, delivered in January 1976, shortly before volume 1 of *The History of Sexuality* went to press, Foucault seems so demoralized by his research trajectory that it comes as little surprise that he abandoned it. He says to his students:

> So what was I going to say to you this year? That I've just about had enough; in other words, I'd like to bring to a close, to put an end to... the series of research projects... that we've been working on for four or five years... [A]nd I realize that there were more and more drawbacks,

for both you and me. Lines of research that were very closely interrelated but that never added up to a coherent body of work, that had no continuity. Fragments of research, none of which was completed, and none of which was followed through; bits and pieces of research, and at the same time it was getting very repetitive, always falling into the same rut, the same themes, the same concepts... [W]e are making no progress, and it's all leading nowhere. It's all repetitive, and it doesn't add up. Basically, we keep saying the same thing, and there again, perhaps we're not saying anything at all. It's all getting us nowhere, as they say.

(Foucault, 2003b, pp. 3–4)

In this lecture Foucault makes repeated references to his work as 'useless knowledge', 'sumptuary knowledge' and 'useless erudition' (pp. 4–5). He admits:

I felt a bit like a sperm whale that breaks the surface of the water, makes a little splash, and lets you believe, makes you believe, or want to believe, that down there where it can't be seen, down there where it is neither seen nor monitored by anyone, it is followed by a deep, coherent, and premeditated trajectory.

(Foucault, 2003b, p. 4)

It seems that Foucault felt that writing five more volumes of *The History of Sexuality* according to his original plan, with at least four of the volumes making the same argument – that sexualities are socially constructed – simply with respect to different kinds of subjects (women, children, 'perverts', etc.), was random, repetitive and useless: not only would he have been making the same point each time, but he would not have been offering his readers any alternative to the picture of modern sexuality that he was describing. He would not have answered the pressing questions: how, beyond agentless 'resistance effects', can we resist biopower and the medicalization of sex? How might we create subjectivity otherwise? Foucault thus abandoned the idea of writing volumes on women, children, 'perverts' and the regulation of reproduction and the race, and, while he did draft a volume on the Christian ministry of 'the flesh', his death in 1984 pre-empted its publication.

Although Foucault's reasons for rejecting his original publication trajectory are fairly clear, it took him a long time to settle on an alternative route, and it was eight years before any additional volumes were published. Indeed, what Foucault intended to do in lieu of his original plan remained confused almost until his death. Even in a late interview with Hubert Dreyfus and Paul Rabinow, Foucault describes a different series of books from what eventually appeared (Foucault, 1983, pp. 229–30): the volume on early Christianity, *Les aveux de la chair* (*Confessions of the Flesh*), was to be volume 3; Foucault claimed that a draft of a volume on sexual ethics in the sixteenth century was completed; and *The Care of the Self* would be 'separate from the sex series' (Macey, 1993, p. 457). At another stage, Foucault thought that the material in *The Use of Pleasure* and *The Care of the Self* would be a single work (Macey, 1993, p. 466). Eventually he settled on publishing *The Use of Pleasure* and *The Care of the Self* simultaneously as two volumes: *The Use of Pleasure* examines sexual ethics in Greece in the fourth century BCE, and *The Care of the Self* is concerned with sexual ethics in Greece and Rome in the first and second centuries CE. *The Care of the Self* was not 'separate from the sex series' after all, but long sections of it do not concern sexual practices at all. The abrupt beginning to volume 3, lacking any kind of introduction, attests to the fact that what was for a while approached as a single book had been sliced in half just prior to publication. *Confessions of the Flesh* is mentioned in the introduction to volume 2 as a forthcoming work, but, like the volume on sexual ethics in the sixteenth century, it has never been published. Some shorter texts that were part of Foucault's work on *Confessions of the Flesh* did appear in print in his lifetime, however, and he delivered lectures on the topic of the 'flesh' for which transcripts survive; by examining these, one can derive a sense of what would have been Foucault's argument in volume 4.[1]

As they were eventually written, volumes 2 and 3 of *The History of Sexuality* have been far less influential than volume 1, and Foucault scholars observe that the final volumes are written in a less forceful and original voice than any of Foucault's earlier books. As David Macey writes,

> The second and third volumes of *Histoire de la sexualité* are by far the most plainly written of Foucault's books. They do not open with dramatic diptychs, and have none of the stylistic flourishes of the earlier works. The writing is plain, almost flat... At times, one has the impression of reading a working draft which should later have been completed and stylistically embellished.
>
> (Macey, 1993, p. 467)

Although James Bernauer and David Rasmussen published *The Final Foucault* in 1988 (Bernauer and Rasmussen, 1988), this was followed by a period of relative neglect, and their edited collection is not focused on *The History of Sexuality* volumes in particular. Many readers of Foucault's work who had appreciated his studies of modern power were disappointed by his leap back in history to ancient Greece and Rome in his final texts, by his apparent turn from politics to ethics and by his focus on relations that privileged subjects (philosophers of ancient Greece and Rome) had to themselves rather than power relations involving marginalized subjects (such as the 'perverts', madmen and criminals of Foucault's earlier books).

While Foucault's works prior to these final volumes have often frustrated readers with their lack of citations and references, volumes 2 and 3 of *The History of Sexuality* rely heavily on discussions of both primary and secondary sources, and these are scrupulously referenced. Unlike volume 1, volumes 2 and 3 of *The History of Sexuality* include bibliographies. Foucault's uncharacteristically careful scholarship and tentative voice in these last volumes reflect the fact that he was working with documents from historical periods in which he lacked expertise and thus confidence; as he notes in an early footnote, he was 'neither a Hellenist nor a Latinist', and thus writing these books required 'modesty' on his part (Foucault, 1985, p. 7). Producing *The Use of Pleasure* and *The Care of the Self* also meant that Foucault 'had painfully to revive the knowledge of classical languages that he had acquired at school' (Macey, 1993,

p. 416). As he describes in his introduction to *The Use of Pleasure*, Foucault also worried that, in working with documents from a distant historical period with which he was relatively unfamiliar, there was a danger of anachronistic projections on his part; that, as he puts it, he 'would run the risk of adapting them, without fully realizing it, to alien forms of analysis or to modes of inquiry that would scarcely suit them' (Foucault, 1985, p. 8). This concern harkens back to an error of historians that Foucault describes in his essay 'Nietzsche, genealogy, history', in which he accuses historians of projecting contemporary norms onto the past, and in this way naturalizing the present (Foucault, 1984, p. 88). This is precisely what genealogy – which stresses contingency, ruptures and difference – seeks to avoid.

As Foucault also argues in 'Nietzsche, genealogy, history', genealogy is political and biased; it seeks discontinuity in the past in order to show that the current state of affairs is not inevitable (p. 87). This raised a second worry with working on ancient texts; by immersing himself thoroughly in classical writings, Foucault ran the 'risk of losing the thread of questions [he] wanted to raise' (Foucault, 1985, p. 8). In other words, while Foucault wanted to avoid projecting the present onto the past, he also wanted to remain motivated by present political concerns, and by the problems raised in volume 1 of *The History of Sexuality* in particular. Foucault thus sought to tread the difficult line between avoiding anachronistic thinking and remaining relevant to the present. It is perhaps as a result of these manifold difficulties that Foucault remarked to his partner, Daniel Defert, that these works on pleasure were the books that he had written with the least pleasure (Macey, 1993, p. 417). Despite all the precautions Foucault took, historians and classicists have not been kind to Foucault's final volumes, and have chastised the philosopher for writing on a topic about which they judge he knew too little (Goldhill, 1995; Nussbaum, 1994, pp. 5–6).

As seen, there are reasons for Foucault scholars to feel dissatisfaction with volumes 2 and 3 of *The History of Sexuality*. Nonetheless, in the last decade considerable attention has been paid to Foucault's final, 'ethical' works. Recent studies drawing on *The Use of Pleasure* and *The Care of the Self* reconsider their position in Foucault's oeuvre, with authors suggesting that these, along with Foucault's shorter writings from the time (Foucault, 1983; 1989e; 1988e), were not a retreat from his earlier concern with modern power relations but a sustained attempt to think through the contingency of modern power, and to explore alternatives, antidotes and strategies of resistance to biopower and psychosexualized subjectivity.

Foucault himself explains the 'modifications' that the *History of Sexuality* series took in his introduction to *The Use of Pleasure*, which is the most cited and, arguably, the most philosophically interesting part of the final two volumes. As he reminds us here, his project in the series was to provide a genealogy of 'sexuality'; that is, his objective was never to write a history of sexual practices but, rather, to provide a critical history showing the contingency and emergence of the *experience of sexuality*, or of the way that we now understand ourselves to be subjects of desire. Foucault observes that his previous books had enabled him to explain how sciences of sexuality and forms of power that regulate sex had emerged, but they had not helped him to examine 'the forms within which individuals are able, are obliged, to recognize themselves as subjects of this sexuality' (Foucault, 1985, p. 4). That is, Foucault's studies in the 1970s had focused on expert discourses and power relations, but had not provided an account of subjectivity – and it was to this topic that he now turned. In particular, Foucault wants to ask: how did modern, Western subjects become desiring subjects, or subjects who see the 'truth of their being' in their desire (Foucault, 1985, p. 5)? How did we become subjects who experience ourselves as having sexualities? What *other* forms of subjectivity have existed or might exist, and what *other* relations to sexual pleasure have subjects had or might they have? As he asked in 1981, 'What are we and what could we be? What forms of new subjectivity can we create that will not originate in subjection?' (cited in Macey, 1993, p. 439).

Finally, in the opening pages of *The Use of Pleasure*, Foucault notes that a fundamental question posed by these last two volumes is

why is sexual conduct, why are the activities and pleasures that attach to it, an object of moral solicitude? Why this ethical concern – which,

> at certain times, in certain societies and groups, appears more impor-
> tant than the moral attention that is focused on other, likewise essen-
> tial, areas of individual or collective life, such as alimentary behaviors
> or the fulfillment of civic duties?... [H]ow, why, and in what forms was
> sexuality constituted as a moral domain? Why this ethical concern
> that was so persistent despite its varying forms and intensity? Why
> this 'problematization'?
>
> (Foucault, 1985, p. 10)

As this series of questions suggests, it is possible to imagine a world in which sex, like sleep, would simply be seen as an unproblematic function of the body, and would not be situated within the sphere of morality at all. We might think that, because sex frequently involves interactions with other people, and can entail domination and violence, it is necessarily a moral issue; nevertheless, Foucault – like a number of feminist scholars – repeatedly asked whether we might not approach these cases simply as problems of violence and domination, without sex per se being problematized (Foucault, 1988b; Brownmiller, 1975). The problem with rape, in other words, may not be that it is sex, but that it is violence. Plausibly, we might argue that sex in itself is not a moral problem.

Even if we think that sex raises intrinsic moral issues, however, we might follow Foucault in questioning why this moral prob- lematization has reached the frenzy that it sometimes has, while other practices, such as eating, go relatively unquestioned. Why are we so much more concerned with the kinds of sex that peo- ple are having than with what they are eating, despite the fact that our alimentary practices almost always involve killing, the exploitation of workers and environmental degradation, and thus are plausibly a higher-stakes moral issue?[2] Why have we so often intervened in people's sexual pleasures – including their solitary ones – while we let people do serious damage to themselves, oth- ers and the environment by relegating food to a personal lifestyle choice rather than a moral and political issue? As Foucault's final writings show, the ancient Greeks were in fact far more concerned with morally problematizing their diet than their sexual pleasures, and it was only slowly, over centuries, that sex eclipsed eating as an ethical issue.

In raising the contingency not only of how we morally problematize sex but of the fact that we do so at all, Foucault's final works provide a genealogy not of sexual practices but of the problematization of these practices. He is not asking what types of sexual activity characterized particular historical periods but, rather, how did sex come to be seen as an ethical problem, and how was this ethical problem posed in different ways in different eras? Most importantly, what were the effects of these problematizations of sex? How did they ultimately constitute us as desiring subjects? And how might alternative ways of problematizing sex allow us to undo the ways that we have been constituted as subjects of desire?

One of Foucault's objectives in *The Use of Pleasure* and *The Care of the Self* is to demonstrate, through the extended example of ancient Greece, that our modern experience of sexuality as an innate psychological identity did not exist in the past and thus need not exist in the future. As volume 1 of *The History of Sexuality* argues in a different manner, the experience we have of ourselves as beings with 'sexualities' is a recent social construction, or the product of a very particular history. Beyond this and more importantly, however, volumes 2 and 3 of *The History of Sexuality* give us a glimpse of an entirely different way in which a sexual life might be experienced, and of more agential ways in which subjectivities might be constituted. While we neither could nor should want to reactivate the sexual ethos of the ancient Greeks, which Foucault observes 'rested on a very harsh system of inequalities and constraints' (1985, p. 253), their understanding of sexual pleasure as one of many practices through which we can fashion the self – and of the self as something to be fashioned – may be an antidote to our present sexual essentialism.

As seen, the purpose of genealogy is to show differences between historical eras and the present, and thus the contingency of our current intuitions, experiences and institutions. Foucault nonetheless opens *The Use of Pleasure* by acknowledging a certain number of resonances between the ways that sex was problematized in ancient Greece, in the Christian tradition and today. For instance, the Greeks, like Christian and modern subjects, idealized sexual austerity and marital monogamy, and had considerable misgivings about sex between men and boys. Like a true genealogist, however,

Foucault notes these resonances only to insist that '[w]e cannot stop there... [T]he prescriptions may be formally alike, but this actually shows only the poverty and monotony of interdictions' (p. 250). Foucault shows us that beneath the monotonous interdictions on extramarital sex and same-sex relations are significant differences in 'the way in which sexual activity was constituted, recognized and organized as a moral issue' (p. 250). Eclipsing the resonances in sexual interdictions, *The Use of Pleasure* and *The Care of the Self* provide evidence of a proliferation of ways in which sex was experienced differently in antiquity compared to later eras in the West. The following sections examine some of the similitudes and differences between ancient Greek, Christian and modern problematizations of sex that Foucault discusses in *The Use of Pleasure* and *The Care of The Self*.

SEXUAL AUSTERITY AND THE MONOGAMOUS IDEAL

To take one apparent similitude between ancient Greek sexual ethics and later, Christian and modern sexual ethics: although there were no laws in ancient Greece that mandated men to be 'faithful' to their wives, many ancient authors expressed admiration for husbands who had sex only with their spouses, thus resisting the temptations of prostitutes, courtesans, slaves and boys. The Greeks even expressed admiration for non-human animals, such as elephants, whom they described as not only monogamous but discreet and moderate in their sexual interactions with their 'spouses'. In what is perhaps the most familiar example of this Greek admiration for sexual austerity, Foucault describes Socrates' 'renunciation' of sexual pleasure in Plato's *Symposium* (Foucault, 1985, p. 245). The *Symposium* (Plato, 1989) portrays a culture in which sexual relations between men and boys were accepted and prized, but it also represents the 'high spiritual value' associated with sexual abstention in classical Greece (Foucault, 1985, p. 245). It includes an exemplary portrait of Socrates, a married man who is not only immune to hunger, fatigue, cold and the effects of wine but is also impervious to the scintillating beauty of Alcibiades. Indeed, as Foucault discusses in the 'True love' chapter of *The Use of Pleasure*, Diotima's speech in the *Symposium* takes sexual austerity to a new level, advocating a love of souls and ideas over the love of bodies. Although there was virtually no inclination in classical Greece to make celibacy, reciprocal monogamy or restriction to heterosexual relations into moral maxims or to embed them in legal codes, it is also true that sexual austerity, while simply assumed on the part of women, was admired in men. We may therefore be inclined to see the moral valuation of sexual austerity, particularly in the form of marital monogamy, to have been a 'universal' of sexual ethics, extending from antiquity through the long Christian era to today, even if we acknowledge that it became more intense in some eras than it was in others.

Against this view, however, Foucault insists that 'Socrates is not a desert Father struggling against temptation' (1985, p. 21). Sex in antiquity was not seen as an evil, to be restricted only so far as it was necessary to the marital relation, as it would be with Christianity. Rather, Foucault emphasizes that the Greeks saw sex as a practice, like exercise and eating, that could be used to cultivate an aesthetic self. In particular, self-restraint and moderation were considered to be important virtues of free men, and sexual abstinence outside marriage on the part of men demonstrated this kind of self-mastery. As such, sexual abstinence – like adherence to a modest diet and regular exercise – was evidence that a man's body was ruled by his mind. While a woman was obliged to be faithful to her husband because she was under his authority, a man was admired for being faithful to his wife because this demonstrated the kind of mastery he exercised over himself. As Foucault writes, 'For the wife, having sexual relations only with her husband was a consequence of the fact that she was under his control. For the husband, having sexual relations only with his wife was the most elegant way of exercising his control' (p. 151).

While we can thus find forms of sexual 'asceticism' in both ancient Greece and the Christian tradition, the ancient Greek man who practised sexual ascetics was thought to be stylizing his freedom, while the 'desert Father' was punishing his flesh and resisting sin. Foucault therefore insists that the Greek admiration for sexual austerity should not be conflated with the 'gloomy and restrictive moralities that succeeded it' (p. 249). As he argues of the Greeks, at least in the classical period: 'One should keep in mind that this "asceticism" was not a means of disqualifying the love of boys; on the contrary, it was a means of stylizing it and hence, by giving it shape and form, of valorizing it' (p. 245).

USING SEX

The notion that sexual pleasure is something one could *stylize* as a means to an end is key to Foucault's discussion of Greek sexual ethics in the fourth century BCE. This utilitarian view of sex gives volume 2 its title. The utility of sex is apparent in advice given to boys in classical Greece. Boys were frequently guided neither to abstain entirely from sex with men nor to give themselves indiscriminately to every suitor. Sex was neither bad nor good in itself. What mattered was how one used it. Foucault cites Plato's *Symposium*, in which a symposiast argues: 'There is… no absolute right and wrong in love, but everything depends upon the circumstances; to yield to a bad man in a bad way is wrong, but to yield to a worthy man in a right way is right' (Foucault, 1985, p. 208). While sex between men and boys would be categorically wrong according to Christianity and modern sexual science, for the Greeks such acts would never be universally condemned, let alone legally sanctioned. For both men and boys, sexual relations and the decision of how and whether to engage in them were opportunities for ethical self-fashioning. Thus, we see that, although certain kinds of abstention were idealized both in antiquity and Christianity, this does not mean that the *forms* of moral problematization were the same. In particular, while sex came to be seen as fundamentally evil in Christianity, it retained a positive function in ancient Greece: sex was instrumental in one's care of the self. The notion of sex as a *practice* that one can use to fashion and refashion the self is to be contrasted not only with the negative ontology of sex in Christianity but also with the modern ontologizing of sex (or sexuality) as something that one *has*, or, even more drastically, as something that one *is*.

SEXUAL ANXIETY

Despite the positive, utilitarian function of sex in classical Greece, in another example of similitude between Greek and Christian problematizations of sex, Foucault notes that numerous texts from antiquity express anxiety about sex, regardless of what form that sex was taking or what kinds of partners it involved. For example, Foucault cites Pythagoras, who, in response to being asked when the best time was to make love, answered: 'When you want to lose what strength you have' (Foucault, 1985, p. 118). Again, therefore, we might be inclined to think that sex has always been seen as 'bad', even if this view was intensified in the Christian era compared to ancient Greece. As Foucault argues, however, although sex has consistently given rise to worry in antiquity, in the Christian period, and today, the worry has not been the same. Once more, sex was not understood as a sign of sin or 'fallenness' for the Greeks, as it would be with Christianity. Rather, the problems with sex were twofold and pragmatic: (1) sex required an expenditure that could deplete a man's or boy's health; and (2), if indulged in excessively, sex could demonstrate a lack of self-mastery on the part of a boy or man.

We see the first worry in Pythagoras' statement that the time to make love was when you wanted 'to lose what strength you have'. The Greeks had, of course, noticed that male ejaculation was necessary to create new life, and they deduced from this that semen was what transmitted life, or soul, to the being who was conceived. It was inferred from this that a man lost a bit of his own life, or a bit of his own soul, by ejaculating. Aristotle argued that this is why men are tired and fall asleep after sex, much as they are tired and in need of rest after bloodletting (Aristotle, 1941, pp. 667–75). Indeed, for Aristotle, male semen was not just the principle of life and vehicle for the soul; it was also a very concentrated form of blood, so finely concocted that it had become small in quantity and transparent. Losing a small amount of this preciously distilled substance was thus the equivalent to losing large quantities of (regular) blood, and blood was also recognized as a principle of life, the excessive loss of which could kill you. As Foucault writes,

[T]he origin of semen remained a topic of debate in the medical and philosophical literature. But no matter what explanations were submitted, they had to account for what enabled semen to transmit life, to give rise to another living creature. And where did the seminal substance get its potency if not from the source of life that was found in the individual from whom it came? The life that it imparted had to have been borrowed and separated from the living being where it originated. In every emission of sperm there was something that issued, and was withdrawn, from the most precious elements of the individual.

(Foucault, 1985, p. 131)

While sex was thus recognized as necessary to procreate, not only did it risk making one lose the self-control that the Greeks so prized, it was also dangerous and strength sapping; indeed, if engaged in excessively, sex – ejaculation, that is – could be life-threatening. Young, healthy men who were full of life, and thus produced abundant semen, could afford to have sex more frequently than older and unhealthy men, who, having less life, produced less semen; nonetheless, all men and boys would be wise to engage in sexual expenditure cautiously (p. 132).

'THE ANTIMONY OF THE BOY'

If there was a certain amount of anxiety about sex in general in classical Greece, this anxiety was intensified when it came to relations between two men and between men and boys. For instance, in a phrase that sounds all too familiar, Plato described sex between males as 'contrary to nature' (Foucault, 1985, p. 222), and Foucault documents extensive debates over whether sex with men dishonoured boys. In *The Care of the Self*, Foucault discusses a popular genre that compares the love of women with the love of boys, debating their relative merits (Foucault, 1986, pp. 189–232). From these facts we might be tempted to deduce that something like 'homophobia' has been a 'universal' of sexual morality in the West, even if these attitudes became more intense in later eras than they were in ancient Greece.

Once again, however, Foucault argues that the differences between the anxiety around sexual relations between men in ancient Greece and in later eras are worth emphasizing. In particular, for the Greeks, the problem was not that a 'sinful', 'abnormal', 'perverse' or 'pathological' form of sex was being engaged in but, rather, that, if two males had sex, one would have to be passive, and since, as Aristotle put it, 'the male, as male, is active' while 'the female, as female, is passive' (Aristotle, 1941, 729b14, p. 676), for a (free) man – or even a *future* (free) man – to be passive was inappropriate. This is why the ideal male–male sexual relationship for the classical Greeks was not between two men of the same age but between a man and a boy – a practice that would be condemned as child abuse and pathologized as paedophilia today. For the Greeks of the fourth century BCE, however, the fact that the passive partner in a sexual relation was not yet a man made his passivity at least somewhat acceptable. Boys, as children, were still expected to be passive in relation to adults, and yet, unlike women and slaves, the boy was not a fully passive subject but an active subject in training; his consent was required for a sexual relation, and thus his agency was acknowledged. While passivity in a boy was more acceptable than it was in a man, the Greeks still worried that it could cultivate womanly or slavish character traits in the boy, which was unacceptable in a subject who was being trained to rule. The Greeks also worried that a man could not respect, and thus love, a boy who had allowed himself to be passive in sex, while the boy would resent, and thus not love, a man who treated him as if he were a woman or a slave. Thus the age differential did not quell all worries, and for a free male adolescent on the cusp of adulthood to practise sexual passivity was still a fraught issue. This anxiety over man–boy relations gave rise to ideals of conduct – which were not always complied with – such as practising intercrural rather than anal sex, and discontinuing the sexual aspect of a man–boy relationship as soon as the boy grew a beard. It also gave rise to a cultural denial of the fact that a passive male partner might derive pleasure. For example, there are no depictions in ancient Greek art of a boy with an erection, even when his penis is being touched by his male lover, whose own erection is invariably shown.

As Foucault writes, the problem 'in this society that accepted sexual relations between men' was caused by the tension between 'an ethos of male superiority and a conception of all sexual intercourse in terms of the schema of penetration and male dominance' (Foucault, 1985, p. 220). The Greeks could not imagine sexual relations in which there was not an active and a passive partner, or in which activity was not superior, masterful and manly while passivity was not inferior, slavish and womanly. Thus, Foucault writes that '[t]he sexual act did not occasion anxiety because it was associated with evil but because it disturbed and threatened the individual's relationship with himself and his integrity as an ethical subject in the making' (p. 136). For the man, the risk of immoderate indulgence in pleasure could undermine his aesthetics of the self and render him passive to his own body. For the boy, immoderation in the form of excessive and indiscriminate sex was one danger, but an even greater danger was the physical passivity that, in the Greek sexual imaginary, was necessitated by the act.

What Foucault wants to stress in this discussion of man–boy sexual relations is that, while we see considerable anxiety around these relations in classical Greece, this should not be assimilated into the blanket condemnations of same-sex relations in Christianity, or into the pathologization of 'homosexuality' that has occurred in modern times. Rather, we might emphasize a series of contrasts between ancient Greek problematizations of sex and those that came later. One of these is that, in contrast to later periods in Western history in which the nexus of sexual problematization was women, for the ancient Greeks the 'sex question' was whether and how to have sex with boys. Foucault calls this 'the antimony of the boy' (p. 221), and, as he notes, it was *this* relationship – and not relationships with women – that 'interested' Greek men the most (p. 225).

That sex with boys was the most obviously interesting kind of sexual relation in the fourth century BCE is apparent in Plato's *Symposium*. When the symposiasts decide to spend the evening making speeches in praise of love, the first thing they do is send away the only female in the room, the flute girl – a slave who would normally be present to provide sexual as well as musical pleasure to the men. Moreover – and without this emphasis ever needing to be made explicit – the majority of the speeches in the *Symposium* are concerned with relationships between men and boys. In startling contrast to our own era, in which heterosexuality is assumed until proved otherwise, and adult–child relations are viewed as decidedly 'abnormal', criminal and pathological, the sexual relationship that first came to mind when (male) classical Greek authors thought of love was relations between men and boys.

In *The Care of the Self*, Foucault contrasts this state of affairs with the situation in the first and second centuries of our own era; while relationships with males continue to be taken for granted in this later moment in Greek antiquity, Foucault argues that the relationship between husband and wife came to be prioritized (1986, p. 163). In particular, the marital relation was increasingly understood as a relation of ideal love, displacing man–boy relations in this respect. Foucault also documents increasing concerns over the 'antimony of the boy' in ancient Rome, and scepticism about whether sex with boys could ever be beautiful. For a freeborn boy to consent to be passive in sex, or for a man to have sex with a freeborn boy through violence, were both options that lacked virtue (pp. 201, 206). Whether it was ever possible to have sexual relations with freeborn boys with grace (*charis*) was thus in doubt (p. 206). As Foucault notes, this resulted in a shift wherein sex with boys came to be practised primarily with slaves rather than freeborn boys or 'ephebes' (p. 190). These sexual relations raised no ethical issues in the first and second centuries CE, since a slave's passivity, like that of women, was never in question.

A MALE ETHICS

Despite some superficial similarities between the problematization of sex in Greek antiquity and in the Christian period, Foucault observes in far greater detail that there were also striking differences. One of these differences is that the entire focus was on male sexual practices in the case of ancient Greece, whereas the Christian tradition was equally concerned with controlling male and female sexuality and thus produced a relatively universal moral code. In fact, Foucault notes that, with Christianity, the paradigm of sexual virtue would become the chaste woman who resists male seduction, whereas in ancient Greece the paradigm of sexual virtue was the man who demonstrates moderation in his use of *aphrodisia* (Foucault, 1985, p. 213). As Foucault writes of classical Greece,

> This is doubtless one of the most remarkable aspects of that moral reflection: it did not try to define a field of conduct and a domain of valid rules – subject to the necessary modulations – for the two sexes in common; it was an elaboration of masculine conduct carried out from the viewpoint of men in order to give form to *their* behaviour.
>
> (Foucault, 1985, pp. 22–3, emphasis in original)

Indeed, as Foucault makes clear, the Greek sexual ethics that he is describing in *The Use of Pleasure* was directed only at an élite subsection of the male population:

> For them, reflection on sexual behavior as a moral domain was not a means of internalizing, justifying, or formalizing general interdictions imposed on everyone; rather, it was a means of developing – for the smallest minority of the population, made up of free, adult males – an aesthetics of existence.
>
> (Foucault, 1985, pp. 252–3)

In Foucault's discussion of dream interpretation in *The Care of the Self*, he similarly notes that it is almost exclusively men's dreams that were interpreted, for dream interpretation was an ethical practice, and such practice required an autonomy that women lacked (1986, p. 20). This was a society in which slaves (whether women or not) and women (whether slaves or not) were unfree, and thus the bodies of these people were considered available for use by free men, so long as they did not belong to other free men. It was taken for granted that women and slaves would be sexually passive, and their desires (and dreams) were of no account. As Foucault observes in *The Use of Pleasure*, even rape was fairly tolerated (1985, p. 146), and,

> [a]ll things considered, the married man was prohibited only from contracting another marriage; no sexual relation was forbidden him

> as a consequence of the marriage obligation he had entered into; he could have an intimate affair, he could frequent prostitutes, he could be the lover of a boy – to say nothing of the men or women slaves he had in his household at his disposal. A man's marriage did not restrict him sexually.
>
> (Foucault, 1985, pp. 146–7)

In contrast, monogamy *was* a social requirement for wives, and yet this wifely chastity was so culturally entrenched that it did not require any ethical problematization on the part of male writers. Moreover, sexual relations between women appear to be of no interest to either the Greek authors or, perhaps consequently, to Foucault.[3] As Foucault writes of Xenophon's *Oeconomicus*, 'In this text devoted to the "masculine" art of governing a household – wife, servants, estate – there is no allusion to the sexual faithfulness of the wife or to the fact that her husband should be her only sexual partner: this is taken for granted as a necessary principle' (1985, p. 163).

In contrast, and particularly in the classical Greece of the fourth century BCE, free men were able to determine the use they made of pleasure. To do so, they were necessarily at liberty to determine the sexual practices in which they engaged. It hence made no sense to forbid free men from having sex with boys or slaves or courtesans. Sex offered such men a forum in which to cultivate their freedom, or to determine the shape that their freedom took. For instance, restricting their own sexual pleasures in any number of ways (marital monogamy, refraining from sex with boys) was a means by which these men could use pleasure to cultivate their freedom in the form of self-rule. This cultivation determined the aesthetic shape of their lives. A man who engaged in promiscuous and indiscriminate sex with many sexual partners would not face legal or religious sanctions, but he would be considered to be leading an ugly life. Since such a man was manifestly incapable of ruling his own body or dominating his own desires, it might also be assumed that he would be a poor ruler of others, and thus a poor choice for a statesman.

While some authors of the fourth century BCE certainly held up marital fidelity as an ideal for men, it is significant to note that, unlike a similar idealization of mutual marital fidelity today, this monogamous ideal had nothing to do with a view of adultery or same-sex relations as immoral, and nor did it have anything to do with reciprocity between the sexes or a concern for the feelings of wives. The 'ethics' that Foucault is describing is not an ethics of interpersonal relations but a relationship of care that one has to oneself. Relations with other people are a means to this self-care, but the end of ethical practice in the Greek sense was to fashion a beautiful self, not to engage in better relations with others. Refraining from sex with boys and slaves thus did not reflect concerns about such forms of sex being inherently wrong or exploitative, or with the emotional consequences of a man's infidelity for his wife. In each case, the ideal was for a man to refrain from sex in order to stylize his own life, and to cultivate a particular kind of aesthetically pleasing self that other men would admire. As Foucault writes,

> It was an ethics for men: an ethics thought, written, and taught by men, and addressed to men – to free men, obviously. A male ethics, consequently, in which women figured only as objects or, at most, as partners that one had best train, educate, and watch over when one had them under one's power, but stay away from when they were under the power of someone else (father, husband, tutor).
>
> (Foucault, 1985, p. 22)

Although the ways that men interacted with women, boys and slaves were thus relevant to and impacted by this sexual ethics, the interests of women and slaves were strictly irrelevant in the kinds of ethical problematizations involved, and the interests of boys were a cause for concern only because they were future free men.

Foucault contrasts this classical Greek sexual ethics with later Greek and Roman ethics in *The Care of the Self*. By the first and second centuries CE we see increasing restrictions on men in marriage, such as interdictions in marriage contracts on the keeping of mistresses (Foucault, 1986, p. 76). In this period, Foucault observes the seeds of sexual symmetry between the sexes being sown, which would be developed further in the Christian and modern eras (p. 172). Nevertheless, Foucault notes that, while an extramarital affair on the part of a man in the second century CE might be viewed as an 'offense', 'it is also a rather minor one', and was expected to occur frequently (p. 174). Moreover, there were no restrictions on the kinds of sex a man might legitimately have before marriage, other than that he should not have sex with another man's wife. As Foucault writes, 'Provided that he exhibits personal moderation and respect for customs, laws, and the rights of others, an unmarried man may very well enjoy his pleasures as he sees fit' (p. 167). Foucault also notes that, in the first and second centuries CE, adultery continued to refer to sexual relations in which the woman was married to another man. As Foucault writes, '[T]he marital status of the man was not relevant' (p. 171). In other words, despite the increasing ideal of mutual monogamy and reciprocal marital obligations, it was still the case in the first and second centuries CE that a man could have extramarital relations without committing adultery, so long as these relations did not involve a married woman. Wives, on the other hand, were counselled to be accommodating and forgetful of their husbands' infidelities, and to ' "refrain from all complaint" ' (p. 174). Furthermore, consistent with the view that ancient Greek sexual ethics were a male sexual ethics, Foucault observes that adultery was conceived in these centuries as a harm that a man inflicted on himself and other men. As he writes, 'It is to himself and to other men, as human beings', and not to women, 'that adultery is injurious' (p. 171).

ETHICS VERSUS CODES

As the preceding discussion suggests, the asymmetrical masculinity of classical Greek ethics may be contrasted with the relative 'universality' of Christian moral codes. The virile ethics of classical Greece is in even more blatant contrast with the norms of sexual morality today, in which interdictions on extramarital sex, sex between men, sex between men and boys, and sex between people in relations of extreme power imbalance are most likely to be problematized because they are considered hurtful, pathological, nonconsensual and exploitative, and not because they do not manifest the ideal relationship a person can have to him- or herself. As this contrast shows, we have moved from a view of ethics as a relationship one has to oneself to a view of ethics as conformity to moral codes regulating our relations with others. This shift is indicative of the distinction Foucault makes between the 'ethics-oriented morality' of ancient Greece and the 'code-oriented moralities' that coexisted and developed under Christianity.

For Foucault, ethics-oriented moralities are about relations that the self has to the self, while code-oriented moralities involve the dictation of moral maxims or universal moral rules. Although the Greeks and Christians would both advocate marital fidelity, it is significant that the Greeks envisaged this fidelity as a means (for men) to cultivate an ethical self, and such ethical self-care was strictly voluntary and tailored *to* the individual *by* the individual. In contrast, the Christian tradition would make marital fidelity a moral rule that applied to everyone in the exact same way, and it was a rule that could be enforced by ecclesiastical and civil law. Likewise, while both the Greeks and the Christians felt anxiety about man–boy sexual relations, the Greek anxiety manifested itself in voluntary restrictions that men and boys might use to fashion themselves through engagement in these pleasures. In contrast, the Christian tradition would codify such relations as a sin and a crime and, at least in theory, would punish anyone who transgressed these codes.

SCALE

Another striking difference between problematizations of sex in ancient Greece compared to problematizations in later Christian and contemporary eras is their disparity in scale. While Foucault shows that the Greeks *did* worry about sex, they worried far *less* about it than Western subjects would do in later historical periods. Moreover, the Greeks worried far less about sex than they worried about other ways in which they could cultivate their freedom, such as their diet and exercise. As Foucault states in an interview, the Greeks

> were not much interested in sex. It was not a great issue. Compare, for instance, what they say about the place of food and diet. I think it

is very, very interesting to see the move, the very slow move, from the privileging of food, which was overwhelming in Greece, to interest in sex. Food was still much more important during the early Christian days than sex. For instance, in the rules for monks, the problem was food, food, food. Then you can see a very slow shift during the Middle Ages when they were in a kind of equilibrium... and after the seventeenth century it was sex.

(Foucault, 1983, p. 229)

In *The Use of Pleasure* Foucault describes sexual activity in classical Greece as part of a larger 'regimen' or 'dietetics'. This regimen was concerned with all the ways in which one exerted and rested one's body (exercise, sleep, baths) and with everything that went in and out of one's body (food, drink, sweat, vomit, semen). The regimen needed to be adjusted according to the individual in question, his age, the season, the climate and similar factors. Sex fell naturally into this regimen, since, like exercise, it involves an exertion of the body, and, like vomiting, entails an evacuation from the body. As Foucault writes in *The Use of Pleasure*, amidst scrupulous attention to the preparation and consumption of foods, the types of exercise taken, bathing, emetics and sleep, 'sexual activity (*lagneiē*) is barely mentioned – between baths and oilings on one side, and vomitings on the other' (1985, p. 110). Of one detailed Greek guidebook on regimen, Foucault observes that sex is only mentioned at all because it is a kind of exercise that warms, moistens and fatigues the body, and because it eliminates a substance from the body and may thus cause weight loss. As Foucault stresses, 'As far as the thinking on dietetics was concerned, the question of foods...was a good deal more important than sexual activity' (p. 114). Thus '[t]he physical regimen of [sexual] pleasures and the economy it required' were not a privileged subject in ancient Greece, as they would become later in Western history; they were but one 'part of a whole art of the self' (p. 139).

As Foucault describes in *The Care of the Self*, this 'art of the self' expanded in the first and second centuries of our era to include numerous spiritual exercises, such as meditation, education, reading, conversation and writing exercises (1986, p. 51). At this point sex plays only a small role in the care of the self, and, indeed, long sections of *The Care of the Self* do not concern sexual practices at all. For Galen, for example, we see sex situated once again as part of a healthy regimen, with the second-century Greek physician primarily approaching sex as a form of bodily evacuation, similar to the expulsion of phlegm. Such evacuations, for Galen, are therapeutic in treating a range of physical and spiritual ailments, ranging from respiratory obstructions to hysteria and melancholy (p. 118). As Foucault stresses, however, we must not exaggerate the importance of sex to the first- and second-century guidelines on sexual regimen, as 'the place they are allocated is limited in comparison with other regimens – particularly in comparison with the dietary regime'. For an example, Foucault offers: 'When in the 5th century, Oribasius comes to edit his great collection of medical texts, he will devote four entire books to the qualities, disadvantages, dangers, and virtues of the different possible foods and to the conditions in which one should and should not consume them. He will give only two paragraphs to sexual regimen' (pp. 140–1).

POSITIONS AND PARTNERS

Ancient Greek problematizations of sexual pleasure are also notable for what they did *not* concern themselves with, including, for the most part, sexual positions and partners. In *The Use of Pleasure* Foucault observes that

> the preoccupation with regimen was never focused on the *form* of the acts: nothing was said about the types of sexual relations, nothing about the 'natural' position or about unseemly practices, nothing about masturbation, nor anything about the questions – which would later become so important – of coitus interruptus and methods of contraception.
>
> (Foucault, 1985, p. 114, emphasis in original)

There was, for instance, no prescription of the so-called 'missionary' position in classical Greece, nor any condemnation of non-'missionary' positions and non-reproductive acts, as can be found in the Christian literature and in the modern sexological tradition. As Foucault writes,

> The division is between lesser and greater: moderation or excess. It is rather rare, when a notable personage is depicted, for his preference for one form of sexual practice or another to be pointed up. On the other hand, it is always important for his moral characterization to note whether he has been able to show moderation in his involvement with women or boys.
>
> (Foucault, 1985, p. 44)

As this passage suggests, even one's choice of partner ('women or boys') was of scant importance to the Greeks in the classical period discussed in *The Use of Pleasure*. Once again, the concern was with moderation and limiting one's sexual expenditure, no matter how or with whom.

The lack of concern in ancient Greece regarding masturbation is noted again by Foucault in *The Care of the Self*, in which he remarks on 'the very modest place that masturbation and the solitary pleasures occupied' in the writings on regimen. As Foucault also observes, when masturbation arises as an issue in these medical writings at all, 'it is in a positive form: an act of natural elimination, which has the value both of a philosophical lesson and a necessary remedy' (1986, p. 140). For instance, Diogenes' famous act of masturbating in the marketplace is discussed by Galen as an example of how one might rid oneself of a humour, similar to coughing up phlegm (p. 139). Like scratching one's leg when it itches, masturbation was seen by the Greeks as a natural response to an irritation, and utterly unproblematic. As Foucault writes, this acceptance of masturbation is in complete contrast with the Western literature on autoeroticism 'beginning with Christian monasticism', in which 'masturbation remains associated with the chimera of the imagination and its dangers. [For the early Christians, masturbation] is the very form of unnatural pleasure that humans invented in order to exceed the limits assigned to them' (p. 140).

Despite the acceptance of 'solitary pleasures' throughout Greek antiquity, Foucault's discussion of dream interpretation in *The Care of the Self* suggests a dawning of concern with positions and partners by the second century CE. For example, Foucault describes condemnations of sex between women in Artemidorus's treatise on dreams, although 'sexual relations between men appear to be taken for granted' (p. 35). Moreover, non-'missionary' positions and fellatio were also condemned by Artemidorus, with the latter described as a 'wasteful discharge of semen'. Dreams of oral sex thus portended useless expenditures or loss of fortune in waking life for Artemidorus (pp. 23–4, 35). In contrast, however, Foucault notes that both Rufus and Galen – writing in the first and second centuries CE, respectively – remain relatively unconcerned with what sexual positions and partners are taken (p. 124). As for their fourth-century BCE predecessors, for Rufus and Galen the frequency, moderation and timing of sexual activities are more significant than the positions taken and what partners are involved. Moreover, much more is said by these authors about the relationships between personal temperament, diet, exercise and sex than about sexual partners or postures.

SEXUAL BINARIES

Another difference between ancient and Christian ways of conceptualizing sex that Foucault notes is that, whereas the sexual binary in Christianity would become that between man and woman, in ancient Greece the binary was between the active and the passive partners. While free men were always assumed to be the sexually active partner (the lover, or *erastes*), a range of subjects – boys, girls, women and slaves of either sex – were understood as sexually passive (the beloved, or *eromenos*). While extramarital sex between men and (some categories of) women (such as courtesans) was socially accepted, as was sex between men and slaves and between men and boys, it was problematic if a free man took the passive role in any of these types of relationships. As Foucault writes in *The Use of Pleasure*, 'For a man, excess and passivity were the two main forms of immorality in the practice of the *aphrodisia*' (1985, p. 47). This point is repeated in Foucault's discussion of ancient Greek dream interpretation in *The Care of the Self*. Describing the meaning of sexual dreams involving servants and slaves, he writes,

> The sex of the partner makes little difference of course; girl or boy, what matters is that one is dealing with a slave. On the other hand, Artemidorus does bring out an important distinction concerning the position of the dreamer in the sexual act. Is he active or passive? To place oneself 'beneath' one's servant in a dream, thus overturning the social hierarchy, is ominous; it is a sign that one will suffer harm from this inferior or incur his contempt.
>
> (Foucault, 1986, p. 19)

In his discussion of dreams of incestuous sex, Foucault again notes that the ominousness of the dream depended in part on whether the social hierarchy was overturned: a dream in which a father was passive to his son was a negative sign, whether the dreamer was the father or the son (p. 21).

While the Greeks were consistent with later historical eras in associating sexual activity with masculinity and sexual passivity with femininity, other aspects of how they experienced what we now call 'gender' in relation to sexual practices are counter-intuitive to modern readers. For instance, whereas in the nineteenth century same-sex relations came to be theorized as 'inversion', and men who had sex with other men were understood as 'effeminate', in ancient Greece an opposite conclusion was drawn. As Foucault observes, in Aristophanes' speech in Plato's *Symposium* it is suggested that men who love men are two halves of an all-male whole, and hence completely masculine. On the other hand, men who love women are two halves of an androgynous whole, and thus as much feminine as masculine. Aristophanes thus argues that the most masculine men will be attracted to other men, and it is womanly men who will be attracted to women. According to this logic, being manly means liking manly things, including men, whereas being womanly means liking womanly things, including women. While this argument is surely coherent, it runs counter to persistent constructions of homosexuality as 'inversion'. It also runs counter to current heteronormative sexual intuitions, according to which 'opposites attract', and thus to be masculine is to be attracted to feminine subjects, while to be feminine is to be attracted to masculine subjects. Along similar lines, Foucault notes that a man who dresses in feminine clothes or adorns himself like a woman might have been seen as showing his taste for women in ancient Greece, whereas today such behaviour would be read as 'gay' (1985, p. 85).

Also running counter to modern intuitions about the relationship between what we now call 'gender' and 'sexuality', Foucault notes that, today,

> [n]o one would be tempted to label as effeminate a man whose love for women leads to immoderation on his part... In contrast, for the Greeks it was the opposition between activity and passivity that was essential, pervading the domain of sexual behaviors and that of moral attitudes as well; thus it was not hard to see how a man might prefer males without anyone even suspecting him of effeminacy, provided he was active in the sexual relation and active in the moral mastering of himself. On the other hand, a man who was not sufficiently in control of his pleasures – whatever his choice of object – was regarded as 'feminine.'
>
> (Foucault, 1985, p. 85)

The fact that a man had sex with other men did not make a man 'effeminate' in ancient Greece; rather, what made a man feminine was being in a passive sexual role or being overly indulgent (and thus passive to his desires) with sexual partners of either sex. A man who had exorbitant numbers of women sexual partners would thus be considered 'feminine' in ancient Greece, whereas, in striking contrast, today that man would be considered to have demonstrated his masculine prowess or virility. What determined whether a man was 'manly' or 'womanly' in ancient Greece was not the sex of his sexual partners but the restraint he exercised over his desires.

SEX AND HEALTH

The Greek problematization of sexual pleasures was also different from later Christian and modern problematizations of sex with respect to how sex was situated as a health matter. Sex was an issue about which doctors offered guidance in both antiquity and today, and yet the *way* that sex was conceptualized as a health issue was different. Today sex is situated as a health matter not only in that some sexual practices are risky (though not for the reasons the Greeks believed), but in that some 'sexualities' are deemed abnormal and thus pathological. In contrast, in ancient Greece sex was situated as a health matter in the same manner as diet and exercise. That is, attention to sex, like attention to diet and exercise, was seen as a preventative health measure: sexual practice or abstinence was a way to avoid ill health or could be a curative measure. Sex was a practice that could be used to remain healthy or to regain one's physical strength, rather than a symptom or pathology. A doctor in ancient Greece would thus encourage a patient to use sexual practices in healthful manners, and to avoid excessive sexual expenditures, much as doctors then and now encourage patients to exercise, eat a healthy diet and avoid excessive alimentary indulgence. Although the Greek doctor might recommend sex, along with other kinds of exercise, he would no more quarantine a patient who failed to follow his advice about sex than he would quarantine a patient who ignored his advice about exercise. This is in contrast to what would happen when a disease model was applied to sex, at which point patients could be removed from society for the pathologized sexual practices in which they engaged.

SEX WITHOUT PSYCHOLOGY

As Foucault makes clear, the Greeks did not see sex as something mysterious, complicated or in need of expert decipherment and interpretation. Unlike moderns, they did not psychologize sex. As Foucault writes, '[W]hen philosophers are laughed at for claiming to love only the beautiful souls of boys, they are not suspected of harboring murky feelings of which they may not be conscious, but simply of waiting for the *tête-à-tête* in order to slip their hand under the tunic of their heart's desire' (1985, p. 41).

In *The Care of the Self*, Foucault is probably fascinated by Artemidorus' book on dream interpretation because this work is in striking contrast with the psychoanalytic interpretation of dreams, and with Sigmund Freud's 1899 work *The Interpretation of Dreams*, in particular (Freud, 2008). While for Freud the interpretation of dreams – including dreams with no explicit sexual content – revealed unconscious sexual (and primarily incestuous) desires, Foucault emphasizes that, for Artemidorus, dreams were of interest for their auspiciousness or inauspiciousness, or for whether the foretold good or bad social fortune. Artemidorus interprets dreams primarily as predictive of whether one will gain or lose social status, and whether one will have economic and political success or failure. Even explicitly sexual dreams, including dreams of incest, are not interpreted by Artemidorus to be about sex, or to reveal unconscious Oedipal desires. Rather, for Artemidorus, because the mother represented trades and one's native land, to dream of having sex with her portended that one was going to attain prosperity in one's profession or have success in political life (Foucault, 1986, p. 22). As Foucault writes, 'In such dreams the subject is indeed seen in a position of activity with respect to a mother who gave birth to and nurtured him, and whom he ought to cultivate, honor, serve, maintain and enrich in turn, like a piece of land, a native country, a city' (p. 32). A dream in which a father has sex with his daughter could have a variety of meanings, including that he was going to be required to provide his daughter with a dowry (pp. 32–3). A dream of father–son incest, on the other hand, was inauspicious if it portended a reversal of social hierarchies, but, like the dream of father–daughter incest, was not interpreted as a revelation of unconscious or incestuous desires. As Foucault writes, the 'guiding thread' of dream interpretation for Artemidorus was whether or not the dreamer was going to maintain his social standing, as suggested primarily by the status of the person he has sex with in the dream, and whether he was active or passive in the sexual act (p. 33).

While dreams were not psychologized, so for the ancient Greeks the forms of sex one engaged in in waking life were not taxonomized into psychosexual types. The kinds of sex one had and the types of partners one chose were not pathologized, and nor did they make one a particular kind of person, such as a 'homosexual' or a 'paedophile'. This is in contrast to the modern era, in which, as Foucault discusses in volume 1 of *The History of*

Sexuality, our choice of sexual partners and our preferences with respect to positions and styles of sex are constituted as keys to our psyches, with many psychosexual profiles being considered abnormal or diseased. While some choices of partners could result in social disapprobation in ancient Greece, they were never deemed 'abnormal' or 'sick'. As Foucault writes, the Greek problematization of sexual pleasures 'did not lead to a drawing of distinctions among those acts, their possible forms and varieties, in order to decide which ones were admissible and which were harmful or "abnormal"' (1985, p. 136). As Foucault reiterates in an interview, ancient Greek sexual ethics were not normalizing, in contrast to sexual ethics today (1983, p. 230). For instance, while a man who had many sexual partners might be considered immoderate and thus to be leading an 'ugly' life, he would not find his behaviour problematized because of the 'abnormal' number of sexual partners he had, and he would not be diagnosed as a 'sex addict' as he might be today. It is crucial to Foucault that in ancient Greece sexual preferences were not framed in terms of medical taxonomies or 'normalcy', as they would be in the modern era.

A result of this non-pathologizing, non-normalizing and non-taxonomizing approach to sex is that Greek subjects did not experience themselves as 'subjects of desire', or as subjects with 'sexualities'. Foucault opens part IV of *The Use of Pleasure* by noting that ancient Greece is 'a society that is believed to have "tolerated" what we call "homosexuality". But perhaps it would be just as well if we avoided those two terms here' (1985, p. 187). In particular, Foucault thinks that we should avoid the term 'homosexuality' when speaking of ancient Greece because it would be anachronistic to speak of ancient Greek men as 'homosexuals' as we understand this category today. As Foucault writes:

> [T]he notion of homosexuality is plainly inadequate as a means of referring to an experience, forms of valuation, and a system of categorization so different from ours. The Greeks did not see love for one's own sex and love for the other sex as opposites, as two exclusive choices, two radically different types of behavior.
>
> (Foucault, 1985, p. 187)

He goes on, 'The enjoyment of boys and of women did not constitute two classificatory categories between which individuals could be distributed; a man who preferred *paidika* [boys] did not think of himself as being "different" from those who pursued women' (p. 190). We may also note that a man who preferred boys in ancient Greece was not seen as 'different' from those who pursued adults. Just as they had no notion of 'homosexuality' or 'heterosexuality', the Greeks had no concept or experience of what we now call 'paedophilia'.

Foucault also rejects as anachronistic the labelling of the Greeks as 'bisexual': although ancient Greek men would commonly have relationships with both boys and women, they had no concept of what we understand as 'bisexuality' today. As Foucault writes,

> We can talk about their 'bisexuality', thinking of the free choice they allowed themselves between the two sexes, but for them this option was not referred to a dual, ambivalent, and 'bisexual' structure of desire. To their way of thinking, what made it possible to desire a man or a woman was simply the appetite that nature had implanted in man's heart for 'beautiful' human beings, whatever their sex might be.
> (Foucault, 1985, p. 188)

While modern sexologists such as Krafft-Ebing thought they were merely labelling sexualities that had always existed, and that they could identify 'homosexuals', 'bisexuals' and 'paedophiles' in the past through retrospective applications of these categories, Foucault's argument is that nothing like the modern experience of homosexuality, bisexuality or paedophilia existed in ancient Greece. These experiences were produced through the creation and application of medical labels to living subjects, and their application to long-dead subjects is nonsensical.

THE USE OF *THE USE OF PLEASURE*

The objective of *The Use of Pleasure* and *The Care of the Self* is to show that how the ancient Greeks problematized sex was entirely unlike our own experience of 'sexuality'. This demonstration serves at least two purposes. First, it reaffirms Foucault's argument in volume 1 of *The History of Sexuality* that the medicalized experience of 'sexuality' is a recent invention. It also shows that the ways that we situate sex as a moral problem are contingent. As Foucault states in an interview, volumes 2 and 3 of *The History of Sexuality* are intended to make us 'wonder' whether our current experience of sexuality isn't 'an historical event, one which was not at all necessary, not linked to human nature, or to any anthropological necessity' (1983, p. 234). Put otherwise, the goal of these two books is to make us wonder if our sexualities are really our essences, and if we really need to moralize sex.

Second, *The Use of Pleasure* and *The Care of the Self*, like the brief reference to the *ars erotica* in volume 1 of *The History of Sexuality*, give us a glimpse of a society that experienced sex without sexuality. Volumes 2 and 3 provide an example of an entirely different way that we might approach sex – even if, as discussed below, the Greeks did not provide an alternative that we either could or should want to 'get back to'. That is, while today, as volume 1 of *The History of Sexuality* has shown, our focus is on sexual desire and how it can reveal the truth of the self, the focus in ancient Greece was on the *aphrodisia* and how they could be used to fashion the self in new, ethical and aesthetic ways. As seen, Foucault ends volume 1 by invoking 'bodies and pleasures' rather than 'sex-desire'; the Greeks provide an example of a culture that saw sexual acts, pleasures and desire as a whole, and did not single out desire as a particular locus of attention. This is in contrast with the Christian doctrine of the 'flesh', which would separate out desire and demote pleasure, and the modern, medical approach to sex, which taxonomizes and pathologizes desire and forgets about pleasure altogether (Foucault, 1983, pp. 242–3). Moreover, the Greeks did not see the *aphrodisia* as an experience that would reveal the 'truth' of a sexual self, and they did not develop a moral or legal code around the *aphrodisia* as Christianity did around 'the flesh' and moderns have done around 'sexuality'; rather, the *aphrodisia* were a set of practices that could be used to fashion an ethical self and a beautiful life, *if* and *to the extent that* a free (male) subject chose to do so. An innate self with a 'sexuality' deciphered through an analysis of desire was not presupposed in ancient Greece; rather, the self was something that an individual actively created through his practices, including his practices of sexual pleasure.

It is clear that Foucault found much to criticize in the masculinist, misogynist, slave-owning sexual ethics of the ancient Greeks, and he goes so far as to call this ethics 'disgusting' (1983, p. 233). Rejecting the suggestion that the Greeks offered an 'attractive' substitute for contemporary sexual morality, Foucault reminds his interviewer that '[t]he Greek ethics was linked to a purely virile society with slaves, in which the women were underdogs whose pleasure had no importance' (p. 232). In the same interview, Foucault insists that the Greeks cannot provide us with an 'alternative' to our sexual present, since 'you can't find the solution of a problem in the solution of another problem raised at another moment by other people' (p. 231). Slightly later, he states that 'there is no exemplary value in a period which is not our period… It is not anything to get back to' (p. 234). Nevertheless, Foucault modifies these claims, suggesting that the Greeks do at least provide us with a 'treasury' of 'tools' that we might draw upon in revising our present:

> My idea is that it's not at all necessary to relate ethical problems to scientific knowledge. Among the cultural inventions of mankind [sic] there is a treasury of devices, techniques, ideas, procedures, and so on, that cannot exactly be reactivated, but at least constitute, or help to constitute, a certain point of view which can be very useful as a tool for analyzing what's going on now – and to change it. We don't have to choose between our world and the Greek world. But since we can see very well that some of the main principles of our ethics have been related at a certain moment to an aesthetics of existence, I think that this kind of historical analysis can be useful.
>
> (Foucault, 1983, p. 236)

In particular, Foucault thought that the Greek approach to ethics could be useful for us today, because we are disillusioned with code-based sexual moralities that the Greeks never imagined and thus did without. As he states,

> I wonder if our problem nowadays is not, in a way, similar to [that of the Greeks], since most of us no longer believe that ethics is founded in religion, nor do we want a legal system to intervene in our moral, personal, private life. Recent liberation movements suffer from the fact that they cannot find any principle on which to base the elaboration of a new ethics. They need an ethics, but they cannot find any other ethics than an ethics founded on so-called scientific knowledge of what the self is, what desire is, what the unconscious is, and so on. I am struck by this similarity of problems.
>
> (Foucault, 1983, p. 231)

In particular, the Greeks offer the modern sexual liberation movement a model for sexual ethics without sexual morality, and without resorting to scientific claims about what sexuality is. While the masculinism and oppressiveness of Greek ethics would need to be rejected, Foucault suggests that the Greek notion that the self is something we can fashion through sexual pleasure, rather than something revealed (to doctors) through (a medical deciphering of) sexual desire, is appealing. Indeed, this notion might be taken up as an antidote to the psychologizing and biopoliticization of our sexual lives today.

In particular, the Greeks indicate at least the outline of a way in which we might approach our own sexual ethics with agency, and without pathologizing other people as abnormal or perverse. As Foucault writes, for the Greeks sexual ethics was 'a personal choice', and 'the reason for making this choice was the will to live a beautiful life, and to leave to others memories of a beautiful existence. I don't think that we can say that this kind of ethics was an attempt to normalize the population' (1983, p. 230). In other words, although ancient Greek society did not exist apart from power – and we can, for instance, describe the authority of husbands and slave owners as sovereign power – their sexual ethics arguably functioned without disciplinary power or biopower, or any kind of normalizing power at all. It is possible, for Foucault, that we might take up the Greek idea of ethics as 'the will to live a beautiful life', and situate our sexual self-fashionings within this ethics, even while rejecting virtually everything that the Greeks considered 'beautiful' – such as their fixation on mastery, their misogyny and their failure to imagine reciprocal pleasure. As Foucault states,

> Greek ethics is centered on a problem of personal choice, of aesthetics of existence. The idea of the *bios* as a material for an aesthetic piece of art is something which fascinates me. The idea also that ethics can be a very strong structure of existence, without any relation with the juridical per se, with an authoritarian system, with a disciplinary structure. All that is very interesting.
>
> (Foucault, 1983, p. 235)

In sum, Greek ethics cannot and should not be 'reactivated', because we are not Greeks and we are not ancients, and because we should not want to revive an ethics that requires slaves and the oppression of women, in which sex must involve an active and a submissive partner, and the latter's pleasure is of no concern. Though not 'attractive' as a whole, Greek ethics is at least 'interesting' and useful to us today, however, because it indicates a way to approach sexual ethics without extending the normalizing logics of both disciplinary power and biopower.

In the introduction to *The Use of Pleasure*, Foucault suggests that volumes 2 and 3 of *The History of Sexuality* do not only describe ancient Greek technologies of the self, but may also function as such technologies for the modern reader. Had Foucault stayed with his original plan for the sexuality series, he implies that he would merely have been repeating what he – and his readers – already knew, and thus remained the same kind of thinker that he already was. By immersing himself instead in an entirely different set of texts, and by allowing himself to be struck by their difference, Foucault was able to think differently from how he had beforehand. His hope is that the books he wrote might serve a similar function for his readers. However difficult these books may have been to write – and, for many readers, however difficult they may be to read – for Foucault they had value because they resulted in 'the knower's straying afield of himself'. 'The object' of these last two books 'was to learn to what extent the effort to think one's own history can free thought from what it silently thinks, and so enable it to think differently' (Foucault, 1985, p. 9). Although the task was hard, and meant many years of delay in his publication schedule, Foucault writes: 'There are times in life when the question of knowing if one can think differently than one thinks, and perceive differently than one sees, is absolutely necessary if one is to go on looking and reflecting at all' (1985, p. 8). Indeed, Foucault argues that such an 'endeavor to know how and to what extent it might be possible to think differently, instead of legitimating what is already known', is what philosophy should be (p. 9).

NOTES

1 Macey notes that Foucault's essay 'Le combat de la chasteté', published in *Communications* 35 in May 1982, was presented as part of the forthcoming volume *Les aveux de la chair*.

2 For a more detailed discussion of Foucault's discussions of food, and applications of Foucauldian thought to food ethics, see C. Taylor (2010; 2012; 2014).

3 Foucault says virtually nothing about relations between women in *The Use of Pleasure*, aside from a few parenthetical comments that observe that the Greek acceptance and prizing of same-sex relations applied only to those between men. Foucault does not see fit to explore this topic, and he opts to discuss neither Sappho nor her reception in the period (approximately 200 years after her death) on which *The Use of Pleasure* focuses. In *The Care of the Self* there are only a few, brief mentions of relations between women. See Foucault (1986, pp. 24–5, 221).

SUGGESTIONS FOR FURTHER READING

Foucault, Michel. 1989. 'History and homosexuality', in Sylvère Lotringer (ed.), *Foucault Live: Collected Interviews, 1961–1984*. New York: Semiotext(e): 363–70.

——. 2005. *The Hermeneutics of the Subject: Lectures at the Collège de France 1981–1982*. New York: Picador [first published in French in 2001].

——. 2011. *The Government of Self and Others: Lectures at the Collège de France 1982–1983*. New York: Picador [first published in French in 2008].

——. 2012. *The Courage of Truth: The Government of Self and Others II: Lectures at the Collège de France 1983–1984*. New York: Picador [first published in French in 2008].

Halperin, David. 1990. *One Hundred Years of Homosexuality: And Other Essays on Greek Love*. New York: Routledge.

Heyes, Cressida. 2007. *Self-Transformations: Foucault, Ethics, and Normalized Bodies*. Oxford: Oxford University Press.

Taylor, Dianna, and Karen Vintges (eds.). 2004. *Feminism and the Final Foucault*. Chicago: University of Illinois Press.

Zeitlin, Froma, John K. Winkler and David Halperin (eds.). 1991. *Before Sexuality: The Construction of Erotic Experience in the Ancient Greek World*. Princeton, NJ: Princeton University Press.

References

Adler, Amy. 2001. 'The perverse law of child pornography', in *Columbia Law Review*, vol. 101, no. 2: 209–73.

Alcoff, Linda. 1996. 'Dangerous pleasures: Foucault and the politics of pedophilia', in Susan J. Hekman, ed., *Feminist Interpretations of Michel Foucault*. University Park, PA: Pennsylvania State University Press: 99–135.

——. 2000. 'Phenomenology, post-structuralism, and feminist theory on the concept of experience', in Linda Fisher and Lester Embree, eds., *Feminist Phenomenology*. Dordrecht: Kluwer Academic: 39–56.

——. 2007. 'Epistemologies of ignorance: three types', in Shannon Sullivan and Nancy Tuana, eds., *Race and Epistemologies of Ignorance*. Albany, NY: State University of New York Press: 39–58.

Anon. 1966. *My Secret Life*, 11 vols., Gershon Legman. Secaucus, NJ: Grove Press [first published in 1888].

Ariès, Philippe. 1988. *Centuries of Childhood: A Social History of Family Life*. New York: Random House [first published in French in 1960].

Aristotle. 1941. 'On the generation of animals (Book I)', in Richard McKeon, ed., *The Basic Works of Aristotle*. New York: Random House: 665–88 [first published in Greek *c*. 350 BCE].

Augustine. 1950. *The City of God*. New York: Doubleday [first published in Latin *c*. 425].

Ball, Kelly H. 2013. '"More or less raped": Foucault, causality, and feminist critiques of sexual violence', in *philoSOPHIA*, vol. 3, no. 2: 52–68.

Bartky, Sandra Lee. 1988. 'Foucault, femininity, and the modernization of patriarchal power', in Irene Diamond and Lee Quinby, eds., *Feminism and Foucault: Reflections on Resistance*. Boston: Northeastern University Press: 61–86.

Beauvoir, Simone de. 2010. *The Second Sex*. New York: Knopf [first published in French in 1949].

Bell, Vikki. 1993. *Interrogating Incest: Feminism, Foucault and the Law*. London: Routledge.

Berggren, Erik. 1975. *The Psychology of Confession*. Leiden: Brill.

Bergman, Ingmar. 1987. *Laterna Magica*. Paris: Gallimard.

Bernauer, James, and David Rasmussen. 1988. *The Final Foucault*. Cambridge, MA: MIT Press.

Birman, Joël. 2007. *Foucault et la psychanalyse*. Lyon: Parangon.

Black, Edwin. 2004. *War against the Weak: Eugenics and America's Campaign to Create a Master Race*. New York: Four Walls Eight Windows.

Bonnet, Henry, and Jules-Amédée Bulard. 1868. *Rapport médico-légal sur l'état de Charles-Joseph Jouy, inculpé d'attentat aux mœurs*. Nancy: Vve Raybois.

Bordo, Susan. 2004. *Unbearable Weight: Feminism, Western Culture, and the Body*. Berkeley, CA: University of California Press.

Brewis, Joanna. 2001. 'Foucault, politics and organizations: (re)-constructing sexual harassment', in *Gender, Work, and Organization*, vol. 8, no. 1: 37–60.

Brodie, Janine. 2012. 'White settlers and the biopolitics of state-building in Canada', in Smaro Kamboureli and Robert Zacharias, eds., *Shifting the Ground of Canadian Literary Studies*. Waterloo, ON: Wilfrid Laurier Press: 87–108.

Brooks, Peter. 2000. *Troubling Confessions: Speaking Guilt in Law and Literature*. Chicago: University of Chicago Press.

Brownmiller, Susan. 1975. *Against Our Will: Men, Women, and Rape*. New York: Simon & Schuster.

Bruinius, Harry. 2007. *Better for All the World: The Secret History of Forced Sterilization and America's Quest for Racial Purity*. New York: Vintage.

Butler, Judith. 1999. *Gender Trouble: Feminism and the Subversion of Identity*. New York: Routledge [first published in 1990].

——. 1993a. *Bodies that Matter: On the Discursive Limits of Sex*. Abingdon, UK: Routledge.

——. 1993b. 'Sexual inversions', in John Caputo and Mark Yount, eds., *Foucault and the Critique of Institution*. University Park, PA: Pennsylvania State University Press: 81–98.

——. 1997. *The Psychic Life of Power*. Stanford, CA: Stanford University Press.

——. 2004. 'Is kinship always already heterosexual?', in *Undoing Gender*. New York: Routledge: 102–30.

Cahill, Ann J. 2000. 'Foucault, rape, and the construction of the feminine body', in *Hypatia: A Journal of Feminist Philosophy*, vol. 15, no. 1: 43–63.

Califia, Pat. 1981. 'Feminism and sadomasochism', in *Heresies*, vol. 3, no. 4: 30–4.

Campbell, Timothy. 2013. *Biopolitics: A Reader*. Durham, NC: Duke University Press.

Castiglia, Christopher, and Christopher Reed. 2011. *If Memory Serves: Gay Men, AIDS, and the Promise of the Queer Past*. Minneapolis: University of Minnesota Press.

Childs, Donald J. 2001. *Modernism and Eugenics: Woolf, Eliot, Yeats, and the Culture of Degeneration*. Cambridge: Cambridge University Press.

Cisney, Vernon, and Nicolae Morar, eds. 2015. *Biopower: Foucault and Beyond*. Chicago: University of Chicago Press.

Clare, Eli. 1999. 'Freaks and queers', in *Exile and Pride: Disability, Queerness, and Liberation*. Boston: South End Press: 71–84.

Clausewitz, Carl von. 1984. *On War*. Princeton, NJ: Princeton University Press [first published in German in 1832].

Cohen, Cathy J. 1999. *The Boundaries of Blackness: AIDS and the Breakdown of Black Politics*. Chicago: University of Chicago Press.

Corbin, Alain. 1990. 'Cries and whispers', in Michelle Perrot, ed., *A History of Private Life*, vol. 4, *From the Fires of Revolution to the Great War*. Cambridge, MA: Harvard University Press: 615–67.

Cunningham, Hugh. 2005. *Children and Childhood in Western Society since 1500*. Harlow, UK: Pearson Longman.

——. 2006. *The Invention of Childhood*. London: BBC Books.

Davidson, Arnold I. 2004. *The Emergence of Sexuality: Historical Epistemology and the Formation of Concepts*. Cambridge, MA: Harvard University Press.

Davis, Angela Y. 1983. 'Racism, birth control and reproductive rights', in *Women, Race and Class*. New York: Vintage: 202–71.

Deckha, Maneesha. 2012. 'Toward a postcolonial, posthumanist feminist theory: centralizing race and culture in feminist work on nonhuman animals', in *Hypatia: A Journal of Feminist Philosophy*, vol. 27, no. 3: 527–45.

Diamond, Irene, and Lee Quinby, eds. 1988. *Feminism and Foucault: Reflections on Resistance*. Boston: Northeastern University Press.

Donzelot, Jacques. 1979. *The Policing of Families*. New York: Random House [first published in French in 1977].

Dreyfus, Hubert L., and Paul Rabinow. 1982. *Michel Foucault: Beyond Structuralism and Hermeneutics*. Chicago: University of Chicago Press.

Duggan, Lisa. 2002. 'The new homonormativity: the sexual politics of neoliberalism', in Russ Castronovo and Dana Nelson, eds., *Materializing Democracy: Toward a Revitalized Cultural Politics*. Durham, NC: Duke University Press: 175–94.

——. 2003. *Twilight of Equality? Neoliberalism, Cultural Politics, and the Attack on Democracy*. Boston: Beacon Press.

Duggan, Lisa, and Nan D. Hunter. 2006. *Sex Wars: Sexual Dissent and Political Culture*. New York: Routledge [first published in 1996].

Duncan, Carol. 1973. 'Happy mothers and other new inventions in French art', in *Art Bulletin*, vol. 55, no. 4: 570–83.

Duschinsky, Robbie, and Leon Antonio Rocha, eds. 2012. *Foucault, the Family and Politics*. Basingstoke, UK: Palgrave Macmillan.

Dworkin, Andrea. 1981. *Pornography: Men Possessing Women*. New York: Perigee Trade.

——. 2006. *Intercourse*. New York: Basic Books [first published in 1987].

Ehrenreich, Barbara, and Deirdre English. 2005. *For Her Own Good: Two Centuries of the Experts Advice to Women*, 2nd edn. New York: Anchor Books [first published in 1978].

Epstein, Steven. 1998. *Impure Science: AIDS, Activism, and the Politics of Knowledge*. Berkeley, CA: University of California Press.

Erevelles, Nirmala. 2014. 'Crippin' Jim Crow: disability, dis-location, and the school-to-prison pipeline', in Liat Ben-Moshe, Chris Chapman and Allison C. Carey, eds., *Disability Incarcerated: Imprisonment and Disability in the United States and Canada*. New York: Palgrave Macmillan: 81–100.

Eribon, Didier. 2013. *Réflexions sur la question gay*. Paris: Flammarion.

Feder, Ellen. 1997. 'Disciplining the family: the case of gender identity disorder', in *Philosophical Studies*, vol. 85, nos. 2/3: 195–211.

——. 2007. *Family Bonds: Genealogies of Race and Gender*. Oxford: Oxford University Press.

Ferguson, Ann. 1984. 'Sex war: the debate between radical and libertarian feminists', in *Signs*, vol. 10, no. 1: 106–12.

Foucault, Michel (ed.). 1975. *I, Pierre Rivière, Having Slaughtered My Mother, My Sister, and My Brother...: A Case of Parricide in the Nineteenth Century*. Lincoln, NE: University of Nebraska Press.

——. 1976. *Histoire de la sexualité*, vol. 1, *La volonté de savoir*. Paris: Gallimard.

——. 1977. *Discipline and Punish: The Birth of the Prison*. New York: Vintage.

——. 1978. *The History of Sexuality*, vol. 1. New York: Vintage [first published in French in 1976].

——. 1980a. *Power/Knowledge: Selected Interviews and Other Writings*. New York: Pantheon.

——. 1980b. *Herculine Barbin: Being the Recently Discovered Memoirs of a Nineteenth-Century French Hermaphrodite*. Brighton, UK: Harvester Press.

——. 1983. 'On the genealogy of ethics: an overview of work in progress', in Hubert Dreyfus and Paul Rabinow, eds., *Michel Foucault: Beyond Structuralism and Hermeneutics*, 2nd edn. Chicago: University of Chicago Press: 229–52.

——. 1984. 'Nietzsche, genealogy, history', in Paul Rabinow, ed., *The Foucault Reader*. New York: Pantheon: 76–100 [first published in French in 1971].

——. 1985. *The History of Sexuality*, vol. 2, *The Use of Pleasure*. New York: Random House [first published in French in 1984].

——. 1986. *The History of Sexuality*, vol. 3, *The Care of the Self*. New York: Random House [first published in French in 1984].

——. 1988a. 'About the concept of the "dangerous individual" in nineteenth-century psychiatry', in Lawrence D. Kritzman, ed., *Michel Foucault: Politics, Philosophy, Culture: Interviews and Other Writings, 1977–1984*. New York: Routledge: 125–51.

——. 1988b. 'Confinement, psychiatry, prison', in Lawrence D. Kritzman, ed., *Michel Foucault: Politics, Philosophy, Culture: Interviews and Other Writings, 1977–1984*. New York: Routledge: 178–210.

——. 1988c. 'Sexual morality and the law', in Lawrence D. Kritzman, ed., *Michel Foucault: Politics, Philosophy, Culture: Interviews and Other Writings, 1977–1984*. New York: Routledge: 271–85.

——. 1988d. 'On power', in Lawrence D. Kritzman, ed., *Michel Foucault: Politics, Philosophy, Culture: Interviews and Other Writings, 1977–1984*. New York: Routledge: 96–109.

——. 1988e. 'An aesthetics of existence', in Lawrence D. Kritzman, ed., *Michel Foucault: Politics, Philosophy, Culture: Interviews and Other Writings, 1977–1984*. New York: Routledge: 47–53.

——. 1989a. *The Order of Things: An Archaeology of the Human Sciences*. New York: Routledge [first published in French in 1966].

——. 1989b. 'Sexual choice, sexual act', interview with J. O'Higgins, in Sylvère Lotringer, ed., *Foucault Live: Collected Interviews, 1961–1984*. New York: Semiotext(e): 322–34 [originally published in 1982 in *Salmagundi*, nos. 58/59: 10–24].

——. 1989c. 'Friendship as a way of life', in Sylvère Lotringer, ed., *Foucault Live: Collected Interviews, 1961–1984*. New York: Semiotext(e): 308–12.

——. 1989d. 'Sex, power and the politics of identity', in Sylvère Lotringer, ed., *Foucault Live: Collected Interviews, 1961–1984*. New York: Semiotext(e): 382–90.

——. 1989e. 'An ethics of pleasure', in Sylvère Lotringer, ed., *Foucault Live: Collected Interviews, 1961–1984*. New York: Semiotext(e): 371–81.

——. 1989f. 'History and homosexuality', in Sylvère Lotringer (ed.), *Foucault Live: Collected Interviews, 1961–1984*. New York: Semiotext(e): 363–70.

——. 1994. '"*Omnes et singulatim*": toward a critique of political reason', in James D. Faubion, ed., *Essential Works of Foucault*, vol. 3, *Power*. New York: New Press: 298–325.

——. 1996. 'Foucault, Michel, 1926– ', in Gary Gutting, ed., *Cambridge Companion to Foucault*. Cambridge: Cambridge University Press: 314–20 [first published in French in 1984].

——. 2003a. *Abnormal: Lectures at the Collège de France 1974–1975*. New York: Picador [first published in French in 1999].

——. 2003b. *'Society Must Be Defended': Lectures at the Collège de France 1975–1976*. New York: Picador [first published in French in 1997].

——. 2005. *The Hermeneutics of the Subject: Lectures at the Collège de France 1981–1982*. New York: Picador [first published in French in 2001].

——. 2006a. *History of Madness*. Abingdon, UK: Routledge [first published in French in 1961].

——. 2006b. *Psychiatric Power: Lectures at the Collège de France 1973–1974*. New York: Picador [first published in French in 2003].

——. 2007. *Security, Territory, Population: Lectures at the Collège de France 1977–1978*. Basingstoke, UK: Palgrave Macmillan [first published in French in 2004].

——. 2011. *The Government of Self and Others: Lectures at the Collège de France 1982–1983*. New York: Picador [first published in French in 2008].

——. 2012. *The Courage of Truth: The Government of Self and Others II: Lectures at the Collège de France 1983–1984*. New York: Picador [first published in French in 2008].

REFERENCES 249

Freud, Sigmund. 1964. 'Analysis terminable and interminable', in James Strachey, ed., *The Standard Edition of the Complete Works of Sigmund Freud*, vol. 23. London: Hogarth Press: 211–53 [first published in German in 1937].

——. 1976. 'The dissolution of the Oedipal complex', in *On Sexuality*, ed. Angela Richards. London: Penguin Books: 313–22 [first published in German in 1924].

——. 1990. *Civilization and Its Discontents*. New York: Norton [first published in German in 1930].

——. 2001. 'The psychogenesis of a case of homosexuality in a woman', in James Strachey, ed., *The Standard Edition of the Complete Psychological Works of Sigmund Freud*, vol. 18, *1920–1922: Beyond the Pleasure Principle, Group Psychology and Other Works*. London: Vintage: 145–72 [first published in German in 1920].

——. 2008. *The Interpretation of Dreams*. Oxford: Oxford University Press [first published in German in 1899].

——. 2011. 'The sexual aberrations', in *Three Essays on the Theory of Sexuality*, ed. James Strachey. New York: Basic Books: 1–38 [first published in German in 1905].

Freud, Sigmund, and Joseph Breuer. 1978. *Studies on Hysteria*, eds. James and Alix Strachey. London: Penguin Books [first published in German in 1895].

Gay, Peter. 1984. *The Bourgeois Experience: Victoria to Freud*, vol. 1, *The Education of the Senses*. New York: Norton.

Gilchrist, Kristen. 2010. '"Newsworthy victims"? Exploring differences in Canadian local press coverage of murdered/missing aboriginal and white women', in *Feminist Media Studies*, vol. 10, no. 4: 373–90.

Golder, Ben, ed. 2013. *Re-Reading Foucault: On Law, Power and Rights*. Abingdon, UK: Routledge.

Golder, Ben and Peter Fitzpatrick. 2009. *Foucault's Law*. Abingdon, UK: Routledge.

Goldhill, Simon. 1995. *Foucault's Virginity: Ancient Erotic Fiction and the History of Sexuality*. Cambridge: Cambridge University Press.

Gossett, Che. 2014. 'We will not rest in peace: AIDS activism, black radicalism, queer and/or trans resistance', in Jin Haritaworn, Adi Kuntsman and Silvia Posocco, eds., *Queer Necropolitics*. Abingdon, UK: Routledge: 31–50.

Gould, Deborah B. 2009. *Moving Politics: Emotion and ACT UP's Fight against AIDS*. Chicago: University of Chicago Press.

Grekul, Jana Marie. 2011. 'A well-oiled machine: Alberta's eugenics program, 1928–1972', in *Alberta History*, vol. 59, no. 3: 16–23.

Grosz, Elizabeth. 1994. *Volatile Bodies: Towards a Corporeal Feminism*. Bloomington, IN: Indiana University Press.

Guenther, Lisa. 2016. 'Life behind bars: the eugenic structure of mass incarceration', in Hasana Sharp and Chloë Taylor, eds., *Feminist Philosophies of Life*. Montreal: McGill-Queens University Press: 217–38.

Hacking, Ian. 1995a. *Rewriting the Soul: Multiple Personality and the Sciences of Memory*. Princeton, NJ: Princeton University Press.

——. 1995b. 'The looping effect of human kinds', in Dan Sperber, David Premack and Ann J. Premack, eds., *Causal Cognition: An Interdisciplinary Approach*. Oxford: Oxford University Press: 351–83.

——. 2002. *Mad Travelers: Reflections on the Reality of Transient Mental Illness*. Cambridge, MA: Harvard University Press.

Halley, Janet. 2006. *Split Decisions: How and Why to Take a Break from Feminism*. Princeton, NJ: Princeton University Press.

Halperin, David. 1990. *One Hundred Years of Homosexuality: And Other Essays on Greek Love*. New York: Routledge.

——. 1995. *Saint Foucault: Towards a Gay Hagiography*. Oxford: Oxford University Press.

Haraway, Donna. 1989. *Primate Visions: Gender, Race, and Nature in the World of Modern Science*. New York: Routledge.

Harris-Zsovan, Jane. 2010. *Eugenics and the Firewall: Canada's Nasty Little Secret*. Winnipeg: J. Gordon Shillingford.

Hekman, Susan J., ed. 1996. *Feminist Interpretations of Michel Foucault*. University Park, PA: Pennsylvania University Press.

Hengehold, Laura. 1994. 'An immodest proposal: Foucault, hysterization, and the "second rape"', in *Hypatia: A Journal of Feminist Philosophy*, vol. 9, no. 3: 88–107.

Heyes, Cressida. 2003. 'Feminist solidarity after queer theory: the case of transgender', in *Signs*, vol. 28, no. 4: 1093–120.

——. 2006. 'Foucault goes to Weight Watchers', in *Hypatia: A Journal of Feminist Philosophy*, vol. 21, no. 2: 126–49.

——. 2007. *Self-Transformations: Foucault, Ethics, and Normalized Bodies*. Oxford: Oxford University Press.

Hobbes, Thomas. 1981. *The Leviathan*. London: Penguin Books [first published in 1651].

Holloway, Lewis, and Carol Morris. 2007. 'Exploring biopower in the regulation of farm animal bodies: genetic policy interventions in UK livestock', in *Genomics, Society and Policy*, vol. 3, no. 2: 82–98.

Holloway, Lewis, Carol Morris, Ben Gilna and David Gibbs. 2009. 'Biopower, genetics and livestock breeding: (re)constituting animal populations and heterogeneous biosocial collectivities', in *Transactions of the Institute of British Geographers*, vol. 34, no. 3: 394–407.

Hook, Derek. 2007. *Foucault, Psychology and the Analytics of Power*. Basingstoke, UK: Palgrave Macmillan.

Hubbard, Ruth. 2013. 'Abortion and disability: who should and who should not inhabit the world?', in Lennard J. Davis, ed., *The Disability Studies Reader*, 4th edn. New York: Routledge: 74–86.

Huffer, Lynne. 2009. *Mad for Foucault: Rethinking the Foundations of Queer Theory*. New York: Columbia University Press.

Irvine, Janice. 2005. *Disorders of Desire: Sexuality and Gender in Modern American Sexology*. Philadelphia: Temple University Press [first published in 1990].

Jahme, Carole. 2000. *Beauty and the Beasts: Woman, Ape and Evolution*. London: Virago.

James, Allison. 1997. *Constructing and Reconstructing Childhood: Contemporary Issues in the Sociological Study of Childhood*. Abingdon, UK: Routledge.

Jiwani, Yasmin, and Mary Lynn Young. 2006. 'Murdered and missing women: reproducing marginality in news discourse', in *Canadian Journal of Communications*, vol. 31, no. 4: 895–917.

Jordan, Jan. 1997. 'User pays: why men buy sex', in *Australian and New Zealand Journal of Criminology*, vol. 30, no. 1: 55–71.

Joyce, James. 1916. *A Portrait of the Artist as a Young Man*. New York: D. W. Huebsch.

Kaan, Heinrich. 1844. *Psychopathia Sexualis*. Leipzig: Leopold Voss.

Kim, Claire Jean. 2015. *Dangerous Crossings: Race, Species, and Nature in a Multicultural Age*. Cambridge: Cambridge University Press.

Kinsey, Alfred C., Wardell P. Pomeroy and Clyde E. Martin. 1948. *Sexual Behavior in the Human Male*. Philadelphia: Saunders.

Kinsey, Alfred C., Wardell P. Pomeroy, Clyde E. Martin and Paul H. Gebhard. 1953. *Sexual Behavior in the Human Female*. Philadelphia: Saunders.

Knowles, Caroline. 1996. *Family Boundaries: The Invention of Normality and Dangerousness*. Peterborough, ON: Broadview Press.

Krafft-Ebing, Richard von. 1894. *Psychopathia Sexualis: With Especial Reference to Contrary Sexual Instinct: A Medico-Legal Study*. Philadelphia: F. A. Davis [first published in German in 1886].

Kral, Michael J., and Lori Idlout. 2009. 'Community wellness and social action in the Canadian Arctic', in Lawrence J. Kirmayer and Gail G. Valaskakis, eds., *Healing Traditions: The Mental Health of Aboriginal Peoples in Canada*. Vancouver: University of British Columbia Press: 315–34.

Kral, Michael J., Patricia K. Wiebe, Kari Nisbet, Catherine Dallas, Looee Okalik, Nubiya Enuaraq and James Cinotta. 2009. 'Canadian Inuit community engagement in suicide prevention', in *International Journal of Circumpolar Health*, vol. 68, no. 3: 292–308.

Kukla, Rebecca. 2005. *Mass Hysteria: Medicine, Culture and Mothers' Bodies*. Lanham, MD: Rowman & Littlefield.

Kymlicka, Will, and Sue Donaldson. 2014. 'Animal rights, multiculturalism, and the left', in *Journal of Social Philosophy*, vol. 45, no. 1: 116–35.

Laqueur, Thomas. 1990. *Making Sex: Bodies and Gender from the Greeks to Freud*. Cambridge, MA: Harvard University Press.

Larcombe, Wendy. 2002. 'The "ideal" victim v successful rape complainants', in *Feminist Legal Studies*, vol. 10, no. 2: 131–48.

Lemke, Thomas. 2011. *Biopower: An Advanced Introduction*. New York: New York University Press.

Lenon, Suzanne. 2011. 'Why is our love an issue? Same-sex marriage and the politics of the ordinary', in *Social Identities: Journal for the Study of Race, Nation and Culture*, vol. 17, no. 3: 351–72.

——. 2012. 'White as milk: Proposition 8 and the cultural politics of gay rights', in *Atlantis: Critical Studies in Gender, Culture and Social Justice*, vol. 36, no. 1: 44–54.

Levine, Judith. 2002. *Harmful to Minors: The Perils of Protecting Children from Sex*. Minneapolis: University of Minnesota Press.

Macey, David. 1993. *The Lives of Michel Foucault*. New York: Vintage.

MacInnes, Teresa, and Kent Nason. 2013. *Buying Sex*. Montreal: National Film Board of Canada.

MacKinnon, Catharine. 1982. 'Feminism, Marxism, method, and the state: an agenda for theory', in *Signs*, vol. 7, no. 3: 515–44.

——. 1991. *Toward a Feminist Theory of the State*. Cambridge, MA: Harvard University Press.

McLaren, Margaret A. 2002. *Feminism, Foucault, and Embodied Subjectivity*. Albany: State University of New York Press.

McNay, Lois. 1992. *Foucault and Feminism*. Cambridge: Polity Press.

McWhorter, Ladelle. 1999. *Bodies and Pleasures: Foucault and the Politics of Sexual Normalization*. Bloomington, IN: Indiana University Press.

——. 2009. *Racism and Sexual Oppression in Anglo-America: A Genealogy*. Bloomington, IN: Indiana University Press.

——. 2011. 'Decapitating power', in *Foucault Studies*, no. 12: 77–96.

Mader, Mary Beth. 2011. 'Modern living and vital race: Foucault and the science of life', in *Foucault Studies*, no. 12: 97–112.

Malacrida, Claudia. 2015. *A Special Hell: Institutional Life in Alberta's Eugenic Years*. Toronto: University of Toronto Press.

Marcuse, Herbert. 1955. *Eros and Civilization: A Philosophical Inquiry into Freud*. Boston: Beacon Press.

——. 1964. *One-Dimensional Man: Studies in the Ideology of Advanced Industrial Society*. Boston: Beacon Press.

Marsh, Ian. 2010. *Suicide: Foucault, History and Truth*. Cambridge: Cambridge University Press.

Medina, José. 2011. 'Toward a Foucauldian epistemology of resistance: counter-memory, epistemic friction, and *guerrilla* pluralism', in *Foucault Studies*, no. 12: 9–35.

Mills, Charles W. 2007. 'White ignorance', in Shannon Sullivan and Nancy Tuana, eds., *Race and Epistemologies of Ignorance*. Albany, NY: State University of New York Press: 11–38.

Minois, Georges. 1999. *History of Suicide: Voluntary Death in Western Culture*. Baltimore: Johns Hopkins University Press.

Mitchell, David T., with Sharon L. Snyder. 2015. *The Biopolitics of Disability: Neoliberalism, Ablenationalism, and Peripheral Embodiment*. Ann Arbor, MI: University of Michigan Press.

Mohr, Richard. 1992. *Gay Ideas: Outing and Other Controversies*. Boston: Beacon Press.

Morgan, Robin. 1974. 'Theory and practice: pornography and rape', in *Going Too Far: The Personal Chronicle of a Feminist*. New York: Open Road Press: 163–9.

Nichols, Robert. 2010. 'Postcolonial Studies and the Discourse of Foucault,' in *Foucault Studies*, no. 9: 111–144.

——. 2012. 'Empire and the disposif of queerness', in *Foucault Studies*, no. 14: 41–60.

——. 2013. 'Of first and last men: contract and colonial historicality in Foucault', in Amy Swiffen and Joshua Nichols, eds., *The Ends of History: Questioning the Stakes of Historical Reason*. New York: Routledge: 64–83.

——. 2014. 'The colonialism of incarceration', in *Radical Philosophy Review*, vol. 17, no. 2: 434–55.

Nietzsche, Friedrich. 1998. *On the Genealogy of Morality*, eds. Maudemarie Clark and Alan J. Swensen. Indianapolis: Hackett [first published in German in 1887].

Nimmo, Richie. 2010. *Milk, Modernity, and the Making of the Human: Purifying the Social*. Abingdon, UK: Routledge.

Nussbaum, Martha. 1994. *The Therapy of Desire: Theory and Practice in Hellenistic Ethics*. Princeton, NJ: Princeton University Press.

Oksala, Johanna. 2011a. *Foucault, Politics, and Violence*. Evanston, IL: Northwestern University Press.

——. 2011b. 'Sexual experience', in *Hypatia: A Journal of Feminist Philosophy*, vol. 26, no. 1: 207–23.

——. 2016. *Feminist Experiences: Foucauldian and Phenomenological Investigations*. Evanston, IL: Northwestern University Press.

Oliver, Kelly. 2007. *Women as Weapons of War: Iraq, Sex, and the Media*. New York: Columbia University Press.

Palmer, Clare. 2001. '"Taming the wild profusion of existing things"? A study of Foucault, power and human/animal relationships', in *Environmental Ethics*, vol. 23, no. 4: 339–58.

Pateman, Carole. 1988. *The Sexual Contract*. Cambridge: Polity Press.

Patton, Cindy. 1985. *Sex and Germs: The Politics of AIDS*. Boston: South End Press.

Piepmeier, Alison. 2013. 'The inadequacy of "choice": disability and what's wrong with feminist framings of reproduction', in *Feminist Studies*, vol. 39, no. 1: 159–86.

Plato. 1989. *Symposium*, intro., ed. Alexander Nehamas and Paul Woodruff. Indianapolis: Hackett [*c*. 370 BCE].

Plaza, Monique. 1978. 'Nos dommages et leurs intérêts', in *Questions féministes*, no. 3: 93–103.

Puar, Jasbir. 2007. *Terrorist Assemblages: Homonationalism in Queer Times*. Durham, NC: Duke University Press.

Raymond, Janice. 1979. *The Transsexual Empire: The Making of the She-Male*. Boston: Beacon Press.

Rehn-DeBraal, Merritt. 2013. 'Translating Foucault: a critique of sexuality for trauma survivors', in *philoSOPHIA*, vol. 3, no. 1: 69–83.

Reich, Wilhelm. 1945. *The Sexual Revolution*. New York: Farrar, Straus and Giroux [first published in German in 1936].

Rich, Adrienne. 1980. 'Compulsory heterosexuality and lesbian existence', in *Signs*, vol. 5, no. 4: 631–60.

Roach, Tom. 2012. *Friendship as a Way of Life: Foucault, AIDS, and the Politics of Shared Estrangement*. Albany, NY: State University of New York Press.

Rose, Nikolas. 2006. *The Politics of Life Itself: Biomedicine, Power, and Subjectivity in the Twenty-First Century*. Princeton, NJ: Princeton University Press.

Rousseau, Jean-Jacques. 1953. *The Confessions*. London: Penguin Books [first published in French in 1781].

Rubin, Gayle. 2006. 'Thinking sex: notes for a radical theory of the politics of sexuality', in Peter Aggleton and Richard Parker, eds., *Culture, Society, and Sexuality: A Reader*, 2nd edn. New York: Routledge: 143–78 [first published in 1984].

Rubin, Gayle, and Judith Butler. 1994. 'Sexual traffic', in *differences: A Journal of Feminist Cultural Studies*, vol. 6, nos. 2/3: 62–99.

Ruggiero, Guido. 1980. *Violence in Early Renaissance Venice*. New Brunswick, NJ: Rutgers University Press.

——. 1995. *The Boundaries of Eros: Sex Crime and Sexuality in Renaissance Venice*. New York: Oxford University Press.

San Francisco Globe, 'How daughter with Down syndrome changed dad's life for the best', in *San Francisco Globe*, 19 December 2014, http://fbarticle.sfglobe.com/2014/12/18/hYr/?src=mcal_30025.

Sanders, Teela. 2008. *Paying for Pleasure: Men Who Buy Sex*. Cullompton, UK: Willan.

Sawicki, Jana. 1991. 'Identity politics and sexual freedom', *in Disciplining Foucault: Feminism, Power, and the Body*. New York: Routledge: 33–48.

——. 2005. 'Review of *Abnormal: Lectures at the Collège de France 1974–1975*', in *Notre Dame Philosophical Reviews*, vol. 1, http://ndpr.nd.edu/news/23977-abnormal-lectures-at-the-college-de-france-1974-1975.

Saxton, Marsha. 2013. 'Disability rights and selective abortion', in Lennard J. Davis, ed., *The Disability Studies Reader*, 4th edn. New York: Routledge: 87–99.

Schotten, C. Heike. 2014. 'Homonationalist futurism: "terrorism" and (other) queer resistance to empire', in *New Political Science*, vol. 37, no. 1: 71–90.

——. 2015. 'Against totalitarianism: Agamben, Foucault, and the politics of critique', in *Foucault Studies*, no. 20: 155–79.

——. 2016. 'Homonationalism: from critique to diagnosis, or, we are all homonational now', in *International Feminist Journal of Politics*: 1–20, http://dx.doi.org/10.1080/14616742.2015.1103061.

Scott, Joan. 1991. 'The evidence of experience', in *Critical Inquiry*, vol. 7, no. 4: 773–97.

Schrift, Alan. 2008. 'Effects of the *agrégation de philosophie* on twentieth-century French philosophy', in *Journal of the History of Philosophy*, vol. 46, no. 3: 449–74.

Sedgwick, Eve Kosofsky. 1990. *Epistemology of the Closet*. Berkeley, CA: University of California Press.

Sheth, Falguni. 2011. 'The war on terror and ontopolitics: concerns with Foucault's account of race, power sovereignty', in *Foucault Studies*, no. 12: 51–76.

Shotwell, Alexis. 2014. '"Women don't get AIDS, they just die from it": memory, classification, and the campaign to change the definition of AIDS', in *Hypatia: A Journal of Feminist Philosophy*, vol. 29, no. 2: 509–25.

Sniderman, Andrew Stobo. 2012. 'Aboriginal students: an education under-class', in *Macleans*, 13 August: 20–1, www.macleans.ca/news/canada/an-education-underclass.

Snyder, Sharon L., and David T. Mitchell. 2006. *Cultural Locations of Disability*. Chicago: University of Chicago Press.

Spade, Dean. 2011. *Normal Life: Administrative Violence, Critical Trans Politics, and the Limits of Law*. New York: South End Press.

Spargo, Tamsin. 1999. *Foucault and Queer Theory*. New York: Totem Books.

Spivak, Gayatri Chakravorty. 1988. 'Can the subaltern speak?', in Cary Nelson and Lawrence Grossberg, eds., *Marxism and the Interpretation of Culture*. Champaign, IL: University of Illinois Press: 271–315.

Stein, Edward. 2001. *The Mismeasure of Desire: The Science, Theory, and Ethics of Sexual Orientation*. Oxford: Oxford University Press.

St. Pierre, Joshua. 2012. 'The construction of the disabled speaker: locating stut-tering in disability studies', in *Canadian Journal of Disability Studies*, vol. 1, no. 3: 1–21.

Stoler, Ann Laura. 1995. *Race and the Education of Desire: Foucault's* History of Sexuality *and the Colonial Order of Things*. Durham, NC: Duke University Press.

Stoller, Nancy E. 1998. 'Foucault in the streets: New York City act(s) up', in *Lessons from the Damned: Queers, Whores, and Junkies Respond to AIDS*. New York: Routledge: 113–34.

Stone, Brad Elliott. 2011. 'The down low and the sexuality of race', in *Foucault Studies*, no. 12: 36–50.

Sullivan, Shannon. 2007. 'White ignorance and colonial oppression: or, why I know so little about Puerto Rico', in Shannon Sullivan and Nancy Tuana, eds., *Race and Epistemologies of Ignorance*. Albany, NY: State University of New York Press: 153–72.

Taylor, Chloë. 2009a. *The Culture of Confession from Augustine to Foucault: A Genealogy of the 'Confession Animal'*. New York: Routledge.

——. 2009b. 'Foucault, feminism, and sex crimes', in *Hypatia: A Journal of Feminist Philosophy*, vol. 24, no. 4: 1–25.

——. 2010. 'Foucault and the ethics of eating', in *Foucault Studies*, no. 9: 71–88.

——. 2011. 'Disciplinary relations/sexual relations: feminist and Foucauldian reflections on professor–student sex', in *Hypatia: A Journal of Feminist Philosophy*, vol. 26, no. 1: 187–206.

——. 2012. 'Abnormal appetites: Foucault, Atwood, and the normalization of an animal-based diet', in *Journal for Critical Animal Studies*, vol. 10, no. 3: 130–48.

——. 2013. 'Foucault and critical animal studies: genealogies of agricultural power', in *Philosophy Compass*, vol. 8, no. 6: 539–51.

——. 2014. 'Foucault and food', in Paul B. Thompson and David Kaplan, eds., *The Encyclopedia of Food and Agricultural Ethics*. New York: Springer: 1042–9.

——. 2015. 'Female sexual dysfunction, feminist sexology, and the psychiatry of the normal', in *Feminist Studies*, no. 1, vol. 42: 259–92.

Taylor, Dianna. 2010. 'Monstrous women', in *PhaenEx*, vol. 5, no. 2: 125–51.

Taylor, Dianna, and Karen Vintges, eds. 2004. *Feminism and the Final Foucault*. Chicago: University of Illinois Press.

Thierman, Stephen. 2010. 'Apparatuses of animality: Foucault goes to a slaughter-house', in *Foucault Studies*, no. 9: 89–110.

Tiefer, Leonore. 2004. *Sex Is Not a Natural Act and Other Essays*. Boulder, CO: Westview Press.

Tierney, Thomas. 2010. 'The governmentality of suicide: Peuchet, Marx, Durkheim, and Foucault', in *Journal of Classical Sociology*, vol. 10, no. 4: 357–89.

Tremain, Shelley. 2013. 'Educating Jouy', in *Hypatia: A Journal of Feminist Philosophy*, vol. 28, no. 4: 801–17.

——. ed. 2015. *Foucault and the Government of Disability*, 2nd edn. Ann Arbor, MI: University of Michigan Press.

Triechler, Paula A. 1999. *How to Have a Theory in an Epidemic: Cultural Chronicles of AIDS*. Durham, NC: Duke University Press.

Truth and Reconciliation Commission of Canada. 2015a. *Canada's Residential Schools*, vol. 1, *The History, Part 1: Origins to 1939*. Montreal: McGill-Queens University Press.

——. 2015b. *Canada's Residential Schools*, vol. 1, *The History, Part 2: 1939 to 2000*. Montreal: McGill-Queens University Press.

——. 2015c. *Canada's Residential Schools*, vol. 5, *The Legacy*. Montreal: McGill-Queens University Press.

Tuana, Nancy. 2004. 'Coming to understand: orgasm and the epistemology of igno-rance', in *Hypatia: A Journal of Feminist Philosophy*, vol. 19, no. 1: 194–232.

Twine, Richard. 2010. *Animals as Biotechnology: Ethics, Sustainability and Critical Animal Studies*. London: Earthscan.

van Ussel, Jos. 1970. *Sexualunterdrückung: Geschichte der Sexualfeindschaft*. Reinbek: Rowohlt [published in French in 1972 as *Histoire de la répression sex-uelle*. Paris: Lafont].

Vigarello, Georges. 1998. *Histoire du viol: XVI–XX siècle*. Paris: Seuil.

Wadiwel, Dinesh Joseph. 2002. 'Cows and sovereignty: biopower and animal life', in *Borderlands*, vol. 1, no. 2, www.borderlands.net.au/vol1no2_2002/wadiwel_cows.html.

Warner, Michael. 2000. *The Trouble with Normal: Sex, Politics, and the Ethics of Queer Life* Cambridge, MA: Harvard University Press.

Winnubst, Shannon, and Jana Sawicki. 2012. 'Guest editors' introduction', in *Foucault Studies*, no. 14: 4–6.

Withers, A. J. 2012. *Disability Politics and Theory*. Halifax, NS: Fernwood.

Woodhull, Winnifred. 1988. 'Sexuality, power, and the question of rape', in Irene Diamond and Lee Quinby, eds., *Feminism and Foucault: Reflections on Resistance*. Boston: Northeastern University Press: 167–76.

Woolf, Virginia. 1957. *A Room of One's Own*. New York: Harcourt Brace Jovanovich [first published in 1929].

Yeng, Sokthan. 2013. *The Biopolitics of Race: State Racism and US Immigration*. Langham, MD: Lexington Books.

Zalk, Sue Rosenberg. 1996. 'Men in the academy: a psychological profile of harassers', in Michele A. Paludi, ed., *Sexual Harassment on College Campuses: Abusing the Ivory Power*. Albany, NY: State University of New York Press: 81–113 [first published in 1990].

Zeitlin, Froma, John K. Winkler and David Halperin, eds. 1991. *Before Sexuality: The Construction of Erotic Experience in the Ancient Greek World*. Princeton, NJ: Princeton University Press.

INDEX

Taylor & Francis eBooks

Helping you to choose the right eBooks for your Library

Add Routledge titles to your library's digital collection today. Taylor and Francis ebooks contains over 50,000 titles in the Humanities, Social Sciences, Behavioural Sciences, Built Environment and Law.

Choose from a range of subject packages or create your own!

Benefits for you

» Free MARC records
» COUNTER-compliant usage statistics
» Flexible purchase and pricing options
» All titles DRM-free.

Benefits for your user

» Off-site, anytime access via Athens or referring URL
» Print or copy pages or chapters
» Full content search
» Bookmark, highlight and annotate text
» Access to thousands of pages of quality research at the click of a button.

 REQUEST YOUR **FREE** INSTITUTIONAL TRIAL TODAY

Free Trials Available
We offer free trials to qualifying academic, corporate and government customers.

eCollections – Choose from over 30 subject eCollections, including:

Archaeology	Language Learning
Architecture	Law
Asian Studies	Literature
Business & Management	Media & Communication
Classical Studies	Middle East Studies
Construction	Music
Creative & Media Arts	Philosophy
Criminology & Criminal Justice	Planning
Economics	Politics
Education	Psychology & Mental Health
Energy	Religion
Engineering	Security
English Language & Linguistics	Social Work
Environment & Sustainability	Sociology
Geography	Sport
Health Studies	Theatre & Performance
History	Tourism, Hospitality & Events

For more information, pricing enquiries or to order a free trial, please contact your local sales team:
www.tandfebooks.com/page/sales

 Routledge
Taylor & Francis Group

The home of
Routledge books

www.tandfebooks.com